D1733337

The Patient's Impact
On the Analyst

For Paul

The Patient's Impact
On the Analyst

Judy Leopold Kantrowitz

With a Foreword by
Anton O. Kris

THE ANALYTIC PRESS
1996   Hillsdale, NJ   London

Published by The Analytic Press, Inc.
Editorial Offices: 101 West Street, Hillsdale, NJ 07642

Library of Congress Cataloging-in-Publication Data

Kantrowitz, Judy Leopold, 1938-
The patient's impact on the analyst / Judy Leopold Kantrowitz with a
Foreword by Anton O. Kris.
p.   cm.
Includes bibliographical references and index.
ISBN 0-88163-211-2
1. Psychotherapist and patient. 2. Psychoanalysts–Psychology.
3. Self-analysis (Psychoanalysis). 4. Countertransference (Psychology)
5. Change (Psychology) I. Title.
[DNLM; 1. Professional-Patient Relations. 2. Psychotherapy.
3. Self Assessment (Psychology) 4. Transference (Psychology) WM
62 K161 1996]
RC480.8.K36   1996
616.89′14023–dc20
DNLM/DLC
for Library of Congress   96-38505
                                                                      CIP

Printed in the United States of America
10 9 8 7 6 5 4 3 2 1

The Patient's Impact
On the Analyst

Acknowledgments

My gratitude and thanks are owed to so many people who in various ways have made this book possible that I wish to apologize in advance for any I may neglect to thank specifically.

I want to begin by expressing my appreciation to the analysts who participated in this study. Without their generosity in sharing their thoughts and experiences, the book never would have been written. I am especially grateful to the 26 analysts who volunteered to be interviewed. Their candor and willingness to share their personal and sometimes very painful experiences deepened my own appreciation of the emotional impact that can come from our work. Their examples helped me to expand the ideas that I had when I began this project. The book that I have written has been significantly shaped by their contributions.

I am grateful to the Boston Psychoanalytic Society and Institute for giving me a small research grant to cover the secretarial, statistical, and other miscellaneous costs of this project. My special thanks go to Diane Nugent for the administration of this fund. I wish to thank Karen Smolens for her secretarial help and Frederick Rocco for performing the statistical analyses and patiently guiding me through their interpretations. Lee Brauer, Murray Cohen, Theodore Cross, and Howard Schuman were each generous in taking time to discuss various methodological issues in this work. Anne Menashi found countless references for me and occasionally unearthed some relevant articles with which I was unfamiliar.

Warren Poland was the first to suggest and encourage me to turn this project into a book. Andrew Morrison introduced me to Paul Stepansky and told me of his very positive experience working with The Analytic Press. Robert Gardner provided a similar endorsement. My appreciation to them is great, for working with Paul Stepansky has been a stimulating and gratifying experience.

From the outset, Paul Stepansky has been supportive and encouraging. He was willing to read drafts of this book even in its most primitive form and offered clear, constructive suggestions that assisted me in finding direction in continuing my work. He has a fine ear for language and an appreciation of the clinical situation that made clear he knew what I was trying to say and when I was or was not saying it well. I owe the title of the book to his suggestion. He introduced me to authors I had not read and broadened my appreciation of current psychoanalytic thinking. His availability and responsivity were consistent throughout. As a first-time author of a book, I have no basis for comparison, but I cannot imagine that any author could have a better experience. His staff has also been a pleasure to work with. I especially wish to express appreciation to John

Kerr for reading and offering suggestions on specific chapters and to Eleanor Starke (Lenni) Kobrin, who supervised the production of this book.

Many of my friends and colleagues have generously given time and, in some instances, editorial assistance to this work. Natalie Bluestone, Frances Givelber, William Grossman, Dan Jacobs, Anton Kris, Austin Silber, Anna Wolff, and Judith Yanof have all read and offered helpful suggestions for various parts and drafts of this book. I am especially grateful to Anton Kris for reading the entire book in its nearly final form and for contributing its valuable foreword.

My gratitude is, of course, not limited to those who formally contributed to the actual construction of the book. I owe an inexpressibly great debt to my patients. If I had not been aware of how much I had learned from them, I might never have embarked on this study. I am also grateful to my teachers, supervisors, analyst, and therapists for all they have taught me and for enabling me to go on and continue to learn for myself. My friends, some of whom read this work in progress and some of whom did not, have also contributed to what I have come to know and continue to learn. Like the analysts interviewed in this book, I find analytic work and its vicissitudes a continual source of stimulation and consider myself fortunate to have friends with whom mutual sharing is not only possible but welcomed.

My family have been a continuing source of inspiration, support, and encouragement. My parents always believed in me and supported my wish to grow and learn even when the directions were in ways they themselves had not known. My father's capacity for empathy remains a model for my best therapeutic self. His self-discipline and determination to overcome adversity have provided an important source of strength for me to emulate. I wish I had known of the shame he felt about some of his early history. This book may be in part an attempt to do for others what I was unable to do for him. My mother's ever-curious and imaginative mind, her openness to new ideas, her willingness to try new creative means of self-expression well into her mid 80s, as well as her capacity to grow and change in relationships, have also provided inspiration for what is possible.

My gratitude to my children is enormous. I have learned from each of them in a different way. Each has made me feel supported in my work and specifically encouraged in writing this book.

But, most of all, I wish to express my indebtedness to my husband, Paul. Without his support and encouragement, I could not have undertaken this project. He has helped me concretely by listening to and discussing my ideas and by reading and critiquing my writing. I will always be grateful for his patience and understanding about the time and emotional energy this project took. I owe apologies to my friends and family for the times I have not been as available as I would have wished to be during the course of working on this book, but to none as much as to him. His devotion and emotional support provided the sustenance for me to do this work.

Contents

Part III
CHANGES IN THE ANALYST

PART IV
EPILOGUE

Foreword

Anton O. Kris

This marvelous volume, filled with an incredibly rich collection of extensive reports by analysts of their *personal* experiences in doing psychoanalysis, presents the findings of a systematic research project. From that powerful origin, with its focused attention to the effects of analytic work on the analyst, comes an extraordinary, wide-ranging series of clinical accounts, deeply probed and comprehensively considered. Judy L. Kantrowitz demonstrates what analysts *really* do and takes the reader through many of the questions at the cutting edge of psychoanalytic technique and understanding.

Enlisting the anonymous efforts of a large group of psychoanalytic colleagues, initially through the medium of a carefully constructed questionnaire, Kantrowitz has created a body of data bearing on the changes analysts experience as a result of doing analytic work. Her achievement goes far beyond the collection of data, however. In the course of the balanced inquiry into the limits of reliability and applicability of her findings, the reader encounters crucial issues of relevance to the researcher as well as vital concerns of the practicing analyst. The resulting volume excites the imagination as it informs the mind. Every analyst and therapist will be stimulated to consider in a new way his or her experiences and will profit from the broadly based theoretical framework with which to evaluate and understand them. For those who are entering the field, it seems to me to provide a profound, comprehensible guide to the critical terrain of therapeutic interaction.

The deeply moving first-person accounts of analysts' experiences form the heart of this volume. The expectation of anonymity in their presentation undoubtedly contributed to their richness of personal detail. Kantrowitz cautions the reader, however, to recognize the study's bias to report only favorable outcomes of change in the analyst, though some of these come with a considerable emotional price tag. The most extensive and magnificent report carries the analyst from the consulting room to near-death hospital experiences of his own in a *tour de force* of self-analysis before achieving a salutary integration.

From the statistical survey of several hundred analysts and from closer examination of a smaller number of replies with telephone interviews, Kantrowitz draws impressive generalizations. She formulates several categories for the types of "triggers for self-knowledge" and for the modes of reflection and inquiry by which analysts pursue the problems they encounter. Making use of these categories, she helps the reader organize what would otherwise be a mass of powerfully stimulating but overwhelming clinical reports. With her comprehensive knowledge of the analytic literature, she builds on the achievements of recent decades, harnessing an understanding of countertransference and the analyst's participation in the analytic process in the service of delineating the impact of analytic work on the analyst. In doing so, however, she contributes to a clearer understanding of the nature of therapeutic interaction and the interplay of conscious and unconscious influences in the "match" between patient and analyst. To take just one example of new insights offered, we are shown evidence to challenge Freud's widely accepted assertion (of 85 years ago) that analysts cannot help patients go further than they themselves have gone in mastering their resistances (p. 145).

I believe this book substantially advances our understanding of psychoanalytic work, especially in illuminating the interaction between patiernt and analyst in the analytic process. By its method and findings, it also advances the borders of what may be discussed publicly. By its example, it provides a model for psychoanalytic collegiality and discourse.

Introduction

Investigating the nature of psychological change and attempting to explicate which factors facilitate its development have always been central to psychoanalytic concerns. Until the 1980s most American analysts focused their attention relatively exclusively on understanding the psychological changes in their patients. With a few exceptions, analysts' assessments of these changes were based on anecdotal material from their own patients. In the late 1960s, when I began my training at the Boston Psychoanalytic Institute, most of my teachers offered a view of psychoanalysis that if the analyst were well-enough analyzed and trained and the patient carefully enough selected for analytic suitability, the outcome would be positive. Of course, the difficulty in assuring that both these conditions obtained was considerable and was assumed to account for analytic failures. While I believed then, and continue to believe now, that my mentors were correct in stressing the importance of these factors, I also maintained a skepticism about the possibility of attaining "enough" personal self-knowledge and skill in both clinical assessment of analyzability and analytic technique to be certain of achieving positive results. My graduate work had been done in clinical psychology, where I had been trained to think about matters of reliability and validity. If there were not systematic pre- and postanalysis assessments of patients, how could we claim they had changed? What about the effect of observer bias? Having invested so much time and energy in the work, didn't analysts have a personal investment in believing their patients changed that might skew their perceptions? Though, in the late 1960s, patients' views of their change were rarely sought, if they were sought, wouldn't their evaluations also be positively slanted for similar reasons?

Much, if not most, of what could be assessed rigorously required exclusion of the nuance and complexity inherent in psychological organization. Psychoanalytic ideas when studied by the methods that most psychologists then employed were so simplified that, for the most part, they no longer represented in a meaningful way what psychoanalytic theoreticians or clinicians believed. At best, projective tests provided some relatively standardized and objective measure of personality organization, conflict, and level of psychological adaptation that could be replicated over time. But the interpretation of these psychological tests was dependent on the skill of the individual psychologist. Was it only skill? Unreliability of projective test assessments was notorious once psychologists went beyond the scoring of the material. Wouldn't the character and personal conflicts of the psychologist also influence the interpretation of the data and possibly affect administration of the tests as well? Roy Schafer (1954) cogently elaborated this interactional perspective in his book *The Psychoanalytic Interpretation in Rorschach Testing*.

If the character and conflicts of the psychologist affected psychological assessments of patients, why wouldn't these same factors influence analysts in their work with patients? I found it difficult to accept that analysts could be as interchangeable as the theories I was then being taught suggested. While there are, of course, enduring and ever-recognizable characteristics for any person, there seemed a commonsense logic that interactions with different people brought to the fore different aspects of them. Wasn't there likely to be a specificity that evolved in each analytic situation influenced by the character and conflicts of the two participants? Such considerations took me far from the positions that were being taught in most of my institute classes.

Fortunately, in my early years as a candidate, some teachers, such as M. Robert Gardner, offered a more interactional perspective in his inspiring course on analytic technique. Such teachers and exposure somewhat later in my training to literature—mostly, but not exclusively, from the British school of psychoanalysis—made me think some analysts might be receptive to ideas more consonant with my own.

Fortunately, the Boston Psychoanalytic Institute also had a research tradition. Peter Knapp had been influential in establishing a group of analysts who had begun some systematic study of the factors determining analyzability. The research analysts, however, seemed to endorse the same perspective as most of my teachers at the Institute in viewing the analyst as being "objective," a "blank screen." While I had serious research interests, I was always primarily a clinician wishing to explore the psyche in depth.

To test some of the assumptions about analyzability and psychological change, I designed and implemented the Boston prospective, longitudinal outcome study of psychoanalysis. By the time I collected the first set of outcome data, it was the early 1980s, and the intellectual climate both nationally and at the Boston Institute had changed considerably. Countertransference reactions were no longer viewed as responses that could and should be eradicated. They were beginning to be discussed by American analysts as reactions that could be informative to analytic work. Analysts themselves were also no longer assumed to be perfectly analyzed.

The findings from the Boston project that analyzability could not be predicted from the initial assessment of the patient when a preselected population was studied, and that only 40% of psychoanalyses were successful, received support from other independent investigators, Erle and Goldberg, 1979, 1984; Wallerstein, 1986). The data from these studies served to further the trend toward deidealizing the expectations of what psychoanalysis could accomplish. From the data collected, the only factor that seemed related to outcome was the match between the patient and the analyst. Overlapping aspects of character and conflict could both impede and facilitate analysis. Other analysts also noted, anecdotally or parenthetically, the importance of the match (Bachrach and Leaff, 1978; Wallerstein, 1986), but no attempt to investigate its impact systematically was undertaken.

The second follow-up investigation in the Boston outcome project began to address the impact of the match on the outcome of psychoanalysis more systematically. The data on the analysts, of course, were retrospective. The natural next step was a prospective study in which pre- and postanalysis assessments of both patient and analyst, as well as measures of analytic process, were obtained. I designed such a project and found senior analysts who were willing to participate, but by this time funds for this kind of research no longer existed. By the mid-1980s, however, it was clear not only that the analyst had ceased to be regarded as a "blank screen" but that an interactional perspective on psychoanalysis had become a mainstream position. If it were not possible to study the analytic process with the depth and rigor that our present state of knowledge and instruments permitted, at least it was now possible to consider the role of the analyst and the effect his or her character and conflicts had on the analytic work.

Once an interactional point of view became generally accepted, it was apparent that the psychology of the analyst needed to be understood as fully as the psychology of the patient. This gap in our knowledge then began to be addressed. Analysts focused on the analyst's use of the self (Jacobs, 1991), the analyst's transference to the patient (McLaughlin, 1981, 1988), and other related self-analytic phenomena (Poland, 1984; Sonnenberg, 1991; Smith, 1993; Silber, in press). These analysts considered how aspects of themselves may have influenced their patients and affected the analytic work. An interactional perspective must presume a bidirectionality of impact. With the exception of McLaughlin, however, there are very few examples of analysts' describing the effect of the conflicts and characteristics of their patients on themselves.

The present project is a first step in studying the analyst in the role of analyst and the impact of the analytic process on the analyst. It sets out to investigate how analysts view changes in themselves developing from their work with patients. An underlying assumption is that the particular patient–analyst match influences the extent to which the analyst is affected and the psychological changes that occur. This project addresses two important and not well documented areas in psychoanalysis. The first area considered is the perception of analysts about the impact of their work on their conflicts and character. The second, more theoretical, area presented in this project is a formulation of the therapeutic effect of psychoanalysis on the analyst.

From their self-reports, I hope to show how analysts come to recognize an aspect of themselves requiring more self-scrutiny, the manner in which they continue the self-analytic process after their training is completed, and the ways in which they conceptualize how changes in themselves occur as a result of their work with patients. I use the specific data provided by these analysts both to convey their views about topics that have become increasingly a focus of analytic interest, for example, countertransference, self-analysis, the patient's impact on the analyst, and to formulate a theory about learning and the process of psychological change for the analyst.

The data for this study are threefold: (1) survey data based on a ten-item questionnaire returned by approximately 400 graduate analysts, approximately two-thirds of whom are training and supervising analysts, of the American Psychoanalytic Association institutes; (2) written clinical illustrations provided by approximately 200 of these analysts; and (3) telephone interviews with 26 of those analysts who had provided written examples of their experiences.

Before further describing the manner in which I present this study, it is important to clarify some of its limitations and some of the limits in generalizing to clinical theory from its findings. In undertaking this investigation, I am not assuming that self-awareness, the conscious knowing about oneself, is the only route to change. Nor am I assuming that working with patients is the only, or even the primary, way that analysts continue learning about themselves. For many analysts, after having a personal analysis in which they freed themselves from many blind spots and increased their capacities to be self-reflective and self-observant, their personal relationships—primarily with their spouses and children—are the greater source of stimuli for continued self-exploration, self-knowing, and psychological change. Life events—illnesses, deaths, births, personal or professional setbacks or both, and personal or professional achievements or both—all are likely to play central roles in influencing later psychological changes. Relationships with their colleagues and friends (and, for some, less friendly relationships) may also provide important data. As adults, our characters are relatively well formed, and it is unlikely that the changes that occur will be transforming in a dramatic sense. Nonetheless, assumptions about adult development have changed over the years, and a greater plasticity is now assumed (Colarusso and Nemeroff, 1981).

Whatever subtle changes occur in the analyst are likely to lead to some subtle change in his or her analytic work. It is unlikely that the impact of any and all of these other factors will be totally separable from what analysts learn about themselves through their work with patients. For many analysts, however, their work may not the primary place where the stimulus for the self-scrutiny or reworking occurs. The effect of psychological change is likely to be reverberating, starting in one part of the analyst's life—for many, outside the analytic work itself—but inevitably manifesting itself in the nature and quality of work with patients. The perception of changes in the analytic work may then provide a source of data about the self and psychological changes that the analyst thinks have occurred as a consequence of events external to analytic work. The shift manifested in the work based on these usually subtle psychological changes often results in shifts in the patients and their responses. This slightly changed interaction then is a source of new information to analysts about themselves and stimulates further self-scrutiny. The analyst may reflect upon the similarities of what he or she has perceived in work with patients and their manifestations in his or her other interactions. As examples accumulate in both personal and professional arenas, analysts may find data that support their belief in the psychological changes in themselves that they think have occurred.

I have already indicated my awareness about the limitations of self-reports. If analysts value being changed by their patients, then they are likely to be biased in the direction of believing these changes have occurred. This study is not claiming that psychological change has actually taken place. To make such a claim requires some independent, external criteria that are both reliable and valid. No such criteria exist, nor could they exist, for data based solely on self-report. Self-deception, to some extent, is inevitable; we can never know what we do not yet know. Most of us believe that there is always more to know, and therefore, what we "know" now is provisional and open to revision as we come to know more. What is being investigated is not the "truth" of any analyst's claim to have changed psychologically. There is no assumption about the conclusiveness or exhaustiveness of the analyst's "knowing." The area I am delineating for study is only how something that previously was not known comes to be known and what impact this knowing has on the analyst in both subjective and external aspects of his or her life, according to his or her own perception.

The reader's conviction about the "reality" of these psychological changes is, to a large extent, dependent on the analysts' ability to conceptualize and articulate what they believe has occurred and why. There is always the danger that verbal skill, rather than "real" psychological change, is being assessed. It is equally plausible that we will fail to be convinced of psychological changes that are experientially "real" to the reporting analyst because of his or her limited skill in conceptualization or articulations. The limitations of subjective reports are inevitable and need to be kept in mind when we try to make generalizations from these data.

As the data show, the younger analysts, those trained during the late 1970s and in the 1980s, tend to be more open about themselves, about their foibles and vulnerabilities. This shift in attitude about self-exposure seems an outgrowth of shifts in attitudes in Western society. When a belief in authority was strongly placed in doubt in the 1960s, the certainty about previously held beliefs was also shaken. It followed that the expectation of being able to achieve some idealized state of knowing and control was lessened. Once expectations of omniscience and omnipotence diminished, expectations about the attainments from psychoanalysis also became more realistic. If one did not expect to be "perfectly" analyzed, then it also followed that one did not need to feel so ashamed of one's personal limitations. The lessening of shame had the consequence of analysts' becoming freer to reveal their sense of their personal limitations. Acknowledgment of personal limitations and of their intrusion, to some extent, upon analytic work transformed the view of most analysts about the nature of the analytic enterprise.

This changed perspective, however, may also result in changed values. The act of self-revelation itself may now have become revered by some analysts. Self-revelation is, of course, seen as an essential part of a patient's analytic work. Once something becomes a value, then perceiving that it has occurred in oneself is viewed as desirable, and the perception of this occurrence cannot be unbiased. If being changed by an interactional process with patients is now valued, as, previously, not having countertransference reactions to patients was revered, then we as readers of these analysts' self-reports must maintain a respectful suspicion about their conclusions about themselves.

Self-revelations even when presented anonymously may be experienced as affectively charged. Some analysts rereading the accounts of their interview described feeling some discomfort seeing their personal material in printed form. Nonetheless, they wanted it to appear in the book. They believed others might benefit from learning about their experiences. Some analysts, perhaps many analysts, have wanted an opportunity to communicate discoveries that have emerged from their own analytic experiences or self-analytic work without divulging their identities. Some reports by analysts of detailed case material have been later revealed to be disguised presentations of their own experiences. Freud (1899) in "Screen Memories," Anna Freud (1922) in "Beating Fantasies and Daydreams," Karen Horney in many case vignettes (see Quinn, 1987), and Heinz Kohut in "The Two Analyses of Mr. Z" (see Cocks, 1994) are considered examples of this phenomenon. These authors seem to have believed that their self-discoveries offered useful information for others interested in psychological development or psychoanalytic treatment. They wished to present these insights and yet protect their psychological vulnerabilities. If we accept the inevitability of the influence of subjectivity, and if we agree to put aside the question of what is completely verifiable, then what psychoanalytically trained persons report about themselves and their quest for self-knowledge may provide a special kind of data about how we come to know and change.

Theoretical questions about the source of the analyst's conflicts, affective distress, or underlying motives for psychological change are not addressed in this study. This is not because I am indifferent to such questions but because I believe that theories, too, inevitably, are subjective and that the introduction of a theoretical perspective on the data would serve only to confuse the reader. We know each patient in his or her particularity. Then, as clinical theoreticians, we step back and try to generalize from what we see in the individual that may be "true" for the more general, human condition; we try to universalize when we create theories. We say, These are the things that people struggle with, and these are the ways in which they struggle. Our theories are influenced by both the historical moment in which we live and our individual histories (Stolorow and Atwood, 1992).

Since theories are always personal, they are often, at their best, adaptive, providing us a reminder of what we may be disinclined to face in ourselves or compensating for what we may sense, if not consciously realize, are our personal proclivities, reflected in our analytic style. They are one avenue to "knowing" but obviously can be employed defensively to conceal, as well as adaptively to reveal, what we wish not to acknowledge.

If we step back from an attempt to answer questions of causations and accept that our views must inevitably be colored by our own experiences, values, attitudes, and beliefs, then our attention can turn to the more general configurations of the struggle to see what is painful to acknowledge. We are then able to consider the process of self-discovery without getting lost in a particular focus on its content. The focus I maintain in this study is on the process—the process of discovery, the process of exploration, and the perception of the process of change. Descriptions of discovery and exploration have a face validity; descriptions of psychological change do not.

Having stated both some of the limitations of self-reports and the limits of what I am trying to study, I now address some of the reasons that self-reports from analysts about their ways of learning about themselves as an outgrowth of their work with patients may provide a particularly rich source of information.

I have studied a relatively homogeneous group of analysts. These analysts are all graduates of accredited training institutes of the American Psychoanalytic Association; the majority of the participants are training and supervising analysts who are, as a group, considered the most skilled[1] and are probably the most experienced of American psychoanalysts. These analysts, due to their personal analyses, clinical and theoretical training, and intensive and generally long-term experience in the treatment of analytic patients, have a background that should make them relatively skilled at observing and describing (1)

---

[1] Some skilled analysts choose not to become training analysts. Other skilled analysts may have been overlooked in institutes where analysts cannot initiate an application to be considered for the training analyst position.

how they come to know what they know, (2) what they do to expand the impact of this knowledge, and (3) what effect this expansion then has on their lives.

My assumption is that learning most often takes place in some form of interaction. One interaction that all analysts are accustomed to observing, describing, reflecting upon, and learning from is with their patients. Usually, we focus on this interaction to learn about our patients. What I propose is that we may also look at what occurs in this dyad to learn about ourselves. Investigations of how we know and how we change may then be informative about the way our patients change; analysts, of course, were all at first patients themselves. I hope that my findings illuminate not only the analysts' perception of their patient's impact on them but also the impact of the patient–analyst match on the therapeutic aspects of analysis itself.

In the first section of the book, I describe the study in more detail and provide a more extensive rationale for undertaking the project at this time and in this manner. I then describe the context and nature of the survey, the sample, and the overall findings from the questionnaire data. The implications and limitations of findings from the survey data are discussed. The three categories of data—checked items on the survey forms, clinical vignettes provided in written form, and telephone interviews—are described. A brief description of example categories explains the basis on which classifications were made. The factors in the work with the patient that stimulated the analyst to recognize an area for personal work were (1) a similarity between the patient and the analyst, (2) a quality or characteristic of the patient that the analyst perceives as being more developed in the patient than in the analyst and that the analyst aspires to achieve, (3) a patient's interpretation of the analyst or the analyst's countertransference, and (4) a transference-countertransference recognition or a transference-countertransference enactment.

In order not to burden the general analytic reader with numbers and statistics, most of the numerical data are presented in the appendices. A summary of the number and characteristics of those analysts who responded to the survey, including a breakdown in percentage by gender, institutional position, and age for each item is provided to supplement the descriptive material presented in the first chapter.

The second section begins with a chapter that describes some different forms of self-inquiry that analysts employ when undertaking their self-reflective work about themselves in relation to their work with patients. The structure of telephone interviews, based on the written vignette, is described. The characteristics of the analysts volunteering to participate in this part of the study are given. Four interviews are presented to illustrate analysts' different modes of working on personal discoveries in the context of their work with their patients.

The third chapter describes the various triggers in their interactions with patients that analysts reported stimulated them to undertake further self-reflective work. Examples of each of the four categories described in Chapter 1 are given and discussed. A theory about acquiring knowledge of disavowed aspects of the self is offered. The differences in accessibility of self-knowledge and ownership of what is known are discussed in relation to the four different categories previously cited.

The fourth chapter describes the different methods that analysts employ to continue their self-inquiry. Data are taken from the survey forms and from the interviews to elaborate how analysts think about and conduct self-reflective work. The literature on self-analysis is discussed in relation to these findings. The role of the audience in relation to self-analytic work is also considered. Issues of self-exposure, shame, the age of the analyst, the time of training, and changing attitudes about the analyst's participation and countertransference itself are explored in the context of what analysts have reported. Case examples are offered of work in progress in which two analysts describe in detail the process they undergo when personal issues are stirred before self-understanding is sufficiently achieved.

The third section focuses on the analysts' perceptions of their psychological changes as described in their telephone interviews. Chapters 5–8 present the analysts' interviews. The telephone interviews—elaborations of written examples—are the basis for discussion of how, to what extent, and in what ways analysts believe they change as a result of their work with their patients. Change is explored in relation to each category stimulating recognition of an issue needing self-reflection. Similarly, change in relation to the method of exploration is considered. The interviews are organized around the specific triggers in the interaction with the patient that stimulated the analyst's personal reflective work. Chapter 5 presents examples stimulated by similarity of affect, conflict, defense, or situation. Chapter 6 presents illustrations triggered by analysts' admiration for a quality or characteristic in their patients. Chapter 7 presents examples of patients' interpretations of the analyst's character, conflicts, or defenses or of the analyst's countertransference as stimuli for the analyst's personal work. Chapter 8 provides illustrations of analysts' countertransference responses as the incentive for self-reflection. In each of these chapters the qualities of the particular trigger is first described. Some commentary is given for each example.

In Chapters 5–7, the examples are followed by a discussion highlighting the role of the particular trigger in the analytic process for the analyst. Since countertransference as a trigger for self-exploration contains within it aspects of all the other species of triggers and provides the greatest opportunity for examining the parallels between the analyst's and the patient's experience of the therapeutic aspects of analysis, the discussion of the countertransference examples is presented separately in Chapter 9. Chapter 10 reviews some literature on analysts' views about their psychological changes and discusses the issue of change. It provides a theoretical discussion of how the therapeutic process works for the analyst. It is derived from the analysts' descriptions of their personal work given in their interviews and conceptualized in relation to the literature on the therapeutic action of psychoanalysis. In Chapter 11, I offer a relatively brief discussion of changes in a negative direction as an outcome of work with patients and propose some ideas about why this material was generally absent in this survey.

The fourth and final section of the book provides overall considerations about self-report and the nature, extent, and stability of psychological change, with some reference to the psychoanalytic literature on this topic. The relationship among self-discovery, self-analysis, shared communications, learning, and change is discussed. I elaborate on the implications of the impact of the patient–analyst match on the therapeutic process of analysis as it affects the analyst.

PART I

Prologue

CHAPTER 1

The Project

Over the last 15 years, there has been a shift in the way analysts view the analytic process. While many analysts have always seen analytic work as interactional, for several decades ego psychology, the dominant school of thought in America, considered analysts as "blank screens" on whom patients could project their conflicts. The analysts were thought to be relatively interchangeable, and their contribution was primarily the offering of interpretations. In this context, countertransference reactions were seen as intrusions to be analyzed by the analyst and controlled or a reason to go back into analysis. Countertransference was regarded as not providing the data for exploration that offered the opportunity for a greater understanding of the patient through a greater understanding of what had been evoked in the analyst in the interaction. Increasingly, analysts have recognized that they are active participants in the process who influence, and are influenced by, what occurs with their patients (Gill, 1982; Hoffman, 1983).

A belief about personal change resulting from work with patients seems consistent with psychoanalysts' current way of thinking. Analysts now pay greater attention to the impact of the patient on the analyst's functioning to provide more information about the patient (Dorpat, 1974; Gill, 1982; Greenberg, 1986; Modell, 1986; Stolorow, Brandchaft, and Atwood, 1987; Stolorow and Lachmann, 1988; Dorpat and Miller, 1992; Stolorow and Atwood, 1992; Hoffman, 1993; Mitchell, 1993; Skolnikoff, 1993; Goldberg, 1994). The belief that the personal characteristics and conflicts of another person with whom one has been intensely engaged have had an influence on the other has a common-sense face validity. The bidirectionality of this influence also has a commonsense logic.

Once psychoanalysis is viewed as a process influenced by, and impacting on, both participants, it would seem expectable that the analyst, as well as the patient, would be affected by participating in it. Yet, analysts often resist openly discussing and describing such changes in themselves and how they come about. There are, of course, notable exceptions in which analysts openly describe their countertransferences and elaborate their self-analytic process (Kramer, 1959; Calder, 1980; McLaughlin, 1981; Gardner, 1983; Poland, 1984; Eifermann, 1987, 1993; Jacobs, 1991; Sonnenberg, 1991; Margulies, 1993; Natterson and Friedman, 1995; Silber, in press). Nonetheless, when analysts discuss among themselves this phenomenon of their continuing personal change, there seems an uncertainty about how representative or how unique their own experiences are.

Personal change remains a general and abstract concept. It may mean very different things to each analyst. Gaining some new intellectual information and potentially new insight may frequently occur; however, it is not inevitable that these new understandings actually result in psychological shifts. Analysts, like patients, can idealize their own changes. Most statements by analysts about personal change remain general and undocumented (Smith, 1993; Goldberg, 1994).

This project studies how analysts perceive changes in themselves emerging from their work with their patients. It provides a new vantage point for assessing the impact of the analytic process over time on a group of people who have devoted themselves to this process as their life's work. An interactional view of psychoanalysis contains a latent presupposition that analysts change as a result of participating in the process, but this assumption has not been systematically explored or demonstrated. I hope to show how the particular match of patient and analyst may enable the analyst to attain new or deeper understanding; rework specific conflicts or distress or modify characterological adaptations and attitudes. This process can occur when overlapping conflicts or characteristics of the participants become the focus of analytic scrutiny.

For most analysts, the psychological issues that they explored in their personal treatment are not rerepressed, as they might be following termination, but rather are kept actively alive by their work with patients.

As a result, the analyst has the continuing opportunity to rework these issues on a different and potentially deeper level. Every analysis is potentially a reanalysis for himself or herself. The questions are: How often does this actually occur? Under what circumstances does it occur? How do analysts think about, and describe, this phenomenon?

In studying the impact of the patient–analyst match on the outcome of psychoanalysis in the Boston longitudinal project (Kantrowitz et al., 1989, 1990c), it became apparent that analysts frequently believed that they, as well as their patients, changed during the process of analysis. The observations about analysts' personal and professional change were not the focus of this earlier project; in terms of the formal study, the only systematically documented reflections about psychological change were made about the patients. Many of the analysts, however, spontaneously commented how much they thought they had learned and changed as a consequence of their work with these patients. Sometimes their reflections were specific; for example, one analyst described how humbling it had been to be confronted by the limits of his ability to get another person to change. Most comments were more general and less self-revealing; they indicated the analysts' belief that they had been personally affected by their work with their patients but did not detail the area in which this impact had occurred.

One analysand, not formally part of this project, who was interviewed about her views about the impact of the patient–analyst match spontaneously elaborated the ways in which she believed her analyst had changed as a result of their analytic work (Kantrowitz, 1987b). In this instance, the patient believed that her analyst had become more flexible and spontaneous over the years in response to the patient's pain and distress at experiencing her analyst as distanced and formal.

Increasingly in recent years, analysts have openly described their countertransferences and elaborated their self-analytic process (McLaughlin, 1981, 1988, 1993; Boesky, 1982; Gardner, 1983; Spruiell, 1984; Eifermann, 1987a, b; Chused, 1991; Jacobs, 1991; Sonnenberg, 1991, 1993; Schwaber, 1992; Margulies, 1993; Poland, 1993; Renik, 1994; Smith, 1993; Weinshel, 1993; Hoffman, 1994; Natterson, and Friedman, 1995; Silber, in press). Most of these analysts focus on the awareness of affective reactions that are stirred or memories that are reawakened by their patients and their patients' transferences to them. Yet, while there is the suggestion that such reactions lead to psychological changes, with the exception of McLaughlin (1981, 1988, 1991, 1993, 1995) and, less explicitly, Tansey (1994), few analysts openly discuss or describe, at least in print, actual changes in themselves or how they come about.

McLaughlin details the impact of his work with patients on the transformation of his stance toward his work, his personal belief system, and changes in his own comfort. He documents how his failure effectively to reach certain patients and the personal distress aroused in him in the course of these treatments led him to increased self-reflection and led him to return at one time for a reanalysis and at later times to seek consultation on his work. The discoveries that emerged from his intensive self-explorations caused him to reevaluate and then change his relative silent stance in his work. He also relinquished his belief in the analyst's authoritative knowledge, which he came to view as undermining the patient's sense of psychic reality. Specific attention to similarities and differences between his patients and himself served as the stimulus for mutative insights leading him to a new perspective on himself and accompanying shifts in his affect state. The changes that resulted in his actual behavior as a consequence of his shift in outlook were subtle, but he believes they had profound ramifications on his patients' experience in the treatment and on the analytic work. He validates his belief in shifts in himself through observations of the short-term and long-term effects on patients. He confirms his subjective sense of change through the recognition of these changes by his family and long-term friends.

In order to obtain data more extensive than personal anecdotal information, a national survey was undertaken. Questionnaires were sent to 1,100 psychoanalysts who were members of the American Psychoanalytic Association. All 550 training and supervising analysts and a comparable number of graduate analysts from each institute were selected as the sample. The training and supervising analyst group was selected because certain comparability in the rigor of their assessment, if not their actual work, could be presumed; they had all been graduates for at least five years, had seen, at a minimum, four patients in analysis over those years, and had been certified by the American Psychoanalytic Association's Board on Professional Standards. In addition, their clinical work had been reviewed by their local institutes prior to their appointments as training and supervising analysts. The second group was a random sample stratified for age, institute position, and gender.

The purpose of this survey was to explore, first, whether or not and to what extent analysts believe that their analytic work with patients had led to personal change for themselves. When analysts did believe that personal changes had come about as a result of their work with patients, the survey explored what in the patient–analyst interaction triggered this change for the analysts, what method, if any, analysts employed to continue their personal work, and what changes, if any, they believed had occurred.

Some analysts may object to this focus on the analyst as a subject of study. They worry that attention has been turned away from the patient, who, after all, should be the analyst's central concern. Studying changes in analysts, however, opens up another way in which we may learn how psychological change comes about. While analysts' subjective appraisals of how they learn and change have the disadvantage of being self-reports, limited by the subjectivity and blind spots of the particular individuals and lacking any form of external verification, there are also advantages. Analysts were all themselves once analytic patients. They experienced the analytic process and then learned how to provide this experience for others. They learned how to describe what occurs between patient and analyst with a perspective derived from having been in both positions.

Having analysts report on themselves obviates the concerns about confidentiality we have when we report material about our analysands. Full descriptions of what transpires for a patient may sometimes seem an intrusion on privacy and potentially disrupt the solutions that the former analysand has achieved. Many analysts are reluctant to write about their patients for this reason. They want neither to risk disturbing a treatment process to ask permission to publish some aspect of the work nor to chance disrupting the synthesis the analysand achieved after termination (Stein, 1988a, b). When analysts voluntarily describe their own psychological processes and their changes, no such constraints apply.

Many analysts who would be reluctant to self-disclose, nevertheless, admire others who do so. The myth of the perfectly analyzed analyst is fading, but many still hold onto this ideal for themselves and feel shame about not living up to this model. Yet, to the extent to which psychoanalysts have reconceptualized the analytic enterprise as an interactional endeavor, they no longer exclude considerations of their contributions from descriptions of their analytic work. Once a joint contribution is accepted, analysts must then conclude that each analyst's character and residual conflicts, as well as skill and experience, affect his or her patients and the analytic process that develops.

If analysts believe in the codetermination of the analytic process, then they must examine and expose themselves in order to understand the nature of the evolving therapeutic interaction. The analyst's position is then dramatically reversed from its historical one. Not only is the analyst no longer a "blank screen" whose anonymity is desired to facilitate patients' fantasies, but now the analyst needs to be scrutinized in order to understand the analyst's contribution to the development of patient's fantasies.[1] Analysts have, of course, always been the focus of patients' intense interest as transferences develop and deepen, but the shift of attention is to the factors introduced by the particular characteristics of the analyst. While this reorientation involves a loss of comfort and potentially of some privacy for analysts, the benefits come from the potential increase in self-awareness and self-knowledge and the possibility to continue to rework personal issues; however, not all analysts who believe that their patients have an impact on them necessarily subscribe to exploring their patients' perception of their countertransference. Exploration of the patient's perception of the countertransference is only one of the possible stimuli for the analyst's self-reflections.

All retrospective evaluations of the analyst's own contribution to treatment stalemates or transference-countertransference enactments are based on what the analyst remembers and conveys after the fact. Readers should keep in mind that analysts have presented the material from the point of view of what they have *come* to understand. Although it may seem as if what became understandable over time should have been recognized at the outset, it is important to remember that the analysts have selected data that support the conclusions they later reached. In the midst of their struggles and confusion, no such clear-sighted perspective existed.

Analysts who respond to a survey that presumes that their patients have had an impact on them are not necessarily the same as analysts who do not respond. The survey was designed so that analysts were able to provide responses that disagreed with the premise of the study; however, the underlying assumption of the project, that analysts are affected by their work with their patients, was made explicit. It could not have been concealed, since analysts familiar with my work would have been clear about my perspective. The questionnaire provided an opportunity for analysts to indicate how they thought about, and worked on, this issue. While there may have been other reasons for answering the survey, most analysts who did so likely agreed with an interactional point of view that presumes that the analyst is affected by

---

[1] This is not implying self-disclosure to patients. The current controversy over self-revelation within the treatment situation (Ehrenberg, 1992) is outside the issues explored in this study. The focus here is the analyst's self-examination and his or her commitment to encouraging patients to explore their perceptions of his or her impact and countertransference, as well as the analyst's willingness to explore and expose this aspect of the analytic process to colleagues.

participating in the process, or they would not take the time to reply. The analysts who answer, then, cannot be taken to be representative of analysts in general.

Although this survey was sent only to analysts who were trained in American Psychoanalytic Association institutes in order to have a relatively homogeneous population, the fact is that even within the American Psychoanalytic Association, there are great variations in its members' training experiences, attitudes, beliefs, and actual manner of practicing psychoanalysis. Some of these differences are related to the personal histories and characteristics of the individual analysts. Other factors are related to the decade in which the analysts were trained and to the analytic atmosphere in particular geographic locations. For example, analysts trained in the 1950s and 1960s in Washington, D.C., were heavily influenced by Harry Stack Sullivan and Frieda Fromm-Reichmann, who subscribed to an interpersonal perspective on analysis. These analysts long ago have accepted the importance of the personal characteristics of the analyst as having an impact on analytic work and have at least some appreciation of the patient's impact on the analyst. In contrast, and possibly in reaction to these influences in an adjacent city, analysts trained in the Baltimore Institute during the same period held to a strict, "classical" stance and viewed analysts as interchangeable.[2] These analysts would be less likely to think of their doing psychoanalysis as a source for their self-exploration. Considerations of the representativeness of the sample of respondents to this study for analysts in general are taken up later in the chapter.

A written survey, of course, is not the ideal form to obtain in-depth data. Many will object that it is schematic, open to misinterpretation and misrepresentation, lacks verifiability, and is subject to all the other limitations of self-reported data (Schuman and Kalton, 1985). Nonetheless, a survey is a good place to begin. The value of the study undertaken here is that it provides an overview of the perspective of a large number of people. As Schuman and Kalton (p. 639) point out, a survey is the only method of investigation that can provide information about a large population. Psychoanalysis has perhaps relied too heavily on single case anecdotal reports for most of its data. A good reason for focusing on individual case studies is that in-depth exploration of psychological experience and organization can be obtained only in this way. Yet, the question of how generalizable the findings are persists. A survey gives an opportunity to compare experiences

---

[2] There are, of course, exceptions, such as Samuel Novey (1968).

more systematically. It also allows people to reveal personal experiences more readily, since they are guaranteed anonymity.

The present survey suffers from the difficulty of not separating general experiences from specific examples. The questionnaire, however, was intended to offer an open-ended format for analysts to describe their views, their manner of undertaking self-exploration if they engaged in this activity, and their belief in changes in themselves if they thought they had occurred, rather than limiting the nature of their responses. The survey did not provide an operational definition of personal change for a similar reason; if the analyst believed that change occurred, such a definitive description might have set a constraint on how change might be construed. Instead, the questionnaire provided specific items that could be checked indicating if the analyst believed intrapsychic and interpersonal changes had taken place. It was left as optional for the respondent to offer a brief example that illustrated this process or any other experience of change that the survey had not captured in more detailed, personal, anecdotal material to supplement the general information asked for in the survey. If they chose to do so, analysts were asked to supply an example illustrating what triggered the recognition of their need to undertake further self-exploration, the method used to conduct this self-inquiry, and the psychological or behavioral change that occurred. Analysts who provided such illustrations offered specific data that supported the general information they had given when they checked items on the questionnaire about their views and actions in relation to their work. The opportunity to describe this process in an extended interview on the telephone provided the possibility for the more usual in-depth explorations of psychological processes.

The survey (Appendix A), then, provides three kinds of data: (1) a series of items that have been checked and, therefore, allow comparisons among analysts in relation to the requested identifying information about gender, age, and institute position; (2) brief written examples that supplement the more general answers and provide data that allow comparisons about the kinds of triggers for self-inquiry, the nature of the process, and the definitions of psychological change among analysts (in addition, the varying degrees of depth and complexity in these illustrations provided a basis for selecting a smaller number of analysts for telephone interviews); and (3) 26 telephone interviews allowing a more intensive examination of the analysts' process in all of the areas described.

In other words, the analysts were asked the most general question first, whether or not they believed that psychological changes occurred for them as a result of their work with their patients. If they considered this an irrelevant or uninteresting question, it was likely, but not inevitable, that they would not bother to fill out and return the survey. Therefore, it was not anticipated that there would be many negative responses to this first question. If they thought they had changed, what sorts of occurrences stimulated these psychic reworkings, and what sorts of changes did they think resulted? In addition, if the analysts believed that they had changed, and if they believed that these changes involved certain regular phenomena, were there particular qualities of experience that the analyst could specify that would indicate that change had occurred?

The survey, then, is used to provide an overall context for the more usual in-depth explorations of psychological processes. Because of the relatively large sample, it has the unique advantage of assuring that very personal data could be published while the analyst's anonymity is retained. It was hoped that under these circumstances analysts would be willing to communicate more openly how they think and work.

THE RESULTS

Of the 1,100 analysts surveyed, 399 returned their questionnaires. A return rate of approximately one-third of the questionnaires meets the average expectation for returns on a survey when there has been a single contact (Schuman, 1995, personal communication). Follow-up reminders are needed to obtain a higher proportion of respondents (Herberlein and Baumgartner, 1978). Follow-up letters could not be used because there was no record of which analysts had and had not responded. For the purpose of the present survey, it seemed more important to retain anonymity for those who desired it than to try to raise the rate of response substantially.

The results of the responses to the survey questions follow (Appendix B presents the percentage of responses based on gender and institute position for each answer on the questionnaire):

1. Belief that their analytic work with patients resulted in their personal change

> Overall, the respondents strongly endorsed the idea that analytic work with patients led to personal changes for themselves.

2. Belief that these personal changes were the result of (a) self-reflective exploration undertaken in relation to their work with patients, (b) some affect or area that resonated and opened or expanded in the context of shared affective experiences with their patients, or (c) some affect or area where differences with their patients' experiences opened or expanded their own awareness or state

> Almost all of the analysts believed that their personal changes were the result of self-reflective exploration in relation to their work with patients. Increased openness and expansion of experiences were also frequently viewed as the result of a shared affective experience with patients. Less frequently, but still to a notable extent, the experience of differences in an affect or area of experience with patients opened and expanded the analysts' experiences.

3. The area of interaction with the patient that triggered this psychological work

> Transference–countertransference recognitions were the most common trigger for personal psychological work emerging from the analytic setting. Recognition of a shared area of difficulty, transference–countertransference enactments, patients' pointing out something about the analyst or shared area of affect, and the impact of attitudes, values, and beliefs that are different from one's own were all cited as other stimuli for self-inquiry.

4. The method the analysts used to deal with an area of difficulty when it came up in their work

> The most common way, by far, for analysts to deal with difficulties that came to their attention was through self-analytic work. The other frequently pursued solution was exploration of personal distress and self-discoveries through discussion with a colleague. This colleague was most often described as also being a close personal friend. Self-reflection during the hour when emotionally charged reactions occurred was also frequently reported. Considerably less frequent, but still notable in number, were consultations in relation to the patient. Personal consultations for the analysts also occurred but were still less

frequent. Seeking personal therapy was an even rarer outcome.

5. The method the analysts used to undertake self-analytic exploration

> Dream analysis was the most frequent way to undertake self-exploration. Again, talking with a colleague who was also a close personal friend was another frequent method. Sometimes the confidant was a spouse who had been analyzed, and/or worked in a related field. Active self-reflection, sometimes intentional but often occurring spontaneously, was another commonly cited technique for self-inquiry. Some analysts described these thoughts as being most easily available when they were engaged in some form of automatic activity, such as walking, gardening, or shaving. A still smaller number of analysts found that intellectual ideas generated from reading were the stimuli for extending self-inquiry. Study groups also stimulated self-exploration. An even smaller number of analysts reported systematically writing down their thoughts and associations.

6. The extent to which the analysts' self-exploration was systematic and frequent

> Most analysts reported that they undertook this kind of personal self-inquiry frequently, especially when they were aware of some difficulty being stirred in the work with a patient. A much smaller number reported doing self-analysis daily. Others undertook self-inquiry only occasionally, but very few analysts stated that self-reflection was rare.

7. The results of self-analysis

> Analysts reported the most frequent outcome of self-exploration was a new understanding. The next most frequent outcome was a change in their work with the patient with whom the difficulty arose. Increased self-acceptance frequently accompanied the new understanding. Decreased experiences of conflict and changes in

other relationships, which included greater freedom of expression and greater comfort, were also reported as frequent outcomes. Other notable changes reported included recovery of memories or previously repressed affects around memories and general changes in manner of working with patients. A relatively small number of analysts sought further personal treatment as a result of their self-analysis.

8. The analysts' awareness of the particular transference–countertransference context or affective experience that stimulated the self-inquiry

The great majority of analysts reported being aware of a particular transference–countertransference context or affective experience that stimulated their self-exploration. Only a relatively small number were unaware of a specific stimulus.

9. The analysts' newly discovering an affect or conflict or rediscovering one that had been previously explored

Analysts reported that the particular stimulus to their self-reflection was most often in an area that had been previously explored in their analysis. Almost 50% of the respondents also cited newly discovered aspects of themselves as a result of material stimulated by work with their patients. Analysts also reported having previously discovered in other nontreatment contexts the same areas raised in work with their patients.

10. The interrelationship between the self-discovery or change in self-experience of the analyst and the patient's psychological conflicts, defenses, life situation, attitudes, values, and beliefs

Self-discoveries or changes in self-experience occurred most frequently in areas where analysts recognized a shared conflict with a patient. Identification or counter-identification with the patient or a central figure in the patient's life was cited as the next most frequent source for analysts' increased self-knowledge; recognition of disavowed aspects of the self and of previously unacknowledged attitudes, values, or beliefs was also commonly reported. Similar life situations provided another major stimulus for self-discovery, leading most notably to new understanding, more self-acceptance, and new perspectives but also, though less frequently, to recovery of affect and recovery of memory. Shared areas of pain by analyst and patient were reported to become less painful through analyzing the patient's painful affects. Both differences between the analyst and patient and the experience of a patient's unfamiliar life situation led many analysts to change some attitudes, values, or beliefs.

WRITTEN CLINICAL EXAMPLES

Of the 399 analysts who responded to the survey, 49% provided an example of interactions with their patients that they believed resulted in their personal change. Approximately 50% of each of the groups—men, women, training analysts, and members—who responded to the survey provided examples. A slightly smaller percentage of the faculty members responding to the survey, 42%, gave clinical examples. Only 53% of the analysts who provided examples described the process they engaged in that facilitated the change and the change that they believed occurred. The remaining 47% of the analysts offered examples illustrative only of recognition of personal issues.

Certain types of situations occurring in the analytic work turned out to be frequently reported stimuli for analysts to embark on self-reflective inquiries. Based on the analysts' responses, four different situations were delineated.

In the first situation analysts became aware of having a shared area of conflict or concern with their patients. Perceptions of similarities regularly led analysts to explore their own parallel issues with reawakened interest. Approximately 30% of analysts described examples of similar conflicts or issues with their patients as stimuli for their self-scrutiny.

The second situation occurred when analysts perceived some admired quality that the analysts wished to have themselves. The patient was seen as having adaptive strengths that the analysts either felt they lacked or believed to be more highly developed in the patient than in themselves. Through participating in the analytic work, the analysts hoped to develop some of this quality in themselves, possibly through a process of identification. Approximately 8% of the analysts described examples of the recognition of an admired quality in their patient that they believed was more developed in the patient than in themselves and that served as a stimulus for their personal work.

The third situation occurred when patients communicated their perceptions of the analyst in the transference. These perceptions led analysts to recognize aspects of themselves that were the triggers for, or hooks on which the patients supported, the patients' views of their analysts. The newly recognized or previously known, but discovered again, aspect of themselves then became a focus for the analysts' self-reflections. Approximately 10% of analysts described patients' communication of their perceptions of them as stimulus for their self-exploration.

In the fourth situation analysts found themselves caught in transference–countertransference reactions with their patients. The transference–countertransference experience stirred affects, memories, and new discoveries, which analysts pursued in their self-exploratory work. By far the largest number of examples given as a trigger for personal exploration was in the category of transference–countertransference recognitions. Sixty-one percent[3] of analysts who offered examples provided illustrations of affective awareness of a transference–countertransference conflict.

These transference–countertransference situations were identified in two different forms. In one situation, 56% of these analysts were aware of conflicted affects stirred in themselves in reaction to their patients' characters, conflicts, behaviors, or transferences to them. In the other situation, the analysts became aware that such reactions had been stirred in them only by their uncharacteristic behavior with the patient. This latter situation was considered an enactment by analysts. Five percent of analysts found their own enactments of transference–countertransference reactions in the analytic situation were the trigger for self-reflection. Overall, very few analysts described using enactments as the source for their personal work.

Both forms of transference–countertransference situations led analysts to be aware of some conflict or disowned aspect of themselves that then became the focus of their self-scrutiny. These situations are more fully described later when I elaborate on the triggers for the analysts' self-exploration (Chapter 3) and how the analysts think about their changes in relation to their work with their patients (Chapters 5–8).

In the clinical examples, sometimes the analysts described revisiting an area previously known and worked on that was now reopened and

---

[3] Analysts often provided more than one illustration; therefore, the percentages for each category when added together exceed 100%.

worked through to a different level; sometimes a previously explored difficulty was recognized again as a conflict area—for example, "Oh, that again"—and the recognition permitted the analysts to be freed from its grip; sometimes there was a newly discovered affect associated with a previously known conflict; and sometimes there was a newly discovered conflict or issue. Some analysts described only a recognition of conflict or distress. Other analysts described a recognition and reworking of an experience of affect or an understanding that deepened. Another group of analysts described a recognition, a description of process, and a change that occurred following the occurrence of one of these triggers in their work with a patient.

Psychological change for analysts, if it was described, was reported to occur in relation to work with patients, in relation to the analyst's personal development, and, for some analysts, in relation to both work with patients and their own personal development.

In addition to these specific anecdotal accounts, 3% of the analysts offered general experiences with patients rather than specific instances as stimulus for change. Ten percent of the analysts described other factors and life experiences that led to psychological changes for them and in their way of working with patients. Examples of the effect of other life experiences were not requested in the questionnaire. I can only assume that these analysts believed it was worth my having on record that they found that the vicissitudes of life, rather than particular patients and their interactions with them, were the vehicle for their psychological changes.

Twenty-three percent of the analysts offered their names and volunteered to be interviewed in greater depth around the examples they offered. The analysts selected for the 26 telephone interviews were chosen on the basis of clinical examples describing phenomena that suggested they believed they had undergone some form of psychological shift as a result of the situation(s) they reported.

OVERVIEW AND IMPLICATIONS

It is necessary to consider to what extent generalization can be made from these findings to those analysts who did not respond to the survey. Among those who did respond, it seems reasonable to assume that they were interested in this topic and believed the questions being posed had relevance for their work and value for psychoanalysis as a field. A few analysts expressed written enthusiasm that this investigation was being undertaken. As stated earlier in this chapter, it seems likely that the analysts who responded to the survey viewed psycho-analysis as an interactional process and shared a belief that a potential outcome of analytic work with patients can be a positive psychological change for the analyst. Not all changes, of course, are in a positive direction. Change, by definition, is bidirectional. There was a striking absence of reports of the negative psychological impact from work with patients. Analysts who have experienced negative psychological changes may have been less likely to respond to this survey. While not responding to the survey cannot be taken as an indication that the non-respondents had negative experiences or disagreed with the point of view espoused by most who responded, neither can we assume that they would necessarily agree. Some respondents may have been merely conscientious and replied because they were asked. In other words, we cannot generalize the findings to conclude that most analysts believe they are personally changed by their work, even if most of the analysts who returned the survey state that this represents their belief. What we can conclude, however, is that a large percentage of analysts believe that their work with patients changes them and see a value in relating their personal experiences. To the best of my knowledge, data confirming that a large number of analysts believe they are personally changed by their work with patients have not been available previously.

Based on the responses of those analysts who participated in this survey, we can conclude that gender, institute position, and the number of years since graduation do not meaningfully discriminate among this group in terms of their views about how treating patients can lead to the analysts' personal change. Age alone meaningfully differentiated among the respondents, and only on three items. Younger analysts were more likely to discuss their self-discoveries with colleagues, more likely to seek consultations for themselves, and more likely to find their self-discoveries in areas that had been explored previously, most often in analysis (Appendix C).

Discussing self-discoveries with colleagues and seeking consultation for oneself, while they may reflect a need to find external support due to relative inexperience, may also indicate that younger analysts tend to be more open about themselves. The climate in psychoanalytic education has changed radically in the last 15 years. Although, previously, analysts might have been more reluctant to acknowledge areas of difficulty that remained following their training analyses, currently, it is more accepted that learning about oneself is a continuing and lifelong process.

Training analyses, like analyses in general, have also changed over the years. While there were certainly exceptions, analysts formerly emphasized oedipal over preoedipal conflicts and analyses of defense over recognition of adaptive strategies. Undoubtedly, current analyses are also neglecting or overemphasizing some particular aspect of conflict or affect state; it is always difficult to assess the particular tilt of theory and technique when we are engaged in the process. We stand too close to see with perspective. Analysts in their informal discussions, however, seem to agree that, currently, analyses tend to be more comprehensive than they were 20 years ago. Analysts in anecdotal reports often state that the analyses they undertake with their patients cover narcissistic and other preoedipal issues that they believe were underemphasized in their own analysis. While the average length of analyses varies in different parts of the United States, in most areas, analyses in the 1980s and 1990s tend to be somewhat longer than in earlier times. Therefore, it would not be surprising if analysts who had the benefit of these broader and longer analyses found that what they were experiencing as triggers for the need for further self-exploration occurred in areas with which they were already familiar.

One striking finding is that, although at the beginning of the questionnaire the vast majority of analysts stated that they believed that personal change had resulted for them from doing analytic work, many of the analysts, though not the majority, who offered examples to illustrate this point did not describe personal changes. They described a *recognition* of countertransference, of affects stirred and conflict mobilized, but they did not actually describe, and often did not even refer to, how they used these recognitions for personal work or whether, or to what extent, personal change resulted from this work. This was the case despite the fact that they themselves had checked items that indicated they believed that psychological changes had occurred for them, often in both intrapsychic and interpersonal spheres and in both professional and personal areas. The survey did specify that the example offered should include an illustration of the personal psychological change. It is possible that this request should have been highlighted more, since almost half the number of analysts who offered illustrations in response to this request did not include descriptions of psychological change as part of their examples. The failure to include data supporting their change does not, of course, mean that it did not occur, but neither can we assume that it did. It may be that, despite their belief in their personal change, these analysts were unable to find specific examples to illustrate that this had occurred.

Recognition of reactions is a necessary first step to reflection, working through, and change. Such recognition may be sufficient for analysts to get back on track with their patients and become alert to what has interfered or might potentially interfere with the patient's analytic work, but it is not the same thing as using this recognition to open up a process of self-exploration or using it as a stimulus leading to a personal change.

From the data, it appears that most analysts answering this survey do see themselves as actively engaging in self-inquiry, at least some of the time, and believe that psychological changes have come about for them as a result of this work. Some also describe their belief that psychological changes come about as a result of their work with patients without their undertaking any active efforts at self-understanding. Why, then, do so many of these analysts not describe their personal change if they, in fact, believe it occurs and are willing to offer examples?

There are several possibilities. Perhaps, as Kramer (1959) and Eifermann (1987b) suggest, the reports of self-inquiry and psychological change are self-deluding and reflect only partial recognitions that may be substituting for fuller recognition of the depth of conflict and pain. Perhaps the failure to offer detailed examples of personal change reflects a continuing reluctance and self-consciousness about fuller exposure even when anonymity is assured. Perhaps, just as some analysts believe they have changed as a result of their work without any articulated process of self-exploration, many analysts believe that they have changed in small and subtle ways that are also difficult to articulate. The ways in which analysts have changed may be difficult to detect by an outside observer, but, nonetheless, these psychological changes may have a profound impact on the analysts' self-experience.

The finding that many analysts state that they changed but do not illustrate it applies to the analysts' written examples; it was not characteristic of the material from those analysts who were interviewed. The analysts, however, who were selected to be interviewed were chosen precisely because their written examples either indicated or suggested that they were aware of, and could describe, psychological changes in themselves. These two groups of analysts cannot be differentiated from each other or from the overall group of respondents based on any of their demographic data. We would need considerably more detailed and personal information about the respondents in order to determine the differences between those analysts who report and describe personal and professional change and those analysts who report they have changed but describe only a recognition of a reaction to the patient.

This overview of the attitudes and experiences of these 399 analysts is offered as a background for a more in-depth reflection on the vignettes and case illustrations provided by a smaller number in this sample and presented in the following chapters.

PART II

Ways of Knowing

CHAPTER 2

Forms of Self-Exploration
Different Analysts, Different Modes of Exploration

In general, the interviews with the analysts provided the most in-depth material for this project. In these more elaborated, personal communications it became possible to appreciate how patients affected their analysts. In this chapter, I offer illustrations of four different ways analysts describe and think about their self-discoveries. These examples are provided to convey differences in style and approach. The first analyst describes a gradual increase in self-awareness that accrues over time and is not related to any specific patient. The second analyst describes experiential transformations that emerge primarily from interactions with patients. The third example illustrates an analyst's using the work with several patients for first discovering and then exploring different aspects of a personal issue. The fourth analyst describes work with patients that leads to a gradual increase of his awareness around a defended area and culminates in a breakthrough of an unconscious impulse in the context of a countertransference response. The specific contents and psychological changes in the analyst are not the focus of this chapter. Illustrations that elaborate the analysts' understanding and changes are provided in the second half of the book.

The four interviews presented in this chapter are more detailed and more fully elaborated than most others in this study. They were selected because these analysts' observations most clearly illustrated the process of their work and had a fluency of presentation that did not occur to the same extent in most of the other interviews.

Before presenting these illustrations, I wish to place the interviews in the context of the interviewing process and describe how it was undertaken and the nature of the material that evolved.

THE INTERVIEWS

At the end of the written survey, the analysts were asked if they would be willing to provide more detailed information or examples and if they would be willing to be interviewed. Twenty-six analysts out of the 92 analysts who volunteered to be interviewed were selected for in-depth interviews. Analysts whose written examples clearly conveyed their understanding of how they used the patient interaction as a trigger for their self-exploration and seemed aware of how this led to their personal change were selected. The aim was to have an equal number of men and women (though this turned out not to be possible, due to the smaller number of women respondents, the number does reflect the percentage of women eligible) and reasonable representation of both age and institute positions. The depth and relevance of process presented in the written vignettes were, however, the central factors determining the choice of participants.

The telephone interviews, conducted in an open-ended manner, took 30–60 minutes, depending on the analyst's material and wish to elaborate. These interviews were tape-recorded,[1] and written notes were also taken during the interview. In addition to offering an account of their personal example, analysts were asked whether they shared their process or findings from their exploration with anyone. They were asked why they chose to share or not share the process or discoveries. If they did communicate their reflections to others, how did they think this affected what they learned?

The analysts were informed that these illustrations would be written in a manner that assured confidentiality and would be shown to each of the participants for their permission before any public presentation. As much as possible, each analyst's tone, terms, theories, and ways of recognizing a difficulty, describing what has been understood, and docu-

---

[1] One analyst requested not to be taped. In this instance the material presented in the book relies exclusively on the notes taken during the interview.

menting the resulting personal change are conveyed in the words of that particular analyst.[2]

Of the twenty-six analysts interviewed, eighteen were male, and eight were female. Of these analysts, fourteen of the men and five of the women were training and supervising analysts; the analysts' ages had the following spread: five in their 40s, ten in their 50s, five in their 60s, and six in their 70s.

The initial part of the interview had a relatively standard form. I explained what I wished the analysts to describe, left it to them to do so in their own particular style, and asked questions only when some area was omitted. Once the basic material had been presented, however, what transpired between us had great diversity. Depending on the particular analyst's responsivity and interest, I sometimes probed more deeply. On most occasions, my responses remained primarily exploratory and empathic. Sometimes, though, I offered parallel examples from my own work with patients as a natural outgrowth of the dialogue that had evolved between the analyst and myself.

The analysts were all extremely generous with their time, and many were generous in their willingness to be forthcoming about themselves. As would be expected, the depth, range, and openness of the material they offered had considerable variety. Some analysts presented the specific example they had in mind and did not seem to want to engage in a dialogue about it. They had already considered the impact of the incident or the work with a particular patient on themselves and were intent merely on providing data for the survey. These analysts described themselves as less often discussing their self-reflections with others; therefore, it is not surprising that they were less likely to use the occasion of the interview to enter more openly into further exploration about themselves.

In contrast, other analysts used the interview to continue their self-exploratory process. They described the material they had planned to present but then continued to think out loud in the manner of free association. Again the depth, range, and openness of this process varied. During the course of the interview, some analysts expressed their excitement about the process that was occurring in the course of the dialogue. A number of analysts found themselves stimulated by the interview to further personal reflection after it.

After I wrote up the interviews and my reflections about what the analysts had described, I sent each analyst a copy of what I had written.

---

[2] Some of the taped recordings were considerably less audible than others and required a greater reliance on my written notes. As a consequence, these interviews have less detail and fluency and more filling in by me to create clarity.

I wanted to be sure that I had understood and represented them accurately. I also wanted to offer them the opportunity to add any further thoughts or reactions they might have had. Two analysts corrected my misunderstanding of aspects of what they had said. The rest of the analysts stated that they believed I had accurately represented their thoughts and reactions. Some analysts used this second contact to convey what had transpired for them following the interview.

A number of analysts found that the interview had opened them to new ideas about the nature of what had occurred between them and their patients. Sometimes the analysts wrote their thoughts in letter form. Other analysts called me. These conversations were not recorded because they had not been a part of the project I had anticipated when designing the study. I took notes on some, but not all, of these second conversations. These analysts who initiated a second contact beyond endorsing or correcting what I had sent described either a deepening awareness of some facet of themselves that emerged after the initial contact or a wish to communicate some information they felt to be somewhat more private and personal than they had initially revealed. Some analysts specified, and on other occasions I understood, that these revelations were for "my ears only" and were not to be included in the book despite the anonymity. As a consequence, I include this information to describe fully the nature of what occurred between the analysts and me, as well as to foreshadow what is described in the chapter on self-analysis, but the actual details of these communications are not reported.

The evolution of the increased intimacy in communication raises the question of the extent to which a transference may develop in the course of these interviews. This construction is, of course, one way of thinking of the analysts' increased willingness to explore and expose themselves in the course of their dialogue with me. I note, however, that the analysts who were most self-revealing were ones with whom I had responded with more personal self-revelations of my own about self-discoveries from my work with patients. We assume that transference is most likely to flourish in the absence of actual information about the other person; if what occurred between us is to be viewed as a transference phenomenon, then we would need to reconsider this assumption. If this phenomenon of increased openness and sense of connection is considered a transference, it is a transference in its nonobjectionable form (Stein, 1981), not regressive in nature. The experiences that the analysts described were often regressive, but the manner in which they observed themselves employed their adult ego functions, their best analytic selves. The motives that propelled the analysts to volunteer for these interviews and the process may be viewed as containing this nonobjectionable aspect of transference. They reflect the sublimated passions that can be brought to work and mutual engagement in adult, intellectual-affective relationships.

It can be assumed that the analysts who volunteered to be interviewed are more likely to be open about themselves than most. They have a relative comfort with self-disclosure, or they would not have offered to participate. They have all, obviously, been analyzed and in some form continue their self-exploration. As described later in the chapter on self-analysis, most, though not all, share their thoughts about themselves with one or two other people whom they trust. For most analysts, these confidants are analyst/friend/colleagues, and the confidences are reciprocal. In nontreatment situations, mutuality is more likely to bring trust. Analysts, like all people, vary in the extent to which they are private or public people and the extent to which openness can be experienced as an enhancing or shaming occurrence. A respected colleague listening to personal reflections can, and for many of these analysts does, provide an opportunity to hear aloud one's own reactions and to become more objective and reflective about them. Reciprocity increases the sense of safety and decreases the likelihood for further regression. It is not to be assumed that this mutual self-disclosure is automatic or occurs in most instances. Whether or not I reciprocated likely had to do with the particular compatibility I felt in response to each analyst. Even in such a select group, it not likely that one would respond with equal openness to everyone.

My experience in conducting these interviews was one of enormous respect for these colleagues. I knew approximately one-third of the group before the interviews. For the most part, I did not know them well. Only one of these analysts is a close personal friend. When I completed the interviews, I felt I had found colleagues around the country to whom I would comfortably refer patients should the occasion arise.

In the following examples, I illustrate a few characteristic approaches to self-exploration stimulated by work with patients.

Analyst 1: Example of Gradual Increase in Self-Awareness not Focused on a Particular Case

The analyst describes that in the early years in his practice he felt

uncomfortable, uneasy, reluctant to work with patients, with men with strong homosexual conflicts. Over the years it improved. I first became aware of this issue or problem of mine in that I seemed to have a lot more success in analyzing women in general. I did have many more men who would interrupt or quit their analysis than women. As I thought more about this problem, I realized I was much tougher with men as an analyst than I was with women. I was perhaps more confronting and confronting of their resistance. I was more tolerant of women and more patient. In my toughness with the men, I was being tough and expecting them to be tough. Being tough meant being intolerant of their passive longings—the whole category of passive longings, needs and wishes, of homosexual longings, longings to be protected and taken care of, or longings to be loved as a woman. I realized gradually that whole sphere of difficulty in my work. Gradually really meant over a period of years. At the same time as these years were going by, I was working with more overtly homosexual men. As I worked with them, I learned to tolerate their intense and overt homosexual transferences and longings; it helped me to work with my not overt homosexual men, my neurotic men patients where these issues and longings were not overt, but hidden and unconscious and resisted against. It was easier to confront these issues and work with them with overt homosexual men because they were overt homosexuals, and it was on the table, not hidden and often not even a matter of such resistance. Mainly, I felt less identification with these men, and it was less threatening to me than with neurotic patients, where it was subliminal, disguised, and defended against. I identified with these men more, and I tended to encourage them to be tough and to hide and defend against those issues. Over the years I became aware of these issues through my failures and difficulties with patients. It prodded me to think about, to work on, to be aware of these feelings and issues in myself that I did not work on enough in my analysis.

For me the self-analysis was not as dramatic as some reports in the literature, papers about analyzing their dreams or some countertransference reaction and realizing and remembering some hidden piece of their history, some great epiphany. It wasn't that kind of thing at all. It was slow, gradual, years of being aware of it, and being aware of it again and again—aware of feelings and momentary issues and experiences in myself and probably piecing it together, remembering and rerembering aspects of my own life, a kind of slow meandering river; nothing that would be so exciting. No great new connections, no new piece of analysis. More revisiting in a deeper and more open kind of way. Examining aspects of myself that I just skidded over in my analysis. It's gotten a lot better, but it's stuff I'm still aware of.

Where I'm aware of it most recently is I've noticed a tendency to interpret too quickly a male analysand's expression of homosexual longings for me as defensive against something else. To show them that it was a shift way from heterosexual anxiety, from aggressive anxiety, or something like that. I realized that in this way I was subtly communicating that these issues stand for something else and not something I want to stay with too long or let develop too intensely or reach full-blown power. I want to deflect it as a reflection of something else. It's not quite the same way. It's a more subtle way or more analytic way, but it is still subtly communicating to the patients that it is an issue I would prefer to avoid. It's not the old, Let's be tough and deal with this. It's more subtle in the service of making a defense interpretation. Really communicating an avoidance. That's the gist of it.

In terms of psychological change, I'm less defensive about macho issues. A zillion different things. Some conflict with my wife could be experienced as threatening to my manhood that stands on this issue. I'm more able to be closer to men. Less fending off closeness, feelings of being too soft or not quite right between real men. It's subtle; it's not so dramatic that people would note this difference in me. I, to some extent, note it in myself. Changes in my analytic work as a result of my self-examination also result in changes in myself. They also translate into changes in my outer life, but the manifestations of that are subtle. It's not like I had no male friends before, and now I have these very close male friends with whom I talk about all this feely stuff. It's a matter of degree. Less of a difference with my original family.

In work, the difference is that, say in this past week, I pointed out to the patient that he experienced my interpreting his homosexual feelings toward me as a defense against something else, as a colluding with him—that he and I would collude against going further with that. I was able to catch myself and realize the experience of that way of interpreting it. So I was both interpreting his defense and mine in our mutual collusion. I can't give a dramatic Hollywood version of it.

[In placing these realizations and changes in a historical context], sometimes I remember specific things, sometimes a general gestalt, experiences in the family, and sometimes with a living family member I will see things more clearly in the kinds of interactions that occur in the present. I was aware of this in my analysis. It's not new; it's a matter of depth. It's how I dealt with it earlier on as an analyst. I didn't deal with it in depth as an analyst because I didn't deal with it in depth in my analysis. I never raised the issues of colluding like this with my analyst because I wasn't aware of it. I'm not sure about this. It may be projecting my own resistance onto him. I did feel he had difficulty tolerating or at least communicating about passive issues. So it made it easier for me to avoid these issues in my own analysis. My analyst communicated difficulties in tolerating passivity in men mostly by not picking up mine, by ignoring my issue in this area—either by not addressing my resistance about pursuing it further or not expressing much interest in it. It allowed me to avoid it. I experienced it as his communicating, what seems to me now, his own difficulty with this area by just not showing much interest in it as an object of resistance or an object of analysis.

Self-analysis is very hard to do. One of the things about being in analysis is you have an analyst to nag you—to nudge, to get past the obstacles and face the difficulties. On your own there isn't a lot of incentive to do that. The incentive for self-analysis, the pushing, comes in a sense from your work, yourself in analysis. You realize you are going to meet up with obstacles and resistances to the work that are brought to your attention by impasses and difficulties that you come across. Patients in their own way help you to become aware of these issues. In self-analysis it has to come from the inside, and that's harder. It's a problem speaking in generalities, [but] to go into specifics, you'd have to know the whole kit and caboodle of my history. I could go into my own history and family situation in detail. [It] may make that easier to understand if you know that, but I don't know if that's necessary.

[Do you share this kind of material with others?] I have a study group I'm quite comfortable with and share things with and with my wife. I learn a lot from my patients who point out my resistances by correcting and criticizing my work.

This analyst has described a process of self-reflective work that took place over a long period of time and resulted in subtle and gradual changes. His interview does not focus on any particular incident or work with any particular patient. Rather, it conveys an awareness of his defenses against the recognition of bisexual concerns and the accompanying anxiety. His avoidance of these issues decreased the likelihood of his working successfully with certain male patients until he better understood the nature of interference coming from himself. He describes the subtle manifestation of the difficulty in his work, the repeated experience of encountering his defense against working on the issue in others, and, over time, the increasing recognition of this avoidance as a defense against working on this issue in himself. The recognition of his defense and what is defended against gradually allows him to confront the issue more fully. He does not describe how he then works on it or the specific nature of what he came to understand, though he suggests that he is aware of this, but it seems too long and complicated to relate. Or perhaps he would rather not. He states that he has shared some of this with his peer group and his wife. The process he describes in the interview is primarily private and self-reflective. He seems to think of it as learning something about himself from what happens with the patient. The assimilation seems to occur primarily preconsciously and apart from the context of specific patients. He believes he has told me as much as I need for the purpose of the study, and he has.

Analyst 2: Example of Encountering a Known Difficulty, Similar to a Patient's Difficulty, with Working Through Occurring in the Analytic Process with the Patient

The analyst illustrates how she immerses herself in the immediacy of her experience with her patients:

> Gradually, as I listen to a patient, I begin to recognize something—a theme we have in common—and I start a process toward considering the ways in which I'm like and different from my patient. I imagine myself in my patient's situation. Then I have to decide on something to respond. I try it out. I don't know if what I'm doing is the best thing or not. Then I say it, and something happens between us. I listen and think about it then, and then as I go about my ordinary life I'll not infrequently review my reaction.
>
> For example, last week one of my patients was angry and gave the impression that she was critical of herself. I interpreted to her that she was being self-critical. She reminded me that when I point out her self-criticism, she feels diminished. Now I have a similar problem with self-criticism. When my analyst interprets it to me, as I have done to her, I find it helpful. Now when you have the experience that something has helped, I think it is an auto-

matic reaction to do the same thing with your patient when it comes up. But she didn't find it helpful, so I had to think about what she was saying. I said to myself she needed to feel hurt and angry and to turn on herself. I acknowledged that she had told me before that I had to let her berate herself, and I had to just listen and let her do it, be critical of herself. She continued her self-hatred throughout the rest of the session, and I had to restrain myself, allowing her to suffer. It was a painful stretch for me because I knew how she felt and have felt very similarly, in a very painful way. Then the next day, she began talking about a patient of hers who brought up self-hating and self-criticism and how difficult she found it. I pointed out to her the dilemma of her suffering and her need to hold on to it and how at the same time it made her feel inadequate or self-destructive, though she got some comfort from it. But I felt I didn't know where it took us. I told her I thought her ability to understand it made it more complex. She said she wished she could see herself through my eyes. Later I thought about the process. My patient found it gratifying; suffering was being tied to someone through pain. That is something that is prominent in my repertoire. So to feel it in relation to my patient—I want to move in and protect my patients from their own suffering. This is confusing to try to conceptualize. It's a much more subtle process than we think, not so easy to locate in time or place or even in a particular part of my own psyche. In my interactions with patients, where I feel stirred, it moves into a territory of a quietly active process, as I did here; it occurs again and again around the same theme.

I had the worst experience years before with another person, a woman who suffered enormously and reproduced that suffering with me. It was very painful for both of us. Although she started off with an idealizing transference, she quickly felt I was torturing her by expecting her to reach into herself and experience something unbearable. She felt a terrible pressure, yet I didn't feel that I was pressuring her. I worked and worked with her. She stopped after a long time. There were gains in her life, but there was an unrelenting melancholy in reaction to her self and to the analysis. In retrospect, I'd offer her antidepression medicine. I guess that testifies to how I still feel a failure in relation to her and her suffering. I have the fantasy of finding her and suggesting that. I agonized over that case.

I feel sure this case will go better. I am more competent now. It's ten years later. My capacity to tolerate negative affect has increased. It's partly practice. I've seen more patients, sat with it more myself. But it's also partly an increase in conscious effort to follow my patients to painful places. Partly I do it because I'm bound by pain but also because I don't have to get stuck in it. I'm so eager for the experience of mastering, of having the experience with my patients. So I really work at it. Whenever I feel pulled back, I try to move where the patient was, especially if it felt threatening. I ease my way through the struggle. I see all these interactions as something constructed in the moment between two people. I never think of it as resolving conflict, just as inter-actional patterns that become less compelling and less toxic . . . and adding other less toxic patterns and more fulfilling ones. Over time I feel more distance from my pain.

With the patient I used to treat I noticed a pattern. She'd come close, and I'd be following her, and then suddenly she'd feel attacked, that I hurt her. She felt me as a destructive force that cre-ated a distressing disequilibrium for her. I had . . . I have my own vulnerability in [affect] state regulation. My capacity has increased partly through my work with patients, partly through my own self-analysis . . . through doing the work, staying with it, with them. I feel an excitement in recognizing the challenge, like going on a roller-coaster ride—scary but fun. I recognize myself as not only high-strung but also thrown off balance. In the context of my work with patients and in other areas of my life, too, it's not only a vulnerability. It allows me to engage in an intense and interesting way. After the hour with the patient, I felt as if I'd been through something . . . not alone, we'd done some-thing together that then became part of our history. It becomes something I enjoy, we enjoy, even though it had been about pain and was painful. Something becomes different because we went through part of a process together. I came with an assumption [that identifying and addressing the patient's self-criticism would be helpful to her], that derived from a context of my own experi-ence that having my own self-criticism identified and addressed by my analyst had been helpful to me, and I just came out with it. Then it didn't work. The something came apart, and I had to scrounge around to discover a new notion. I have to find a new way. When you and the patient have to confront this together, it's a different experience than, say, when a supervisor says, "You should stay with the pain." I'm aware of pain all over the place, in my whole life, in my personal relationships, in my work—some-times much more subtle, but I'm always aware of it. The dilemma is inescapable in dyadic relationships. The issue is who is going to be helped. This woman is characterologically like me. She's ultra-responsible, quite repressed. A focus on pain is central in our work because she and I make it so. She and I recognize how we are alike.

With other patients where I'm not so like them I can feel similar experiences of being together and things happening to both of us. I can always find a part of myself in a patient, but in a different way. The more I know a patient, the more I recognize the ways we are alike, even if on the surface we are totally different. We establish points of communality. One of my patients now knows that I'll react differently from the way he reacts both in general and specifically, that I'll react differently to him than he reacts to himself, and that is useful to both of us but in a different way [compared with working with patients who are more similar to us]. Each time I've been through it, I'm a little different.

I used to share a lot more of this with my peer group. I still do some, but now a lot more of it seems to be worked out in relation to the patient directly. I used to think more about genetic origins of these things, but now I think of it more as a part of me that I'm not in control of. It becomes something I can recognize and use now. I've handled it so many times before.

This analyst views herself and her work in an interactional context. Self and other are discovered through shared themes. The subtle transformations potentially evolve from a mutuality of engagement. The analyst had made an assumption about a similarity between her patient and herself. She had substantial data to support that they shared a struggle with painful affect. It was, however, in the context of confronting the way in which she and her patient were different with respect to the function of pain in a dyadic interaction that the analyst had to stretch her own capacities. In finding that her identification with her own analyst's way of promoting her increased tolerance for, and perspective on, painful affect did not help her patient, she had to discover some new way to increase her own repertoire in dealing with pain. The similarity between herself and her patient created an intimacy and resonance, whereas the difference between them facilitated both the development of a new mode of interaction and a new perspective on the pain.

While this analyst is clear that she makes use of her peers, her analyst, and her own self-reflective process, her emphasis is on the discovery and working through that occur directly in the interactions with the patient. She stresses its subtle quality. The transformations that come to pass are less related to specific conflicts than to shifts in interactive patterns that become less painful and more fulfilling over time. The analyst also describes a conscious change of attitude toward herself. While insight and cognitive understanding may be part of what facilitated these changes, they are not the factors that the analyst describes in this interview. Rather, she has conveyed how the work with her patients, accompanied by other life, analytic, and self-analytic experiences, has helped her to tolerate and modulate her own painful affect. Her increased sense of competence and mastery permits greater emotional risks in her interactions and further stretches her emotional and interactional capacities. Much of the assimilation that occurs seems to take place preconsciously, but, in this analyst's view, it occurs primarily in the interactional context.

Analyst 3: An Example of Self-Discovery Triggered by a Countertransference Enactment with One Patient but then Explored in Relation to Partial Identifications with Several Other Patients

The analyst begins her process of reflection by focusing on a specific patient:

> A number of years ago I terminated with a woman whom I had seen once a week for many years. I had thought she would benefit from analysis, but she had always resisted this idea. We both understood that her need to remain in control made this prospect too frightening, and so we worked with the degree of intensity she felt she could tolerate. She is an only child, a lesbian, and had sought treatment because of her inability to sustain an emotionally and sexually intimate relationship with a woman. Until sometime in latency, she shared a bedroom with her parents. She maintained that her parents were not intimate with each other in any way. I'm not going to describe the patient's history or our work except in relation to my personal discovery.
>
> Fairly far along in her treatment, the patient came across a series of photographs that her father had taken of her parents in bed. He had set the camera up with a time delay and then captured pictures of them coquettishly lying together with sheet pulled up to their chins. She'd been amazed, since it challenged her construction that they were asexual. While she was telling me about this, my eyes closed. My patient was upset, humiliated, . . . feeling she had put me to sleep, that she was boring—

a chronic concern about herself. I wasn't asleep or bored, but I had had no control over my eyes closing. I empathized with her distress and said something was going on between us that I didn't yet understand.

Following this incident, the patient had a memory of being in the bedroom with her parents with her head buried under the covers and her eyes closed. This was not something she had ever recalled before. Was closing my eyes a projective identification where I enacted her role in the primal scene, a shutting of eyes— as denial and then repression of the parents' sexuality? With the recovery of this memory and other work around her feelings about her mother portraying herself as a "have-not," but really having, the patient became freed up to "have" more herself and begin a relationship with a woman. She now lives with this woman. . . . Several other times this material came up . . . and I similarly involuntarily closed my eyes, but the work with my patient and myself around this did not go further. I am embarrassed to say that, while it occurred to me that there was something going on for me, after brief attempts at self-analysis that went nowhere, I let it go and settled for thinking of it only in terms of the patient.

Some years later the patient returned. Her relationship with her partner was satisfying in many ways but not as passionate as she wished. One day she began an hour by saying that she really had nothing to talk about, and I had a fleeting thought about my closing my eyes. She went on to say that her lover often complained that she felt the patient did not want to engage with her, which she acknowledged often was true, though ironic, since it is her lover's distance that she minded. She noted that she was having the thought that I was going to fall asleep. She then told me that she not only felt she was understanding more, but that I was giving her a lot . . . which was a surprise to her, since she had been certain if she made known what satisfied her, I would withhold it. She thought she was becoming less hard on herself, and she then related a satisfying sexual experience with her lover, and I involuntarily closed my eyes! She asked if she'd lost me; I admitted this had happened and apologized for the lapse but asked if we could try to understand what had happened between us. I was struck that both of us had anticipated this happening, and still I could not control my reaction. I'm not going to describe my work with her around this except to say it was very illuminating and fruitful for her.

This time I could not let this go in terms of the part that was mine. I had lots of intellectual theories about something sexual I had repressed, such as being discovered masturbating or having seen my housekeeper, who slept in my room, having sex with her boyfriend. I tried my usual ways to analyze what was going on, but I was really blocked.

I knew I needed to talk with someone to get a perspective on this. So I talked to a friend who is an analyst, who thought of Freud's Wolf Man case and the closing of the eyes. I first thought, "Oh, I'll reread that!" and next wondered if I ever had read it before. As I began reading it, I still wasn't sure until I came to the only line I had underlined in the entire paper—the one that said that this material indicated that what the patient was experiencing was based on a real experience and not a fantasy. Then I came to Freud's describing that the patient had slept in the parents' bedroom at one and a half when he had malaria. And then I had the image of myself in my mother's bed (my parents had twin beds) at age five when I had a serious illness. This was not a new memory, but I hadn't thought of it while I was associating to what I might have seen. I know I slept in their room for two months while I was running a high fever. Having found what I thought was a repressed primal scene memory, the difficulties with the patient receded. I didn't recover the memory, but my eyes stayed open with the patient from then on. Our work was very successful for her. . . .

I found myself thinking a lot about a different patient of mine who was much more similar to me than the first patient. She was a therapist, married, with children, and had an active and satisfying social and intellectual life. She had an early childhood memory related to sexuality that had been repressed prior to her analysis. Since her repression lifted, she'd been much more spontaneous. I won't go into all the details but just say that while she enjoyed her sexuality, she was aware that she inhibited a fullness of response. We worked on that a lot, and after a while—not in any very immediate way—it became clear that things were now different for her. She was describing her experiences of passion vividly. I was somewhat envious. It sounded like her experience was surpassing anything I had known. And I had helped her to overcome her inhibition! I began listening very carefully to what she described when she recognized being inhibited, . . . anxieties and fantasies. Later I would think about this and compare them with my own awareness of times of inhibition and my own anxieties and fantasies. My patient's exploration of her bisexuality stimulated me to consider mine in greater depth than during my analysis. I began to put together childhood fantasies and confusions that I had not previously been conscious of.

At the same time, there was another patient I had begun to see, another basically hysterical woman. She had a wonderful time with men sexually but absolutely could not commit herself to a serious relationship with a man. Now her issues with bisexuality were really blatant. Her father had an incapacitating illness when she was around five. Her fantasies and dreams made it clear that she blamed herself for what happened to him. Unconsciously she had constructed that his incapacity was the result of the sexual contact she fantasized between them . . . this sounds like an early Freud case, but that's the way it was. She was already angry with her mother for working and for having and preferring her younger brother. Males were definitely preferred, she felt. So she stepped into her father's shoes—part out of envy and part as a resolution of the loss of him as he was before he became ill. After a while it became clear she feared if she really committed herself to a relationship with a man, she would no longer have what she felt were the privileges of being a man. Then homosexual issues came out in the transference . . . in a much more intense way than I usually encounter with a nonovertly homosexually oriented patient. So with this patient, as I helped her work and deepen her understanding of herself around these issues, I found I was exploring in much greater depth both my homosexual feelings and my identification with, and envy of, men. . . .

It's not that these issues hadn't come up in my analysis, but they had emotional aliveness now that was much more vivid. I began to write down my dreams and analyze them, something I had done for a while after my analysis but then let it go. I also began talking about what I was figuring out about myself to two friends—one a colleague and one who is not an analyst but, analyzed and wise . . . both friends also confide in me so this is a mutual thing. I also talk with my husband about what I am discovering about myself. I listen to my patients work on these issues and then reflect more about parallels and differences between them and me. I talk with my friends some more . . . when I get clearer about some of my fantasies and reactions, that often helps me get clearer about the patients'. I suspect I have a repressed primal scene memory that still is not recovered, but even without it, I feel different in ways that seem palpable. My husband would confirm that. I'm much freer in my feelings and responses. I don't know if it really shows in social situations, since I never felt that inhibited, but in more intimate ways it's definitely true.

This analyst's approach is somewhat more eclectic than that of the previous two analysts. It involves self-reflection, shared communication, and a focus on the interactional context with patients. In the analytic work, similarities and differences between herself and her patients become a focus for self-scrutiny. The analyst has illustrated the interfering effect of repressive process on therapeutic work. Self-reflective work, along with exploration with colleague/friends, enabled her to regain her equilibrium as the therapist, though the actual repressed memory is not restored. There is no indication that the analyst believes she worked on these issues in relation to the first patient and her difficulties, even though the description of the patient's conflicts suggests there is at least some similarity to the analyst's other patients' struggles and the analyst's own inhibitions. For reasons that are not clear, the analyst has experienced her work with the first patient primarily as sharing a similarity of situation, a place for the analyst to discover a repressed memory in which a conflict resided. With the other two patients, the analyst experiences a more conscious resonance and sense of similarity. She does not detail the process as she did in her discovery but more generally conveys how she works, moving back and forth between exploration and discovery in the interaction with her patients and her self-reflection and shared reflections with others outside her work. The work seems active and intense; the process of assimilation seems primarily preconscious.

Analyst 4: Example of a Gradual Increase of Self-Awareness Culminating in a Breakthrough of an Unconscious Impulse in a Transference–Countertransference Context

The analyst provides a panoramic view of his personal and professional experiences that enabled him to reach an affective insight:

> The example is of rage that I discovered in my work with a patient. . . . There's a whole lot left out or I'm not remembering. What I'm describing is a baseline to somewhere else. It has to do with hatred of women. In growing up I was always more empathic and more sympathetic with women than most boys or men were then, that seemed to hold . . . with little in the way of

anger, except for remarkable jealousy with oedipal things, with dating, but there the anger was with the guy—except anger with certain girls who were blind to not see I was better. It didn't come to any angry fantasies [with women], whereas the fantasies were quite available in terms of the guys. So there was really a great deal of defense operating in terms of defense [against anger] with women.

That held through my analysis pretty much. I had an old-fashioned analyst who was hypermasculine, and he really objected to my respectfulness, which was quite genuine on my part, and that included respectfulness with regard to sexuality with women. He really tried to get me to use pornographic words, which I didn't want to . . . and instead of interpreting, he tried to push it. For me, part of it was identification, not just defense, with my father, who had a gentleman's thorough respect for the ladies, and that was part of his honor system. I was identified with that. My father was the primary strength and set the course of ethics and morality for the family. But my mother was quite hysterical, and sexuality was spread everywhere, because she was quite unable to suppress it . . . I didn't like how in that sector she tended to dominate things.

I had a long stretch of working with borderline patients in residency, and there was a borderline who would demand so much, require so much caring, and that caring was extracted with the hostage being herself. That is, she would kill herself if it wasn't good enough. At the same time I did have a great deal of concern and caring—both empathy and sympathy for her. . . . But I found it awfully difficult. At times I got so stretched and angry at her on the phone that I said she just had to stop it. But even there I noticed only somewhat that I got resentful. What I noticed more was that I got terribly concerned that she would kill herself and especially concerned that she would suicide because I had been inadequate or had felt fed up, and that would show—though I don't think it did show. But mostly I was aware of a deep, deep concern that she would be dead.

I shared that kind of experience with an analytic colleague who is a friend. It was our collective experiences that we talked about and recognized together and analyzed together and got progressively closer to how we hated these patients. Then, the hatred became more prominent. I could see it more . . . but it took the form of, "It's just too much. We are being tortured. We wished they were dead. We'd like to kill them." It was helpful to him and me. We found if we could be honest with ourselves and with each other with how angry we were getting, . . . we were much less likely to act on it. So all that was very useful and put me more in touch.

I saw I got much more angry with the women than with the men who were also borderline. A man that I treated also placed a lot of demands on me; there was some difference in style, and I didn't know it at all then until much later, but I just wasn't reacting as much to him. I had a supervisor who was helping me then who asked why I wanted to work with this woman. I found myself saying she reminded me of my mother. He meant that in the caring vein, and I meant it because she was the same in [area of country], same kind of physical build and style of talk as my mother.

The last time she ever threatened suicide was to my daughter on the phone—and that was it. I stopped treating her for two years, had her hospitalized, but then when she came out, she wanted to start with me again, and I was willing. I had done a lot of processing about it. My consultant helped me see that she was trying to manipulate me into wanting her dead so she could suicide—because she couldn't do it by herself and couldn't do it if I wanted her alive. So she really provoked me, said that I never cared, and stormed out saying I wanted her to kill herself. So I interpreted it. She did not acknowledge that it was correct, but she never attempted suicide again. She settled down, and I've seen her over the years. She manages her life.

Now I've had a male patient who has been unable to connect love and sexuality. He's definitely a heterosexual, but his whole excitement is around milder tortures of women, mostly making them out of their mind and to the point where they can't stand how much they want him erotically. Obviously, this is based on an awful lot of hate that he's out of touch with, and that treatment has never gotten very far in spite of consultations and so on. . . .

But I was treating a young woman who was very competent and likable, in a good marriage, but had a horrendous background. I did not know when I started treating her, but in no time at all she was floridly borderline, but more perniciously than any borderline I had ever worked with. She was in intensive treatment with me. She began to cut herself, and at the same time she intensively was requiring my caring about her. There were many calls. She was very sensitive if in any way I was not closely focused on her. . . . All kinds of dynamics and genetics I could interpret. It was on one level an out-and-out reproduction of a transference of her relationship with her mother, who was much to the patient how she was to me. But understanding that didn't do anything. She was determined to . . . to live it out with me. Her requirements escalated to the point . . . but she was also really miserable. She focused on me as the source, even though she had a good marriage. She was absolutely distraught if she did not have me somehow preoccupied with her.

An interesting thing happened while treating her and another patient not so disturbed, but also with a horrendous background, who expressed more directly that she wanted me sexually. The first [borderline] patient wanted me totally in a caring bond, but she also wanted to possess me and to possess me sexually. That was not so much a problem with the healthy person, but with her it was. The second patient in effect was saying that if you are not mine, I will kill myself. And with the two of them together, it was certainly working its way in me. To my surprise I found that while I was having a very nice time with my wife, I would have associations to their misery in that I felt so sad about their being so deprived in their lives. I was also aware that I regretted that I had to spend so much of my emotional energy with these patients at a time when my kids needed me emotionally. I felt very sorry about that. I was more and more aware how the kind of care they needed took what my children needed and that it made me, and others I talked to about this, hate these patients.

The preoccupation with these patients was such that I would start to feel guilty, began to have a form of guilt about having a nice time in my life, and the associations began to interfere with my most romantic life. I thought, This is serious, and I've to get this thing straightened out, because this won't do. There was countertransference obviously, but not only that; there was a response to the actual need of the patient, so it takes some time to become aware of the countertransference part. But it also required a willingness to let a patient die—now that's an amazing thing to say. Luckily, at that, only one of my borderline patients had ever suicided. But I think to treat this kind of patient, you have to be willing to say in advance that there's a limit, that I'll do everything I reasonably can, but that I have my life, and they do not belong in my life. We can be with them only to the extent we can, and if we can't provide enough—quite disturbing when I found their need, . . . my feeling they need so much could disturb my romantic life. Quite disturbing to me until I got all that worked out; I learned that associations to their need could disrupt my own most intimate relationship. That got worked out. Thank God.

Then the worst thing that ever happened to me, that was really shaking. . . . This woman patient I started telling you about started requiring more and more. She played for keeps. It was psychotic without being actually psychotic. It was psychotic in action. The way she was living it out. She was also very sexually, overly personal, out of line in her assumptions. I don't mind patients' having fantasies of me in any way, sexually, aggressively, or so forth, but when it starts to be used as a kind of torture, and there's a mass refusal to use it to understand themselves. . . . at the same time she had demands of me that I couldn't go along with, such as if I were to go away with my wife that she would cut herself seriously—she meant it. I was to stay home; there was no working on it. It was a point that she should have been hospitalized, but she was recalcitrant. She could also be charming and bright. So I was going nuts. There was no way to support her, no way to interpret, no way to offer understanding, and the understandable hate. No way anything could work. My colleagues whom I talked to could offer no help. So it reached a point of such total insistence on possession and such total sexualization that I was going nuts. One day in the midst of all this while I was running, it just came to me . . . I was seized by a . . . completely by an impulse to kill her phallically in intercourse. It really horrified me, especially since it was not a thought or a fantasy or some association that came to me; it was the real thing. It was terrible. Of course, I realized that this was intense countertransference, that something very primitive, very repressed had been shaken loose. I had no idea that I hated to that degree or that I hated in that sexual mode. Well, that was very helpful when I regained my balance. If we can stand it, it's very worthwhile. Very few, if any, patients I've had have been able to get to me at this level. I know much more what it's about than I used to.

I still can get stressed with things like that. But I'm much more open to reverberating with that kind of anger, sexualized anger, but in other places, too. It's been much less, but I notice I can reverberate with male patients who in themselves have been somewhat sadistic and in the transference are sadistic toward me. I've had associations come up that keep me on guard as a signal in the countertransference but not something that takes me over, not a sexualized vengeance like with this woman.

It's the combination of the erotic with destructive hate that, for whatever reason, stirs in me that wish for retaliation. I'm much more able to use that and not be afraid of it. On the whole that area is more accessible. Kernberg says he considers a certain amount of sadomasochistic behavior in the sexual life of couples to be normal, to the point of saying that actually inflicting bodily pain is a normal part of sexual life. Well, I can understand how that can happen and how that can be part of some people's psychology, but it goes so far from, from what I find acceptable, against my ideals in real life. I would not say that that is normality, but that I can accept and understand more how it is something to be dealt with.

I'm much more readily attuned to that component both in myself and toward men and toward women than I was prior to that experience. I'm more understanding of the horror that you can come across. I think of a movie with Michael Caine where he's a serial killer and kills women in intercourse. . . . It showed a little bit of his relationship with his mother, who is seemingly nice but is, in fact, very dominating . . . and he, in fact, hated. I think I understand more and don't have to divert myself. I have more freedom of being in touch with it in myself. . . . Very important is that I married a woman who in every way is not my mother.

I'm much more comfortable with hating my mother and hating her sexually. She was something.

In the aloneness area—that relates too. I'm impressed that one doesn't have to be borderline or have horrific early loss to know aloneness. I learned that through lots of work with patients. None of it came up in my analysis. To a very significant extent parents don't know you. For me beginning around age three and a half or four and into adolescence and adulthood, just not knowing me— my Dad was better at it, but I had to be too good for him—he was a very good guy—I couldn't measure up to be that good. I really acted up in college, and that was needed. I couldn't swear around him and things like that, but at the same time he was glad for me to be myself. He was glad for me to be male.

My mother was a hysteric—and maybe there really does need to be a change in thinking about penis envy as a concept . . . but she needed to be sure that she had more power to attract. She did not really want me to enjoy progress and achievement in all kinds of ways. If she did enjoy it, it was more to show off that she had that kind of children. It was difficult to come to a place of realizing that she mostly needed to use us—now I'm painting a picture of her as more pathological than she was, because this wasn't all there was to her, but this is true.

So that was very much part of my life, and that required me to leave her because there was no way to be known by her. I was always available to support her or love her. At the same time I long since gave up on having a real relationship with her, because it's not possible. I didn't know I'd hate my mother this way. I'd never had the kind of urge or fantasy that I had with that patient; it was hard. I am aware, however, partly because of what I felt with that patient . . . but because of it I gained a kind of peace or acceptance of what I felt and got to know it more.

One time I was visiting at home and trying to talk to my sister and brother-in-law, but whenever we got into anything of our interests, she'd interrupt and draw attention to herself, and it became blatant that there was no room to move anywhere except to her. I suddenly had this feeling and picture, identification with . . . I had the thought, I understand how someone could simply squat and huddle on a back ward and never move from there; otherwise, they could kill their mother. I really knew it. Fortunately, I had a whole lot more perspective with that one than with the woman patient. I realized what I had suppressed and repressed— that I had sexual anger with my mother. So that I never let anyone, any woman, like her get near me in my personal life. . . . I'm not nearly as ready to feel angry and rejecting of a woman like that now. It's pretty much past stuff. It makes sense to me she had to be dominant in terms of sexuality.

Since that patient, it's become more integrated for me. It's one aspect of my having to leave my mother behind; it's not only that she didn't know, but also basically her sexuality was destructive, that men were objects for her. I didn't like her for that. Part of my anger at her is that she wouldn't recognize my gender identity. I know I feel anger about that, but at the same time I now know that in my unconscious I have feelings toward her like what I had toward that patient, but I've got to let myself go too much to really know them. More and more I feel I'm ready to accept how it was. My mother was so destructive of male sexuality. The saving factor was a deep love my parents felt for each other. While she wouldn't ever recognize my various pursuits, she did honor my father's pursuits, that was unmistakable, but not his sexuality. That was just how I described it.

There are about four years where a [colleague/friend] and I met essentially every week. It was mutually very beneficial in clearing up a lot of problems from our analyses and then going further in a very beneficial way. My aloneness fits into this, too. Aloneness was extremely important to me, and I didn't understand why I felt I was so interested in aloneness. I hadn't had the kind of early experiences that borderline patients had, and I knew that. So it was only when I began to understand it in relation to older kinds of experiences that it started to make any sense to me. I found that out as I worked with patients. Then I began to think of it differently—related to later experiences. I had to find my identity by myself, without the help of a parent, and as I was saying before, even in opposition to a parent. I found as I worked with patients who would start to feel very alone and described the conditions of it, I suddenly was put in resonance with it over and over.

That tended to shake loose my unconscious, and, as I told you, I had this tremendous caring with my father. This got disrupted when I was four and a half. I was head over heels in love with, enamored with, my Daddy's work. He worked at a power plant, and, as far as I was concerned, it was Daddy's plant. We lived across-river from it. We'd started to go to it one day, and it blew sky-high. The area we lived in was just raining with machinery. My father disappeared right then. He was a hero. The plant had been shut down. The foreman of the plant had fired up the boiler without purging it first or getting rid of any gas that might have been there. So we had a huge gas explosion that killed people instantly. My father ran to the control pipe house that was on our side of the river that contained the valves for the flow of gas. The valves had these huge stems that are controlled by wheels that control them by turning them. The wheels were locked up. My father, who was very strong . . . he with his bare hands . . . [analyst cries] one thing I get from my mother is I feel a lot . . . he shut them off, he saved the plant from further explosion. But I was absolutely terrified. The whole area of attachment and identification with my father became fear of being like him, when what I really wanted most was to be like him. For a period through childhood—through latency and part of adolescence—I really stayed so far away from so much of what would have been my ideal.

So a gulf was created with my father that left me without what I so much needed in terms of being with my Dad, the identification with my Dad that I so much needed. Fortunately, that got retrieved later, considerably. It left me with a certain kind of aloneness in that regard. That was what I got clear about. That was a sudden and quite complete loss. I didn't know the loss part until postanalysis. I got more in tune with it, reverberating with patients. I had had only an isolated memory of living in that house, of looking out the window as I was supposed to go to sleep, and there was this street lamp of an old-fashioned type. Just looking at that, and there was this strange, alone feeling of being in the dark. It was an isolated experience, but an experience of aloneness. And I didn't get it all together until I realized this as I started to feel the feelings in resonance with patients describing their feelings of aloneness. Then the other, the understanding about what being apart from my father had meant, started to come into focus.

And there was another thing that happened shortly before this. My mother had twins and nearly died. She had been unable to care for me. Her sister took over. She was a wonderful aunt, but nonetheless I couldn't have access to my mother. She had hemorrhaged so badly that she was in bed for ages. And being a hysteric, she loved to talk about it, talk excitedly about almost dying in the hospital, almost dying of a hemorrhage. I remember once saying, "Mama, weren't you frightened?" and she was totally oblivious of my fear and said, "Oh, no it was like angels were carrying me away." So these aloneness things along with my mother abandoning me in terms of my developing identity all amounted to an awareness of aloneness as quite vivid for me but had nothing to do with the early nurturance issues. It was helpful to understand.

I've been impressed that most neurotic patients have some area that has predisposed them to a continued difficulty in either incomplete identifications, gender identifications, or completed working out of oedipal conflicts. There are some roots of it in this earlier stuff. Even in the healthiest person I ever worked with, the fear of becoming an adult was a fear of aloneness, which came in this case from a very narcissistic father, who essentially appropriated his son's life for himself without really appreciating where his son was at. There was caring, but he couldn't let the side of himself that was distressed or troubled be known. So there I could catch on that he had had an important experience of aloneness that he had never had anyone understand. What I saw really most clearly then, when it was so apparent with this really most healthy patient, was that aloneness was something—not just from early issues, but later ones and then I really got how these experiences had affected me and made me sensitive and responsive to these feelings in my patients and had made me so interested in experiences of aloneness.

Analyst 4's description of his work is similar to that of Analyst 3; it involves self-reflection, shared communication, and a focus on the interactional context with patients. Analyst 4 has described a dramatic moment of intense countertransference that released his unconscious feelings. He used this new awareness then to trace the earlier manifestations of this issue. He makes it clear that his analyst recognized the inhibition but that his manner of working with it did not free it. He traces his reactions in his earlier work with other patients and relates how he, over time, became freer in recognizing his feelings of hate, his need to protect himself from being used to a point where it was self-destructive. He makes clear that the moment of facing a frighteningly intense sexualized rage and hatred was paved by this earlier work. Nonetheless, he is staggered by his discovery. Once he has the experience, he is then able to recognize and accept how deeply angry he was with his mother. He is even able to entertain the "idea" of his rage in her presence, though it occurs in a displaced form. The vicissitudes of his discovery are perceived mainly in relation to his work, though he also reports that he no longer had to block out these experiences of sexual violence as they were present in the world. As with analyst 3, a specific countertransference moment forcibly dislodged his repression. These two analysts' examples provide a contrast, in that analyst 3 describes this recognition as a stimulus to understand more and undertake self-reflective work in the area uncovered, whereas analyst 4 presents his recognition as the culmination of earlier work that crystallized in this moment.

Analyst 4 then makes clear that not all discoveries come in such dramatic and powerful form. He traces a slow, gradual increase of understanding that came from pursuing his awareness of heightened interest in experiences of aloneness and his resonance with his patients' similar experiences. While his experience of sexualized rage was discovered in his countertransference reactions, his understanding of his feelings of aloneness, an experience that was conscious, came from recognitions of similarities with his patients around this issue. The slow, steady accretion of understanding and clarity about this facet of himself is described as occurring in ways that are somewhat similar to analyst 1's description of learning about his fears of passive longings. It begins with an intellectual recognition that then leads these analysts to trace and deepen their understanding through work with many different patients who shared this experience and struggle with it. Analyst 4, however, is specific and detailed about what he can, and does then, reconstruct of his own history about aloneness. Of all the analysts in this study, he is the most self-revealing and offers the most vivid picture of how work with patients interdigitates with the analyst's own struggles and can facilitate personal growth.

Most of the analysts participating in this project shared a similar theoretical orientation; they retain an appreciation for conflict theory but also view the analyst as an active participant, influencing the process. Each of these four analysts has a slightly different way of thinking about, and approaching, his own residual conflicts and pain in relation to his work with patients. In the chapters that follow, many other styles and approaches are demonstrated.

CHAPTER 3

Triggers for Self-Knowledge
How Analysts Recognize an Aspect of Themselves Requiring Further Self-Reflection

While the personal events in the life of the analyst are undoubtedly the most powerful in creating psychological changes over time, I propose that the analyst's work with patients also has a strong and powerful influence on the analyst's psyche. Almost all of the analysts responding to this survey endorse a similar belief. Analysts do not undertake this work for their personal growth; their focus is on their patients and their patients' conflicts and states. Psychological changes for the analyst, however, are a likely consequence of undertaking each analysis. If this is so, why does it occur? How does it work?

The present survey was undertaken with the hope that it would begin to explore, though certainly not completely answer, some of these questions. In the following chapters, I lay out the steps in this process. The first step is the recognition of conflict or distress. In this chapter, I present analysts' descriptions of their interactions with patients that lead to their discovery of a need for self-exploration. Personal treatment and training make analysts aware of their patterns of reaction, strategies for coping with, or defending against, various affects and conflicts. I propose that analysts' self-knowledge may be enhanced when they discover or refind previously unexplored, partially explored, or rerepressed aspects of themselves through first recognizing, exploring, and helping their patients work on parallel areas.

I provide examples of the four triggers for self-knowledge examined in this study. Each of these stimuli is considered in terms of the relative ease or difficulty with which the analyst can learn from it about himself or herself.

I wish to draw a parallel between how patients and analysts learn about themselves. Just as patients can more readily take in, and make use of, observations and interpretations that are closest to the surface of their awareness, so analysts are more likely to be able to integrate aspects of themselves that are closest to their consciousness. While it seems obvious once it is pointed out, this focus on the parallel of analyst's learning has rarely been addressed. In later sections of the book, I discuss how these triggers are reflected upon and the changes that occur through a combination of self-exploration and assimilation taking place both within and outside the analytic situation. Here I primarily focus on the differences among the various triggers and consider why some triggers more than others provide stimuli that can be more readily assimilated or stimulate further self-reflection. I demonstrate the relative accessibility to the analyst's consciousness that these different forms of engagement represent.

I draw upon both my clinical experience and the analysts' written responses to the survey to offer some preliminary thoughts about how analysts become aware of aspects of themselves that have remained unintegrated or only partially mastered.

LEARNING FROM CONSCIOUS COMPARISONS

What the analyst sees on the outside in his or her patient may begin to be more fully understood on the inside for the analyst. As the analyst becomes increasingly clear how a particular issue that a patient is working on is also a personal one for the analyst, not yet mastered, it also gradually becomes clear how this shared aspect is, in some ways, the same for patient and analyst and, in some ways, different. Something the patient is saying or working on evokes something similar, parallel, or different, but almost always, in some way, related to something in the analyst. These are the experiences of seeing more about oneself from seeing more about the other (Gardner, 1983; Jacobs, 1991; Margulies, 1993; McLaughlin, 1993; Poland, 1993; Smith, 1993; Silber, in press). Sometimes this knowing is already preconsciously near the surface of the analyst's awareness, and the patient's focus on a parallel area pushes it into the center of the analyst's consciousness. Other times the intense focus on the patient's conflicts, the emotional intensity of what is going on between the analyst and the patient as they examine the patient's feelings in relation to the analyst, gradually raises a more deeply buried aspect of the analyst's experience to consciousness. It is not always clear which of these situations leads to the recognition of something previously unacknowledged; it is also hard to determine when an external trigger stimulated an experience of internal recognition and when the recognition of a previously unacknowledged external element occurs because one has already been thinking about it.

Work with patients provides an opportunity to investigate areas of unresolved or partially resolved conflict or distress that otherwise might be avoided. Unacceptable aspects of the self are likely to be more easily perceived in others before they are acknowledged as areas of internal conflict. From the clinician's vantage point, there are data that psychological ownership of these unacceptable aspects often requires that they are first explored through displacement.

When patients experience some affect or conflict or aspect of the self as too unacceptable, it is disavowed and experienced as not belonging to them. The shame and humiliation of acknowledging this unacceptable aspect are unbearable; therefore, in order to help the patient tolerate and accept this disavowed part, it must first be worked on through displacement.

Child analysts most often, and almost always early on, work with their young patients through displacement. Rather than using the transference as a vehicle to see and then interpret directly to their patients their thoughts, feelings, fantasies, and unconscious beliefs, they convey this information through its attribution to a third party, most often done through play. They help their child patients understand their inner processes by seeing them concretely represented outside themselves and attributed to others who they can see struggle with conflicts and feelings that the child cannot yet acknowledge as his or her own. Eventually, as the child, the relationship, and the analytic work develop, it is usual to address these issues more directly.

Similarly, with many patients suffering from narcissistic disturbances, the analyst often begins by working through externalizations (Kohut, 1971, 1977). Other analysts (Blechner, 1992) advocate working in the countertransference with the more severely disturbed patients who cannot tolerate the direct focus on themselves. For the child and the narcissistic and other more severely disturbed patients, seeing, exploring, and coming to understand a not-yet-acknowledged inner struggle in externalization are the first steps toward seeing and integrating something about the self.

Most often, successful work with both children and narcissistic patients begins with learning through displacement; this fact suggests that there may be a developmental progression in how one comes to acknowledge aspects of oneself. For the child, learning is in a state of evolution; for the narcissistic or other more severely disturbed adult, there may have been an arrest in this aspect of development. The point is that we have clinical experiences that support that one learns about what is inside one's self by first seeing something similar outside one's self.

The analyst may or may not be conscious of a similarity between himself or herself and the patient. All that analysts have learned about themselves remains as a backdrop for their work. Analysts' disturbing or disquieting reactions to patients are often precursors to a discovery of a similarity with their patients that the analysts wished they did not share. This is a familiar form of countertransference, in which what the analyst does not want to own is first recognized and "criticized" on the outside. Potentially, the understanding and empathy that then develop for this shared conflict or characteristic make it easier for the analyst to see and acknowledge it in himself or herself. Whether the analyst then continues to make personal use of this awareness is another matter.

EXAMPLES FROM THE SURVEY OF TRIGGERS
FOR SELF-KNOWLEDGE

In the present study, the triggers for recognition of areas where analysts felt a need to inquire more deeply about themselves were categorized in four different groupings based on the stimuli arising from patient–analyst interactions. As previously described, the categories are similarity of conflicts or issues; quality more developed in a patient than in the analyst and admired by the analyst; transference perception of the analyst by the patient; transference–countertransference awareness and enactments by analyst. In each situation, it was then further considered whether or not in these recognitions the analyst describes revisiting an area known and previously explored, working these issues through to a different level or discovering something new, and whether or not personal change, professional change, or both followed. I present illustrations of each of these occurrences for each category whenever a relevant example was provided.

First, I review the overall findings. Some analysts offered illustrations that described only how a recognition of something in the analyst was stimulated by something in the work with a patient and did not indicate what, if anything, was then done with this recognition. Other analysts offered illustrations that also described how this recognition occurred and how some experience of affect or some understanding was deepened but did not indicate what, if any, change occurred in the analyst on the basis of this experience. Still other analysts provided examples that illustrated how a recognition occurred, the experience of affect or under-standing that followed, and what changed for the analyst as a result of this work. These changes were described in terms of the analyst's work, more personal changes, and changes in which the analyst perceived shifts occurring in both professional and personal areas.

Some, though not many, of the illustrations given by the analysts exclusively addressed transference–countertransference reactions and did not include explicit acknowledgment of what, if anything, the ana-lyst saw about himself or herself as a result of the interaction. Examples that did not indicate a recognition of the aspects of the analyst or reso-nance with the analyst's life are not reported in the following chapters.

There is considerable variability in the kind and quality of the ana-lysts' examples. Some of the illustrations are vivid and detailed, while others are presented only in general terms. When the examples describe recognition alone of the triggers to self-discovery, it is relatively easy to understand what has been stirred in the analysts; however, when the analysts introduce the idea of change without elaboration, it is difficult to enter into the analysts' experience of the process and to believe in these psychological transformations. The way most of these written vignettes are presented fails to demonstrate the process in the manner that is possible in longer case reports. These brief examples are provided to create a picture of the kind of issues that arise for analysts and to con-vey a sense of how these experiences are conceptualized by them. The written illustrations should be viewed as a background for the more in-depth reports obtained in the interviews, which are discussed in the sec-tion on psychological change in the analysts.

Illustrations of the different depths of self-explorations—recognition, deepening an understanding or affect, a new discovery, and change of affect, attitude, or behavior—are offered for each category triggering recognition for the need to be self-reflective. In the transference–coun-tertransference category, illustrations for both countertransference awareness and countertransference enactment are given.

SIMILARITY OF CONFLICTS OR ISSUES

The first category, similarity of conflicts or issues, contains illustrations of analysts stimulated to work on their own issues by a patient's work on a similar conflict or distress. The rapidity with which an analyst comes to recognize something about himself or herself through work with a patient may reflect the degree to which this aspect of the analyst is already close to awareness. The degree to which the analyst is already prepared to acknowledge this aspect as part of the self determines whether or not the analyst can maintain a self-discovery in consciousness. The source of recognition for the analyst's response, that is, whether or not the analyst's reaction occurs in the form of a countertransference enactment, a countertransference response, an interpretation of countertransference by the patient, an awareness of an admired and possibly envied aspect of the patient, or a perception of an aspect of similarity with the patient, may convey the extent to which the analyst is prepared to own this aspect as part of the self. Recognition of similarity indicates a consciously owned or more easily accessible problem area.

Analysts provided many different examples of areas of conflict or pain described by their patients that reopened areas of conflict or pain that analysts experienced as familiar and previously explored by them.

One analyst provides an illustration in which the description offered is restricted to the recognition of a similarity:

> Patient going through a very painful loss of career caused by his self-defeating behavior has led to huge pain and shame which has made me aware of my defenses and vulnerability to similar feelings due to my real and imagined shortcomings.

In this example, the analyst reports his awareness of parallels between himself and his patient. The analyst does not indicate if or how this recognition was explored by him or if any personal or professional changes resulted from this awareness.

An illustration of both recognition of conflict and pain based on a perceived similarity as the stimulus for a deepening of an understanding and an experience of an affect was provided by another analyst:

> I had two patients with intense split-off or disavowed sadistic rage. My father's sadistic rage was disavowed and [defended against in other ways, too, like in pacifism], but it leaked out and terrified me. My own rage terrified me, and the depth of my own sadism was only touched on in my analysis—I was very aware with one patient who could have scared me and scared everyone around him and with the other patient who didn't scare me but whose rage terrified himself—I was aware that I had to deepen my understanding and acceptance of my own rage—and that I be able to tolerate and not fear it within myself. I spent some time focusing on this in me and the work was able to progress [with the patients].

The terror stirred in her by the sadism of her patient made this analyst aware that she had to deepen her understanding and acceptance of her own rage in order to be able to tolerate and not fear the sadism in herself. She saw that she could not effectively help her patient before she did this personal work. This analyst elaborated her thoughts about the links among her patient, her past, and herself. She implied that a change in relation to the work with the patient occurred, but neither her process of work nor the change is described.

An illustration of a recognition, a deepening experience, and a change in the analyst's awareness in relation to personal qualities in himself was offered by another analyst:

> Working with a child who had an older brother who died and [whom] he replaced helped me revive memories of a younger brother who died while I was a child. His issue—his fear of dying when he reached seven—triggered memories of anxiety that I might die as my younger brother did. It made me aware of still being anxious at times and where it [these fears] originated. Further, it opened newer areas of masochistic traits that had reemerged after analysis.

In this example, the analyst uses a similarity of situation as a stimulus to reexplore old anxieties, reevoked by the exploration by his patient of this shared experience. Reflection on his old anxieties leads him to be aware of a line of continuity between old and present anxiety and a new awareness of characterological traits.

This analyst was among those analysts who described a change of perspective of themselves; other analysts describe discovering and exploring similarities with their patients that stimulate changes in relation to the analysts' work with the patients as well as personal changes. One analyst described work with a patient whose characterological tendency he recognized as similar to his own:

> I encountered a patient with an angry narcissistic reaction to his son that paralleled a similar trend in myself. Working on this helped me to clarify for myself identifications with my father, who had a similar orientation to me. This allowed me to work more sympathetically with the patient, to think through my relationship with my son, and to be more accepting of him for his good qualities and distance myself from my own narcissistic needs.

In this example the analyst's recognition of a similarity of conflicts and reactions between himself and his patient enabled him to reflect on the origins of his struggle. Understanding his feelings and reactions as an unconscious identification with his own father resulted in a shift of the analyst's affective experience in relation to his patient, his son, and himself.

Some analysts described experiences in which a newly discovered affect associated with a previously known conflict emerged as a result of an awareness of a similarity between a patient and themselves. An example of a newly discovered affect was offered by one analyst whose patient experienced "soul murder" in childhood:

> The patient's experience of "soul murder" in childhood and the recovery of affects, memories, and ego states that are overwhelming lead me to recover affect I have defended against in relation to emotional and physical abuse by my own father. I remember the incidents but successfully defended against the affects/ego states until I recognized that I defended against identifying with the patient's experience.

In this example, the similarity of experience of the patient and analyst triggered the analyst's previously unavailable affective response to remembered events. There is no elaboration of the impact of this freeing of affect on the personal or professional life of the analyst.

Other analysts did elaborate on the effects of recovering previously repressed affect. For example:

> A homosexual [male] patient's awareness of rage toward his seductive mother helped me to become aware that rage toward my own mother was blocking my ability to be creative. Awareness of this in myself and the emergence of this conflict in dreams enabled me to begin writing.

This analyst not only became conscious of a formerly repressed affect but also described the impact of his new awareness. He believed that the availability of his rageful feelings freed him to be able to write, a change that may be viewed as having both personal and professional ramifications.

Some analysts described a newly discovered conflict or issue, in contrast to a newly discovered affect in relation to a known conflict, and became conscious, as a result, of the recognition of a similarity between a patient and themselves.

> The untimely death of the analysand's marital partner led to a temporary analytic stalemate related both to grieving and not grieving the loss. The patient's defense against painful feelings was strongly reactivated and, finally in a timely and appropriate way, could be respectfully linked to much earlier losses. My "empathy" for the patient was more like "sympathy" and based largely upon my own recent and early losses and my characterological way of dealing with

them and defending against my own painful feelings. The "empathy" gave way to irritation with the patient's alternately avoiding and then "wallowing" in the current [and past] misery. I was struck by the dramatic shift in my attitude toward this suffering patient, how different it was from my usual [ideal] image of myself and eventually, with my usual unbidden conversations with myself, I recognized a long forgotten attitude of my mother's toward me and my pain. The issue had come up in my own analysis, long ago, but had found its way back to the cobwebs until called forth by my "peculiar" shift in response to my patient—which response had, by the way, been enacted in an analytic hour by the analysand to me.

In this instance, the analyst offered a description of a similarity, a countertransference reaction, and an unspecified enactment that culminated in the lifting of repression and recovery of memory for the analyst. He does not report the effect of this freeing of memory on his personal or professional life. The example illustrates how, when the analyst's resistance is not too strong, once a process of self-reflection begins, multiple triggers for recognition of conflicts on different levels of consciousness can evolve in rapid succession.

Two examples in which analysts' initial countertransference difficulties quickly gave way to their recognitions of similar conflicts between their patients and themselves are provided as illustrations of conflicts for analysts not in direct awareness but easily accessible to consciousness:

> Analyzing a young adolescent, I found myself unusually intolerant of his resistance/negative transference—I also sensed the underlying/defended against desperate search for a father/mentor. Self-analysis uncovered for me certain aspects of my passive yearnings for my father to be more of a mentor for me in my struggles with puberty/adolescence.

The analyst has described the trigger—the recognition of defended-against longings for a father/mentor during a particular stage of development. Self-exploration reveals a similar experience of his own, but his report goes no further.

A similar experience is reported by another analyst who first perceives a stalemate in his work and then seeks a consultation to understand the difficulty. He describes an expansion of understanding beyond this initial recognition of difficulty that he believed led to some change in his work with the patient:

> Consultation helped me recognize I was having difficulty recognizing the strength of a male patient's yearnings for a more inti-

mate closeness with me. Reflection enabled me to recognize that this resonated with a residual problem of that sort of my own, wanting closeness, yet being threatened by the possibility of obtaining it. I was better able to deal with the patient's conflict.

Here the analyst has perceived the same similarity of wish and defense in his patient and himself as the previous analyst. The difference is that the second analyst reports a greater awareness of conflict in his yearnings and a belief that his increased awareness led him to change in his work with this patient.

From the illustrations, one can see that the depth and complexity of exploration reported vary greatly among analysts. This variation is not limited to any particular stimulus but, rather, is characteristic of the responses in all categories.

QUALITY MORE DEVELOPED IN THE PATIENT THAN IN THE ANALYST

The second category contains illustrations of stimulation of the analyst's self-exploration by a quality in the patient that the analyst admires. A patient has an adaptive strength either that the analyst lacks or that is more developed in the patient than in the analyst. In these instances, the analyst desires some characteristic perceived in the patient to be a greater part of himself or herself. The patient in this respect is seen as a kind of ego ideal by the analyst.

Through participating in the analytic work, the analyst hopes to develop, or believes he or she has developed, some of this admired quality in himself or herself. An illustration of recognition of a desired quality that an analyst aspired to was offered by one analyst:

> The patient, a woman slightly older than myself, described her father's outstretched arms and warm greeting for her. I liked the image and vowed to be more demonstrative toward my own daughter. I also felt encouraged in my work as her analyst, through a lengthy, seemingly slow analysis, as I realized our work was becoming more fruitful since she could now describe him in a way she hadn't before.

In this instance the analyst uses the recognition of his patient's appreciation of her father's warmth to create a model of the kind of father he wished to be. Here he aspires not to the quality of the patient but rather to her internalized image of her father. There were no data given about whether or not or how the analyst explored ideas, feelings, or fantasies about being demonstrative or the extent to which the analyst was able to meet this goal.

Some analysts did report that admired qualities of their patients became their own. For example, one analyst had a patient who was open with, and less afraid of, anger, while the analyst had been more inhibited about expressing angry, rageful feelings:

> A patient who was less afraid than I was of rage directed at the analyst led me to explore my own inhibition in expressing such rage, which had not been adequately addressed in two analyses. I became freer with the expression of my anger.

The patient's directing her rage at the analyst led the analyst to explore her own inhibition in expressing such rage. The analyst believed that the patient's greater freedom with negative feelings facilitated her becoming freer with her own anger. The analyst was aware she aspired to this change and used her patient's freer expression as a model for developing more freedom for herself.

A less conscious process of identification and change was reported by an analyst who admired her patient's sense of humor:

> My first control case was way ahead of me in terms of ego strength and in fact terminated before I terminated my own analysis. She had a wonderful sense of humor about herself, which helped us tremendously during difficult times. My own analyst and I were serious people! Her finishing was very important and sad to me. About a month after her departure, I'm reviewing something painful in my life in a different way. My analyst commented that this was the first time he'd ever heard me laugh at myself. My immediate association was to my patient and how I'd always appreciated this trait in her. A precious part of her I retained—through internalization?

This example is elaborated in the section on change in the analyst.

PATIENT'S INTERPRETATION OF THE ANALYST

The third category contains examples in which the patient has confronted the analyst with an interpretation of his or her character or behavior. In these illustrations, the focus is on how the analysts have responded to their patient's observations as providing information about themselves and not only as transference perceptions, the usual and customary manner in which analysts work. The patient's perception of the analyst in the transference leads the analyst to recognize some aspect of himself or herself that is the trigger or the hook the patient uses to support a view of the analyst.

In these instances, the patient may be more consciously attuned to an aspect of the analyst than the analyst is. Patients' calling attention to their analysts' behavior and its impact is, in effect, offering interpretations to their analysts (Gill, 1982, Hoffman, 1983).

Analysts provided examples in which the patient's perception about them reopened areas of pain, conflict, or previously recognized defensive style that analysts experienced as familiar to them and previously explored.

As a result of the patient's confrontations some analysts described being more aware of the aspects of themselves that their patients select as a focus. It may be, of course, that in these examples what the patients have selected for comment are aspects of the analyst that are already close to the analyst's consciousness. One analyst wrote:

> The patient was a 36-year-old medical researcher in analysis for a year when the incident occurred. Competitive strivings and inhibitions had been prominent features of the analysis but expressed in a muted fashion in the transference until this incident. After a series of escalating albeit mild, challenges, one day he came into the office saying, "Today I want to sit in your chair," but then proceeded to lie on the couch to pursue the topic. The patient continued, "What if I really *did* sit in your chair? What would you do then, smuck?" My own emotional reaction got the best of me [in retrospect only] as I answered: "We couldn't do analysis, then, if you were sitting in my chair." He accurately perceived my comment came under the guise of my wish to analyze the issue, but more from my own discomfort with the growing sense of challenge he was presenting, particularly since I knew realistically there was no danger of this actually happening. He latched on to this incident, largely for his own reasons, and it became a symbol, literally for years, of my vulnerability to his challenging me in earnest.
>
> The incident, and especially the lengthy fallout that all too clearly brought home to me the various elements of my reaction, allowed (or maybe I should say forced) me to think about and rethink my fear of a real competitive battle with this increasingly imposing and, in many ways, powerful man, as well as its connection to my relationship to my father and to my increasingly challenging 13-year-old son. Equally important, I realized my attempt to hide my discomfort behind what seemed at the time to be a "proper" and justifiable analytic intervention.

I appreciated this man's insight into the real meaning of my "We couldn't do analysis then," as it allowed me to consider in a new way the many dimensions of my own struggle with intense rivalries.

The patient's challenge led this analyst to see both that he had been trying to hide from his fear of competitive battles stirred in relation to his patient in their interactions and the defensive mode he employed in his use of an analytic stance. The analyst was aware of these competitive issues and his fears in relation to both his father and his son, but the patient's confrontation made the analyst consider many dimensions of his struggle with intense rivalries in a new way. He does not tell us if or how his self-reflections resulted in personal or professional changes.

Some analysts described a newly discovered conflict or an issue's becoming conscious as a result of the patient's pointing out an aspect of the analyst. In addition, these analysts reported a deepening of an experience of some affect or some understanding and of a change in the analyst in relation to the analyst's personal development, professional development, or both following these recognitions. For example:

A patient whose marginally sociopathic behavior was a major focus of analytic work pointed out that my sometime lateness for his sessions must be due to my disapproval and dislike of him and that I was being subtly sociopathic myself by being late. I had at first considered my lateness as a part of a somewhat "tolerant" attitude toward him, but spurred by his observation, I did some self-analytic work that made me realize a double layering of reaction formation against my envy of his overriding his guilt and allowing himself such "freedom." My hidden reaction of disapproval was further reacted against by a "tolerant" attitude. My self-analytic work included analysis of dreams of forbidden behaviors, variously forgiven and punished, as well as observing differences in my attitude and behavior with him and other patients.

The patient's confrontation served as the stimulus for the analyst's self-explorations, and the analyst reports recognition of the accuracy of the patient's perception and the process by which he works on exploring what he discovered and then reports a change in attitude that he sees in his behavior in his work.

TRANSFERENCE–COUNTERTRANSFERENCE EXPERIENCES

The fourth category contains examples that are generally charged with affective distress for the analyst. Transference–countertransference experiences stir affects, memories, or new discoveries for the analyst. These experiences are divided in two groups: transference–countertransference experiences in which the analyst recognizes his or her reaction to the patient as uncharacteristic and finds it has triggered by his or her past conflicts in which the patient or the patient's transference revives experiences of previously conflicted relationships; and transference–countertransference experiences in which the analyst acts on unconscious affects, fantasies, or conflicts stirred in relation to the patient or the patient's transference with no conscious registration of what is transpiring between them. In this second transference–countertransference expression, defined as an enactment, the analyst's uncharacteristic behavior with the patient leads the analyst to be aware of some conflict or aspect of himself or herself stimulated by the interaction with patient.

The analyst may be aware that he or she has reacted in a familiar way or may even recognize that what stirred the reaction is something familiar. What may not be recognized or owned by the analyst is how or to what extent the aspect of the patient that triggered this response resides within the analyst's self.

An illustration of only recognition of the reopening of earlier conflict or pain was offered by an analyst:

> When a patient derides me as inadequate, a bumbling idiotic analyst (the negative transference used defensively or otherwise) I have to disengage myself and realize my feelings of irritation and/or inadequacy stem from a lifelong struggle to get out from under the shadow of an older brother who did to me what the patient was currently doing in the transference. In the negative transference I am constantly on the lookout for my reactions.

The recognition of the origin of the analyst's reaction, his means of managing his response, and his need to be alert to his reactions are reported. We do not know if he reflects further and deepens his understanding or if he believes any changes occur as a consequence of his recognition.

Recognition of conflict and pain and a deepening of affect and understanding in the analyst are illustrated by another analyst:

> As a male analyst, fear of pointing out a female analysand's disavowal of her sexuality, fearing she would put the focus on me as completely off-base and disgustingly so. Self-reflection led me to memories of my mother's unwillingness to have her character and motivations commented upon, responding with an attack on my perceptions and motives. The memories were more intense

and detailed than they had been in my analysis, and I've connected for the first time to an inhibition in my interpretive work as an analyst.

This analyst, through self-reflection, linked his reaction of inhibition with his patient to its historical roots. He not only understood his transference to his patient but came to perceive a previously unrecognized reverberation from his childhood relationship with his mother.

Another analyst related his understanding of his countertransference reaction to current developmental issues as well as a conflict from the past. He described a change in his experience of conflict and change in his work with the patient following his self-reflection:

> A woman in a conflicted erotic transference evoked distracting reciprocating fantasies and affects in me, out of proportion to the analytic material. Careful reflection over time enabled me to realize that the patient reminded me of a turbulent adolescent love affair, now attached to conflicts about my aging. Further personal exploration contributed to distinct changes in the intensity and character of these conflicts (and to resumed spontaneity with the patient).

Both these analysts believed that, self-exploration in response to their recognition of countertransference reactions enabled them not only to learn more about themselves but also to experience their affects and conflicts differently and, at least in relation to their patients, to behave differently.

In contrast, some analysts believe that, though they are able to recognize their countertransference reactions and to appreciate the historical roots of their responses, their self-exploration is ineffective in attaining any lasting sense of change in self-experience or conflict. These analysts believe that they remain vulnerable to the same reactions over time despite their self-analytic efforts. This point of view was illustrated by the analyst who responded:

> For me it seems to be a continued effort to master undesirable affective responses (e.g., anger and shame) that were improved through my personal analysis—but naturally, not completely resolved, or mastered.

Some analysts were very specific that the countertransferences that arose with the patient they described were directly related to incomplete, sometimes even totally overlooked, areas in their own analyses:

In a recent analysis, a patient complained that she had no feelings of love for me—only hatred. I, in turn, realized that I had only feelings of dislike for the patient. Subsequently I recognized that I was uncomfortable with erotic feelings I was having for her and was making sure that I do nothing to stimulate her in any way. This, of course, led to a very tense, sterile, "classical" analysis. Once recognized by me, I set out to "correct" the situation, finding derivatives of her positive feelings for me and interpreting her defensiveness to these feelings. This led to renewed efforts on her part to deny the existence of such feelings. At this point I recalled being at the very same juncture with the patient very early in the analysis, and we had both retreated to the positions of mutual negativism. For the first time in my life I recognized that this has been a defensive characterological position for me and was untouched by my analysis years ago. My love for the analyst (mother—at times father) was not conscious and remained repressed beneath this rigid, submissive posture I assumed relative to the rigid, no-nonsense "classical" analyst. My patient, fortunately, was less submissive than I and forced the issue to the surface. She gave us two chances, and the second one was successful.

Although the account is offered in this abbreviated form, the analyst has described a complex process of recognition of a countertransference reaction, a similarity of defense, a similarity of conflict, and then a shift in affective experience, and an implied behavioral change.

ENACTMENTS BY ANALYSTS

Examples of enactments by analysts, although they, too, stem from transference–countertransference engagements, are also offered because they depict the analyst when he or she has been most dramatically caught unaware of his or her own psychological reactions and process. While the recognition of uncharacteristic feelings toward a patient is disquieting, the recognition of uncharacteristic, unintended actions toward a patient, though they inevitably occur, is far more distressing to analysts. It means that, for that moment, the analyst is both "out of touch" with, and "out of control" of, himself or herself. Such a recognition usually forces an analyst to come to grips with some unconscious or disowned aspect of himself or herself. Enactments represent communications that have not acquired a conscious representation.

Two illustrations describe a recognition of conflict and pain, a deepening experience of some affect and understanding, and a change in the analyst triggered by the same enactment but different underlying conflicts. Both analysts locked their patients out of the office. In one example:

> Two rebuffs by me of the analysand—locking her out and falling asleep—leading me to introspect, to realize the fright I felt at the power of her unconscious seductiveness. This was reconfirming of the powerful sexuality between me and my grandmother. The new ability I gained [from this understanding] was to help the analysand recognize her own sexual wishes.

Self-exploration revealed to this analyst that his feelings toward his patient had reawakened and reconfirmed for him the powerful experience of seductiveness between him and his grandmother. This understanding enabled him to help the patient recognize her sexual wishes as well as giving him a new perspective. The quality of feeling and conflict in relation to his patient changed following his self-analytic work. The analyst does not indicate whether or not these changes extended into his personal life.

In the second example, an analyst's locking a patient out of the office led her to realize how shut out she had felt by the patient:

> One particular patient had a very sadistic, rageful father. She could not tolerate these affects with herself, and I also had a hard time with these same feelings in me from my father. She would shut me out, and I discovered that I was shutting her out—one time quite completely by locking the door to the waiting room and forgetting her appointment. I remembered five minutes later and found her waiting outside, quite hurt. I did a lot of self-analysis on that one (also went for a consultation about the patient because I had never acted out like that before). Now that I can tolerate my own affects, I can more easily notice her defenses in the area and point them out to her; she can now have her very strong rage, and we both live through it. She is beginning to feel really close to me—a new experience for a woman in her 30s with no intimate relationships.

The analyst was aware that she and the patient were both struggling with identifications with sadistic, rageful fathers. The analyst sought consultation, which helped her tolerate her own affects better. As she gained a better appreciation of her difficulties, she was able more quickly to recognize and address the patient's rage and help her live through it.

In both instances, the analysts unconsciously shut their patients out in their attempt to "shut out" their awareness and experience of their own intense affective responses to these patients. The enactment forced both analysts to face their intense need to defend themselves from "unacceptable" feelings in relation to their patients. Once they saw the intensity of their need to defend themselves, they were able to recognize what they were defending against, to explore the historical source for these experiences, and to regain their professional stance with their patients. In addition, they reported learning more about themselves in relation to the conflict that had been reactivated.

Not all enactments are so stark and dramatic in nature. Some enactments are much more subtle and may go undetected because they are insufficiently recognized or addressed in these more minor forms unless or until they escalate. An example of recognition of a subtle enactment was offered by another analyst who saw she was being too sympathetic to a patient, who experienced the sympathy as infantilizing:

> A tendency to respond "too sympathetically" to a current patient was experienced as infantilizing her. It helped me to see I was not viewing her as "more grown up" and capable and was too identified with the "sufferer."
>
> I learn and relearn the same thing again and again with my patients. I'm not sure of the "permanence" of the insights I get for myself, but luckily I have patients to remind me of what I keep forgetting.

The analyst's recognition that she was too identified with the sufferer was not a new understanding for her. It was rediscovery, which enabled the analyst to regain an analytic stance. This analyst was aware of her difficulty in keeping her self-discoveries conscious. Doubting the permanence of the effect of any insight or affect recognition, she appreciated her work with patients as a means to keep herself from total rerepression.

In contrast to these rediscoveries, another analyst found a depth of new understanding about both his patient and himself from the recognition of a subtle enactment:

> A concerted effort at resistance analysis in a depressed woman patient led to an impasse with the enactment of a dyadic interaction, a strong negative maternal transference, and suicidal impulses. The focus shifted as the patient's complaints intensified. Tension regulation and an intolerance for affect were gradually recognized as central to the experience. My approach was one that set the narcissistic value of conflict analysis above [consider-

ation of] the developmental needs of the patient. My self-analytic effort involved the recognition of experiences in which I felt similarly misunderstood in my own analysis.

The analyst does not specify the exact nature of the enactment, but he described recognizing that he had a narcissistic investment in the theory, which he was putting above the patient's needs. His "self-analytic efforts" also led him to the recognition that he had had an experience in his analysis in which he felt similarly misunderstood. He saw that his imposition of this theory on his patient was an identification with the aggressor, his own analyst.

It is apparent from these examples that the different triggers cannot be viewed as discrete categories. One form of engagement with the patient, such as an enactment, may trigger analysts' awareness of some area in themselves requiring further exploration, while another form of engagement with the patient, such as the recognition of a similarity, may quickly replace the initial stimulus and provide additional information for further self-inquiry. I suggest that finding the surface of awareness of the unassimilated aspect for the analyst is the segue for the recognition and assimilation of more deeply buried aspects, just as it is for patients.

Analysts' perceptions about themselves that are acquired through their recognition of a similarity between themselves and their patient are the easiest to describe and understand. The greatest readiness for ownership is reflected in perceptions of similarity. When an analyst sees that a patient's conflicts or the manner in which the patient struggles is similar to the analyst's conflicts or strategies of adaptation and defense, the analyst is already acknowledging knowing something about this conflict, about the coping mechanism, or about both as his or her own. It may, however, have required an external representation of a conflict, painful state, or adaptive and defensive strategies to attune the analyst to this particular aspect of himself or herself. Students of learning theory know that it is easier to recognize material than it is spontaneously to recall it. So it may be that the analyst is pushed to a recognition about himself or herself by a kind of mirror phenomenon. The analyst sees the patient and essentially says, This looks like me. The extent to which this first recognition of similarity actually reflects overlapping areas for the analyst with this patient may not become clear until much more work is completed by each participant.

Reactions of the analyst that reflect an identification with the patient are what Racker (1968) called concordant countertransferences. Sometimes these identifications are empathic, such as the analyst who recognized yearnings for closeness with his own analyst after he perceived his patient's longing to be close with him. When the analyst's awareness of some aspect of the self is near the surface of consciousness, appreciation and empathy with a patient's struggle around similar feelings frequently allow the analyst to become conscious of a parallel issue in himself or herself. Being empathic to another person who is grappling with strong feelings often permits the analysts to be more sensitive to the presence of similar feelings in themselves.

Most often, however, when analysts learn about themselves through the recognition of a similarity, this new awareness is somewhat more painfully acquired. The issues that the analysts perceive first in the patient and then in themselves are around qualities or behaviors that the analysts do not like about themselves. "Rage," "self-righteousness," "self-pity," "narcissistic investments," "hostility," and "envy" are some of the affects or qualities that the analysts responding to this survey found in themselves as a result of first perceiving them in their patients. Most analysts are less likely to empathize with these more aggressively tinged states than with more benign states, such as a yearning for closeness or other dependent wishes. The degree of self-criticism stimulated by a recognition of previously distanced unacceptable feelings as aspects of themselves depends on the particular history and conflicts of the particular analyst.

A different state of discomfort occurs when the analyst perceives the patient as possessing a quality or ability that the analyst would like to have or have more developed in himself or herself. In these instance, the analyst may, at times, feel envious and competitive with the patient, especially unconsciously. Often, however, analysts consciously admire their patients who have particular attributes that they wish they had. The patient then serves as a model for the analyst in this area.

The analyst may be able to learn through the patient's exploration of the patient's conflicts the factors contributing to the development of this particular strength or perspective. Seeing the patient possess and demonstrate a particular ability can inspire the analyst. It enables the analyst to believe that if it is possible for the patient to develop this particular quality, it may also be possible for the analyst to acquire this attribute for himself or herself. For example, the analyst who admired her patient's free expression of negative feelings aimed to become less constricted in her display of angry affects. This analyst consciously wished for, and tried to emulate, her patient's characteristic. For other analysts no such conscious effort to acquire a desired trait was described. The analyst who acquired the ability to laugh at herself was surprised and pleased when she recognized this new perspective on herself that was similar to her former patient's use of humor, but she had not consciously tried to emulate her patient.

Whether or not analysts are conscious of aspects of themselves that their patients perceive and tell them about also depends on the particular patient–analyst pair and the specific characteristic or conflict that the patient addresses. When patients tell their analysts how they are perceived by them, these communications may function like interpretations from analysts to patients. Although it is understood as a transference perception by the analyst, that is, shaped by the patient's needs and conflicts, nonetheless, it may reflect some real dimension of the analyst. McLaughlin (1991) describes the uncanny accuracy of his patient's perception of his character and conflicts. The readiness of the analyst to see the accuracy of the patient's observations, of course, influences the extent to which the analyst can, and does, take in, and reflect upon, the patient's view. Some analysts, such as Gill (1982), Hoffman (1983), Schwaber (1981), and Blechner (1992), not only welcome such communications but have developed theories of technique where encouragement of these observations by the patient about the analyst is central to analysis of the transference. In these instances, the analyst, though actively seeking the patient to observe and openly communicate what he or she has seen for the sake of the treatment, is relatively more passive in the process of self-discovery than in the other interactions with the patients described in this survey. Here the patient "sees," and the analyst is left to assimilate, refine, or reject the patient's perceptions. Obviously, analysts who reject the validity of their patient's perceptions about them would not have offered responses in this category.

For those analysts who provided illustrative material, the descriptions seemed remarkably similar to the way analytic interpretations work. "Readiness" on the part of the analyst and tact and timing on the part of the patient[1] may be as important in the analyst's ability to assimilate the patient's observations as they are for patients when their analysts offer interpretations. Analysts in this survey were able to recognize their "unavailability," defensive "properness," "narcissistic exploitativeness," "distancing," "manipulativenss and clutching" behaviors, "assaultiveness," "withholding," and being "judgmental" as a result of their patients' observations. The acceptance of such unflattering characteristics and the willingness to reflect upon them as accurate representations of themselves indicate an alliance with, and trust of, their patients, as well as a capacity to be open and undefensive about themselves.

---

[1] It is not, of course, the patient's job to be tactful or to offer sensitively timed observations about his or her analyst. The point is only that tact and timing influence how readily the observations may be accepted by the analyst.

In contrast, if the analyst is strongly defended against the recognition of an aspect of his or her self that the patient has been attuned to, the analyst not only may fail to recognize its accuracy but may respond to the patient's confrontation with a countertransference reaction or enactment. Countertransference reactions, when defined in the narrow manner originally employed by Freud (1910), are always reflecting some less-acknowledged, some less-owned aspect of the self compared with perceptions of any kind of similarity between the analyst and his or her patient. In countertransference reactions, something from the patient stirs an affective response from the analyst that the analyst experiences as coming from the outside. The analyst reacts before he or she is able to recognize the reaction. It requires an additional step to consider and find the way in which an aspect of the analyst is similar to the part played by the patient, the triggering part of the interaction.

Examples of increased self-awareness acquired through transference–countertransference recognitions can be grouped in two different categories. In one category, the analyst becomes aware that his or her reaction to the patient is determined by the patient or the patient's transference similarity to someone emotionally important in the analyst's life. In these instances, the patient has reevoked some previously powerful, affectively charged relationship for the analyst, such as the "belittling" older brother or the "sadistic" or "frustrating" father, and the analyst has responded with affects that occurred in relation to these people in the past. Once each analyst understood whom the patient represented, the affective disruption for the analyst settled down. In these examples, the analyst did not pursue self-reflection further—or at least did not report doing so. The self-analytic work stimulated by the countertransference reaction stopped once the link between the patient and the person in the analyst's life had been established, and analytic work was no longer disrupted.

In the second category of transference–countertransference recognitions, the analysts take a further step in self-exploration. While their initial responses are reactions to their patients as representing "the other"—either historically based, as in the examples cited, or as disavowed aspects of themselves—these analysts pursued their self-exploration until they discovered the source of the feeling that was similar to the patient's feeling. Most often, as in the examples provided of self-discoveries through recognitions of similar conflicts or affect states, the aspect of the self that the analysts found to be common to themselves and their patient or their patient's important objects was one the analysts experienced as dystonic.

Once an analyst is in touch with the experience that underlies a particular countertransference reaction, he or she is usually freed from this reaction. Recalling the experience of "facing the defense against one's own anger," "entitlement," "erotic" interest or fantasies, "performance anxiety," or acceptance of personal "limitations" enables analysts to feel differently about their patients and respond differently to them. In addition, these recognitions of similarity of conflict or affect state most often facilitated the analysts' making personal changes.

Some examples fall between these two categories of countertransference, such as the analyst who feared his female patient's turning on him as his mother had if he were to point out something about her. Reflecting on his countertransference response, he came to perceive his defense against being actively interpretive. The analyst made his recognition and acknowledgment of his inhibition explicit. In taking ownership for his inhibition, he approached, but did not quite reach, a recognition of his defense against his identification with his attacking mother. When analysts stop short of the recognition of the traits or affects they react to in their patients as representing aspects of themselves that they, at best, dislike and, at worst, disavow, it is likely that they remain more vulnerable to countertransference interference than when they own and grapple with these similarities. Countertransference reactions in relation to disavowed aspects of the self because they are further from consciousness may first be recognized through enactments.

The dividing line between what we define as a countertransference reaction and what we define as an enactment may at times be slim. For practical purposes of classification, I limit the label of countertransference reaction to examples in which the analysts described recognition of affective responses that were cognitively contained and did not take a behavioral form but that analysts recognized as shaped, at least in part, by their own histories. I label as enactments examples in which the analysts described a countertransference response that took a behavioral form. These categorizations, however, are dependent on the analysts' capacity to observe the extent to which their affective reactions spill over and become behaviorally observable. Minienactments are likely occurring all the time without the analyst's or the patient's being aware of their occurrence until they take more dramatic form. For example, the illustration in which the analyst recognized she was being "too sympathetic" was brought to light by the patient's making clear she felt infantilized. Had the patient not stated her reaction, the analyst might have recognized the excessiveness of her response but might not have known it was perceptible in her behavior. If the example had been

described in those terms, it would have been conceptualized as a countertransference rather than an enactment.

Enactments catch the analyst's attention; they rapidly lead the analyst to be aware that a countertransference reaction not only has been
stirred but has also been defended against. Most of the time, the analysts then become aware that they unconsciously have registered that
some aspect of themselves is resonating with something similar in their
patients. For example, when the analyst locked his patient out and fell
asleep during her session, this analyst was startled into an awareness
that some powerful affective response had been stirred in him in relation to his patient. Such an intense affective engagement with a patient
that becomes apparent through an action by the analyst, rather than
through a cognitive registration of the affect experience, indicates to the
analyst that a countertransference not only has developed but is being
resisted by the analyst. The analyst, now alerted to the presence of this
intense unconscious force, reflects about both the patient and himself.
In this illustration, the analyst first turned his attention to trying to
understand what he was feeling in relation to the patient that would
lead him so forcefully to shut her out. Recognizing that he was very
frightened of his sexual attraction to her, he then scanned his own history to find when he had previously had a similar experience. The
memories of similar feelings for his grandmother were not new discoveries, but neither were they directly in his awareness; they were
"reawakened and reconfirmed" by this similar response to his patient.
The analyst's attraction to his grandmother was experienced as reciprocated by her. It was "a powerful experience of seductiveness
between" them. The analyst, having now understood what was evoked
and having found its origin in his history, could refocus his attention on
the patient and help her recognize her sexual wishes that she was not
acknowledging.

In this analyst's self-awareness the process in which elaboration
grows through self-reflection is familiar to most analysts. It is how we
both monitor and use ourselves in our work with patients. In the example given by the analyst whose patient was grieving the loss of the marital partner and the revival of other losses, the analyst's self-reflection
began when he first recognized a similarity between himself and his
patient. He also had "recent and earlier losses." They had a similarity
both of situation and of affect: they were both experiencing grief. The
analyst began by overidentifying with his patient; he viewed himself as
"more sympathetic than empathic." He then developed a countertransference reaction—irritation toward the patient, whose way of coping
with loss he viewed as maladaptive. In other words, the analyst's cop-

ing strategies were different and, he believed, more adaptive than the patient's; his irritation may be an anger at the patient for giving into regressive wishes that he would not permit himself. In any case, while he was conscious of his irritation, this recognition did not serve to contain his feelings, and there was an unspecified enactment with the patient. The enactment then, as in the previously offered example, provided a stimulus for the analyst to recall his "long forgotten" memory of his mother's attitude toward his pain. Presumably, the analyst is saying that he identified with his mother in his reaction to his patient's way of managing her pain and was identifying his patient with his childhood self. The similarity that is then recognized and acknowledged is much deeper than the similarity of situation that he initially perceived; it is, instead, the recognition of a similarity in their response to pain, a similarity that the analyst would wish to disavow. The analyst initially defended against seeing the regressive wish in himself by his disapproval of this wish in his patient. This analyst made a new discovery about himself, that is, that he defended against wallowing in pain and that, like his mother, he could be critical and intolerant of another person's difficulty in dealing with dysphoric affects. He does not tell us what , or if any, psychological changes resulted from these discoveries.

When analysts' enactments result in new discoveries about themselves, it may be that the conflict that is revealed is sufficiently powerful that the analyst is unlikely to pursue exploration beyond this recognition, at least at first. Analysts who reported their recognition of new conflicts in the context of enactments did not report that they had any personal changes; in contrast, many analysts who reported their recognition of new conflicts stimulated by seeing similarities with their patients, by the patients' transference perceptions, and by transference–countertransference reactions reported changes in themselves as a result of what they perceived in these interactions. Since the trigger for an enactment is furthest from consciousness, the enactment is catching the analyst unaware. It may require more time to assimilate what is learned from this situation than from any of the other triggers described.

When analysts become aware that they have engaged in enactments, many different factors complicate their willingness to look clear-sightedly at what has transpired. Since the analyst's intent is to be helpful, she or he must first cope with the painful realization that she or he has failed, albeit temporarily, to accomplish this goal. One way or another, the patient is communicating that what has transpired has, at least for the moment, hurt, not helped. Although analysts know that psychoanalysis cannot be conducted without their patients' experiencing pain in reliving and working through past injury, the pain caused by enactments—even when we acknowledge that these enactments are inevitable—is different from the pain from interpretations.

Besides the analyst's discomfort over his or her failure, the analyst needs to grapple with the content that was affectively sufficiently powerful to disrupt his or her analytic stance. The interpersonal interaction that led to the enactment must have some unconscious intrapsychic representations. The analyst's enactment forces into his or her awareness that some disavowed aspect of his or her self was expressed. If the analyst's anxiety is too great consciously to maintain this self-discovery, an initial understanding of the aspect of the analyst's self that was displayed may be replaced by new and increased resistance on the analyst's part. Under such extreme circumstances, the analyst may retreat rather than use this event as an opportunity to face something new about himself or herself.

Most often enactments reflect conflicts that are neither so easily accessible to consciousness that a mere recognition of their occurrence is freeing nor so deeply repressed that the affective responses require total avoidance and denial. In the more common middle ground, analysts, once they recognize their enactments, realize they need to do considerable self-reflective work in order to discover the source of the analytic disruption. Minienactments, of course, are always taking place, and the more thoroughly they are explored by the analyst, the less likely that the more dramatic enactments will occur.

On the basis of the analyst's written examples, I have summarized and illustrated in this chapter the different forms of patient–analyst interactions that stimulate analysts' self-reflective work. In the next chapter, I describe how these analysts use these experiences of recognition to continue self-reflective work.

CHAPTER 4

Pathways to Self-Knowledge
Private Reflections, Shared
Communications, and Work with Patients

Self-discoveries sometimes occur as discrete insights, arising from a specific, powerful interaction or as a definitive culmination of less conscious previous reflections. More often, however, self-knowledge is acquired through a slow and circuitous process of self-exploration. The manner in which these personal inquiries are undertaken varies. Some analysts are very private about their self-investigations, while others find it beneficial to engage in these endeavors with colleagues, close friends, or a spouse.

While personal analyses teach analysts to recognize, as well as loosen the intensity of, their conflicts, defenses, and vulnerabilities, they do not completely eliminate the effect of early experiences and conflicts or all of the behavioral and experiential manifestations (Abend, 1986). Stimulated by the material of patients, analysts are continually subject to the reappearance of their own potentially distressing material. The reemergence of these conflictual and painful issues creates stress for the analyst, but it is also an opportunity for further integration and reworking.

The material collected in this study provides data about the frequency, method, process, and effect of self-reflective work that supplement anecdotal accounts of self-analysis. Three different kinds of data are presented in this chapter. The first is the report of survey data about frequency and methods for self-inquiry. The second is taken from telephone interviews in which analysts elaborated on their thoughts about self-inquiry and explored their ideas about privacy and self-disclosure in relation to their self-analyses. The third is based on two analysts' written accounts of the process of self-discovery in the course of work with a patient.

The psychoanalytic literature has documented analysts' accounts of private reflections in their continued pursuit of self-knowledge; even so, self-analysis has always been viewed as a controversial activity. Freud (1910, 1914, 1937) both advocated its use and cautioned awareness about its limits (Freud, 1916–17, 1935). The danger is that the analyst will prematurely believe in its completeness, settle too soon for a partial understanding when something more important still remains hidden, and believe instead that there has been sufficient exploration. Nonetheless, most analysts engage in the process of private self-inquiry at least for some period of time or as part of their method of learning about themselves. Some analysts make a daily commitment to analyzing themselves and have a systematic way of conducting their self-investigations (Calder, 1980; Sonnenberg, 1991; Smith, 1993). Others consciously employ self-analysis when they become aware of some particular tension or shift of mood (Engle, 1975; Eifermann, 1987b, 1993; Silber, in press). For still others the process of self-analysis is not conscious; rather, an unconscious process is set in motion that is an outgrowth of a personal analysis (Kramer, 1959). In fact, most analysts describe that self-reflective work overtakes them rather than their actively seeking it (Gardner, 1983; Beiser, 1984; McLaughlin, 1988, 1991; Kantrowitz, Katz, and Paolitto, 1990b; Jacobs, 1992).

When actively exploring something troubling to themselves, some analysts re-create the analytic situation by lying on a couch and free-associating, using the triggering event as a stimulus, wondering why so much affect had been stirred or what affect and fantasy lay behind some unusual piece of behavior. Other analysts undertake a similar process but much less formally. They seek a quiet place or time to themselves where they can follow their thoughts. Some analysts find it easiest to gain access to their thoughts when they are engaged in some form of automatic activity, such as walking, gardening (McLaughlin, 1993), showering, or shaving (Calder, 1980). Again, for some analysts these activities are planned to create a congenial atmosphere for associating; for others, these activities are undertaken for their own sake but seem to be the time when associations are most apt to come unbidden.

Some analysts pay particular attention to the moment their affects become more prominent in relation to particular thoughts (Spruiell,

1984; Weinshel, 1993); others are more alert to when they move away from what they had been thinking (Chused, 1991); others rely on the accompaniment of bodily sensations (Jacobs, 1973) or visual images (Gardner, 1983) as guides for areas of further exploration. Almost all of these accounts describe self-inquiry as a solitary activity. In recent years, both the content and process of many of these privately undertaken investigations have become part of the psychoanalytic literature.

Writing or presenting a description of a self-analytic process alters the solitary or private nature of self-exploration. Eifferman (1987b) describes the fantasies and self-reflections stirred by a particular audience she envisioned. The specific transference evoked in her directly related to these self-created perceptions. Her ability to pursue her self-understanding was deepened by her recognition of who this imagined other was and the role they played in her psychic life. Poland (personal communication, 1994) finds companionship in writing about his self-explorations by evoking thoughts of other authors' doing the same kind of work. For him, these companions are most often found among novelists and poets; Natterson and Friedman (1995) believe that writers use their own writing as "the other." Natterson and Friedman think writing about his subjective process enables him to look at his reactions and "tease out the truths of the situation."

A distinction between "the other" as a transference object and "the other" as a companion may be necessary. Silber (in press) finds that self-analytic work provides him a freedom from the fear of harming the other person. Without the fear of a hurtful impact from the expression of his anger directly addressed to an analyst, he feels able to explore and experience his aggressive feelings in greater depth. While the presence of a transference figure is not desirable, the presence of a real or imagined other as recipient of his thoughts remains important.[1]

SUMMARY FINDINGS ON SELF-ANALYSIS

Frequency of Self-Exploration

According to the results of this survey, a considerable number of analysts (92 analysts, 24%) report that they systematically undertake self-analysis on a daily basis. For many other respondents, self-analysis is a

---

[1] The implication is not that he is reluctant to discuss or explore his reactions and insights about himself with others; his extensive self-revelations about his conflicts and pain indicate his openness and his belief in the healing power of putting experiences into words.

frequent, even though not daily, part of their work (174 analysts, 46%). Although few analysts in this study describe their self-exploration as only occasional (10%) or rare (2%), 15% of analysts state that their self-reflections were not undertaken in a systematic way.

Analysts described their self-inquiries as set off by a variety of stimuli both in their personal lives and in their work with patients. The majority of analysts (318 analysts, 89%) reported that something stirred during the course of an hour with a patient would lead them to explore their own reactions. Unusually intense affective responses to patients' material, uncharacteristic behaviors in relation to patients, dreams of patients, preoccupation with patients, and enactments or impasses with patients are some of the triggers from their work that led analysts to personal inquiries.

Methods of Self-Exploration

Dream analysis was the most frequently employed technique in self-exploration. A majority of analysts reported analyzing their dreams (245 analysts, 62%) and viewed what they learned from dreams as the most reliable and trustworthy data about themselves. In the interviews, many analysts reported that they did not remember their dreams as frequently or fully as they wished, nor did they employ dream analysis as often as they thought they would following the termination of their analyses. Most analysts, however, stated that when they were engaged in trying to work on some particular issue in themselves, they paid particular attention to their dreams.

Some analysts write down not only their dreams but also their thoughts and associations in relation to the dream when engaging in self-exploration (71 analysts, 18%). Some analysts then use these reflections as a springboard for further intellectual exploration in a particular area and in creative work. For a few, new ideas emerge that then are further elaborated in teaching and writing (14 analysts, 4%).

The writing process itself was experienced by some analysts both as a method for teasing out the truths about themselves in the particular situation and as a way to modulate the affects aroused. Writing was described as a way to transform a personal pain into a valuable contribution.

Apart from dream analysis, the most frequently described method for self-exploration was a general form of reflection characterized by "thinking" about the affectively charged topic (160 analysts, 42%). Analysts varied considerably in the extent to which they describe self-reflections as organized, extensive, fleeting, or fragmentary.

THE ROLE OF THE OTHER IN SELF-EXPLORATION

Self-analysis is commonly thought of as a private project. The findings of this survey reveal that the majority of analysts usually began with private self-reflection. They, however, introduced a real or imagined other in the course of trying to learn more about themselves. Most of the respondents discussed their self-explorations (268 analysts, 67%) with a colleague, friend, or spouse. Twenty percent of the analysts (77 analysts) imagined talking with their former analyst or some other person in the course of their self-inquiry. Some analysts sought more formal assistance with the reactions stirred in them; 174 analysts (44%) initiate consultations in relation to the patient, and 160 analysts (42%) initiated personal consultations.

Writing self-reflections to someone, apart from writing-connected dream analysis, was undertaken by very few of the analysts (12 analysts, 3%). For those analysts who write, "the other" to whom their thoughts are directed is often an imagined audience.

THE ROLE OF PRIVACY VERSUS DISCLOSURE IN SELF-EXPLORATION

Questions and Method of Inquiry

From the survey findings, it is clear that many analysts express a need to communicate their experiences to another person. When analysts wrote about or discussed their self-analytic work, they continually mentioned the role that other people played in relation to self-exploration. How were the decisions made to keep self-discoveries private or to share them? When self-insights were shared, at what point in the process did this occur, and with whom? How were the revelations communicated, and how were they received?

Before describing the findings, it is necessary to reemphasize that the analysts who responded to these questions are likely to be different from those analysts who did not return these questionnaires. The respondents are people who are both interested in the question of self-exploration and willing, to some extent, to reveal personal data. The affectively charged responses about self-revelation spontaneously expressed on the questionnaires stimulated interest in learning more about why analysts would or would not be self-disclosing.

Even though anonymity was assured, some analysts expressed concerns about self-revelation. Some analysts wrote that examples were "too personal" to divulge; others, that they were "too defensive" to offer a specific example. A number of analysts provided illustrations that were "for your eyes only." Yet, in contrast, other analysts seemed to welcome the opportunity to communicate intimate material and wrote openly and fully of very personal discoveries.

Approximately half the sample offered written clinical illustrations. A smaller subset of these analysts, approximately 40%, also volunteered to discuss their illustration in greater depth in a telephone interview. As part of the interview, analysts were asked if they shared their struggles or self-discoveries with others. If they did so, what was their reason, with whom did they share it, and at what point in the process did this occur? If they did not communicate their concerns and the insights, why did they make this decision?

The material described in this section is primarily drawn from this last group, the most self-revealing group of these respondents. Therefore, when some of their reluctance to expose themselves is noted, this needs to be viewed in the perspective of a presumably even greater reluctance present in the larger psychoanalytic community.

Analysts' Views About Self-Disclosure

The responses of analysts clustered in four different patterns: (1) analysts who did not confide their self-discoveries to anyone verbally, but some of whom wrote about their self-reflections or wrote about something closely derived from what they had learned about themselves; (2) analysts who used their self-discoveries in teaching and supervising their students; usually, in these instances, the most personal aspects of the discoveries were not disclosed; (3) analysts who communicated their self-discoveries to one or two people with whom they were very close and in whom they had great trust: their spouses, who themselves most often, but not always, were mental health professionals; a close personal friend, who was also most often a colleague, or both; (4) analysts who either participated in peer groups or had a number of friends or colleagues with whom they are mutually self-disclosing. All these analysts also shared their self-discoveries with their spouses. This group of analysts tended to be the youngest in this survey.

The first group, whose self-revelations were generally kept private, comprise mainly older analysts. Some analysts who hesitated about self-revelation expressed concerns centered on competitive anxieties. They worried that if they showed their vulnerabilities, their peers might lord it over them for these frailties—even if just in their heads.

They feared that revealing limitations or anxieties might make them the losers in some fantasized competition.

Some analysts who were reluctant to confide their self-discoveries to others were more ready to risk self-exposure in writing. At first, this seems puzzling. Why would someone who is reluctant to reveal personal matters, even to a few people she or he knows, be ready to communicate them to a wide audience in papers and articles?

One analyst offered an explanation. He described how he would present personal, self-revelatory material abroad that he would not consider presenting locally. Under these circumstances, he would never see his audience again and would have no fears that the material would be used against him in a malicious way.

For example, a self-revelation he offered to a foreign audience revolved around oedipal issues blatantly exposed in a dream. While the analyst stated that he knew we all had such issues, he feared that he would be referred to as "a pervert" if he were to disclose such a dream to his colleagues at home. He stated that he could cite many instances when self-revelations had been used against colleagues. As he grew older, he felt freer to write about some of his more personal discoveries, but very circumspectly.

In the second group, the analysts made a distinction between professional discussions where self-discoveries are recounted to illustrate how they are used in analytic work and the more personal discussions in which they are reported to relieve psychic distress or to facilitate more personal development. While these two forms of discussion are similar in certain respects, and the impact of each of these dialogues may have its reverberations in the other realm, the intent behind the initiation of these discussions, at least consciously, is different.

One analyst describes his view of these two agendas this way:

> When I discuss my work in respect to what I find about myself, I am involved in something so subjective that I find it helpful to see if others think I am on the right track. Their reactions serve as a corrective for me. Other times, I share my experience with colleagues as an unburdening when something has been difficult or troubling. In these instances I am using it in a cathartic way. Then there is also a third reason for sharing with colleagues, and that is to try to understand more objectively how one can make use of these more subjective experiences. It helps to consider how they may be applied and misapplied.

The effect of sharing more personally, with my wife or close friends, is different. They can offer confirmation of what I am discovering about myself. They can cite other occasions where they have observed the same thing I am now seeing. What they tell me adds dimensions to what I have discovered.

This analyst believed that there are not usually reverberations in the personal sphere from the first kind of professional discussion; however, he thought that such discussions with a spouse or close friends were part of a process of continually working through conflictual aspects of oneself. This ongoing process is stimulated by one's work with patients but worked out in other realms as well.

One analyst stated that in professional settings, especially when she taught, she used her self-analytic explorations to stimulate others to undertake more self-reflection. She might offer personal discoveries to illustrate a particular point, for example, using empathy to understand the patient better. While she did not see herself as a self-revealing person, she thought this was not because of an inhibition. Rather, she thought that most people tend to be self-involved and would not really want to know personal material about her. Unless there were real interest, it would be an imposition to be self-disclosing. At times of psychic suffering, she would discuss self-reflections with her husband, who is a colleague, to get his help and insight.

The particular phase of the analyst's development also may influence the nature and function of self-disclosure with friends and colleagues. One analyst describes that when he was in training, he felt an eagerness to get together with his colleagues:

> to tell each other about the amazing experiences we had with patients. There was so much excitement about the endeavor, and there was a wish to recapture and share this excitement about our work.

This analyst has continued to share his reflections about himself in relation to his work, but he now does so in a much more sparing and selective way. He talks with individual friends and colleagues and belongs to a peer group. Part of the reason for communicating what he experiences is cathartic:

> Maybe I need to express my conflicts and their resolutions to get an affirmation, a confirmation, to make sure that I'm on the right

track. But sometimes, just like when I was a resident, I just feel an excitement to share a discovery.

Another analyst described a professional lifetime of talking with one particular friend/colleague whom he trusted and with whom he felt he could be completely open about his struggles, vulnerabilities, and self-discoveries. Whenever something was troubling him, he would "confess and confide" to this friend. He believes that reflection, both alone and then shared with another, leads to the synthesis of one's experiences. The synthesis of personal struggles comes, he suggested, when what we put together inside ourselves is given representation in the world. In his view, part of the consolidation of the process comes with the communication of the process to another.

Another analyst stated that he shares his experiences and self-discoveries but more sparingly than he would wish. This analyst tells his wife about his self-discoveries and has a relationship of mutual sharing with a few colleagues. In their development as analysts he sees that they are having similar experiences or learning about themselves through what they learn with their patients.

> Learning about oneself (through the work with patients) is a real benefit the field offers, not a reward I'd expected. It would be nice to have as much of that as possible . . . to share it. . . . Sharing helps confirm something you think you know. . . . There is also a certain shared enjoyment . . . like a shared meal, much more fun than eating alone.

These shared communications made him think about the issue of trust: trusting his patients, his patients' trusting him, trusting his colleagues, and his colleagues trusting him. He wondered how that trust between patient and analyst gets extrapolated into the world and reflected on a former patient of his who became a businessman "who works without contracts . . . he's known as a man of his word." He wondered how much of that quality the patient had brought to analysis and how much had developed in the process of their work. He wondered how much this patient influenced him and how much he influenced this patient.

The more this analyst considered the question of sharing what his personal discoveries were, the more he found himself thinking he wanted to do so even more. He wondered if he stopped himself because he felt he wanted to be more sure or what he would reveal. He realized that with those people whom he trusted, he already felt "comfortable and fine" about this kind of communication. He reflectd that his reluctance to be more publicly open was the fear that he would not be understood.

This analyst, like many others in the survey, notes that recently many changes in attitudes and atmosphere have taken place in the field of psychoanalysis. He sees an openness today that did not exist when he began his training some 20 years before. He was pleasantly surprised by the self-disclosures of some of his former teachers who he never expected would be willing to reveal so much about themselves. He believes the culture of many institutes has changed and considers the current atmosphere much more facilitating to deeper analytic work.

Many of the analysts state that they needed the communication with other people to do their work most effectively, both in treating their patients and in understanding and monitoring themselves. For these analysts, there was no substitute for discussing personal issues raised for them with another person. Most who emphasized the importance of communication were under 60 years old. One analyst describes that while personal material was both stirred for her and indirectly worked through in the analysis of her patient around their shared difficulties, the consolidation of psychological changes for her came through the discussion of this process with someone else.

Another analyst put it this way:

> Telling another makes it concrete. Sometimes I share what I'm working on and sometimes not . . . sometimes it makes a big difference. I don't do this until a certain point, but when I do it, it makes it more real, solid, and then something changes. . . . Sometimes I just work it through in my own mind and get greater choice and control. . . . It's a question like about mourning—can you do it without saying it out loud. This is lonely work . . . most often I talk to [spouse] . . . sometimes I talk to my analyst in my head. Sometimes I think of going back to actually talk to my analyst, but I haven't. It doesn't feel like what I want or need is more analysis now . . . but I do feel a need to talk about what I feel and find.

Similarly, another analyst described that talking about what she learned about herself through the course of her work was not only relieving to her but also an important way to strengthen her understanding. Being aware of her responsiveness to others' views, she does not bring her quandaries to others until she has first thought them through herself. Once she has thought through her own ideas, she finds her insights about herself are both validated and enriched by communicating them to those she trusts.

> When I put things in words to my husband or close friends it becomes much clearer what I am thinking. Then I can think more of what and where it comes from. When I try to formulate some understanding of myself to another person, it is useful to me.

Learning interpersonally through the reverberations from communicating with others complements the intrapsychic learning acquired through private self-reflection about personal psychological organization. One analyst saw herself as characterologically an open person; she made certain, very specific distinctions about what she shares and with whom. She, like most of the people interviewed, does not discuss material related to patients with noncolleagues. She does, however, tell her husband (who is not in the field of mental health) things she discovers about herself during the course of her work. She gave an example of telling him her recognition that her manner of withdrawing in reaction to a particularly vituperative patient was similar to her response to one of their adolescent children's attack upon her. Her insight into her reaction and her sharing this with her husband she felt, had led her to consider other, perhaps more productive, ways she now might respond to both their child and her patient.

Some analysts focused on the cognitive benefits and intrapsychic changes, while others reflected more on the emotional, interpersonal aspects of communicating self-discoveries. One of the younger analysts (in this group "younger" means in the mid-40s) was in a peer group with whom he reviewed his work. Over the years, they had become more open with each other. He said that it is still difficult for him to share certain feelings, for example, disappointment about not becoming a training analyst, or thoughts that if he were really good enough, he would have had more referrals of analytic patients. He feared that such disclosures would be met by criticism or disdain, though he acknowledges that this might not really occur. He finds, however, that revealing such concerns, along with things that he learns about himself in the course of his work, provides a mutual comfort and increases his closeness with others.

> Sharing what I feel and learn gets other people sharing. We get increasingly involved with each other, increasingly close.

Like other analysts in this study, this analyst notes that

the ideal of being perfect or perfectly analyzed no longer is believed. It makes us able to look at what we do and be more open to look at ourselves and ourselves as agents of change and of changing in ourselves. It is a relief not to have to be perfect.

Another analyst, who talks with his wife and with a psychologically attuned close friend outside the mental health field, wonders whether this urge to share comes from an early dyadic pull to be with another:

It often happens that in talking about something important to me, I learn something new, but it depends on who the other is that I'm talking to. I have a desire to learn and to share together, but I have to have a sufficient sense that the other person will understand and be coming enough from the same place . . . be sympathetic enough with me.

Being with another may make it safer to explore . . . give one more courage to move ahead and think . . . like the experience of having a hand on the back of the bicycle when you are learning to ride.

Reluctance to Self-Disclose

Sociological Factors

A number of analysts who openly and generously communicated their very personal experiences expressed a sentiment that, apart from their spouse or a trusted friend/colleague, they did not trust anyone enough to share their personal discoveries. While it is understandable that analysts, like anyone else, wish to retain their privacy and that both trust and intimacy are necessary for personal concerns to be openly communicated, the depth and extent of sentiment about feeling unsafe with even a slightly expanded group were striking.

While there are undoubtedly other reasons, fear of exposure and shame is one possible reason for the lack of response from many analysts who were sent the survey; openly acknowledged lack of trust in the reactions of other analysts was expressed by some analysts who did return the survey. Do analysts have a greater sense of shame than others? Do those members of our society who are less informed about expectations of how they are "supposed to be" tend to be more self-accepting and therefore more open both with others and with themselves about their impulses and their vulnerabilities? This is a hard question to answer since we do not have any way of collecting systematic data. But some factors might account for why analysts are particularly susceptible to feeling shame.

Analysts may have accepted, and then expected, a certain ideal of health that they may then often, if not always, feel that they do not live up to. Many American psychoanalytic institutes, at least until the 1980s, trained analysts with some very stringent standards about what constituted maturity and mental health. These were the goals to set for patients; analysts could hardly expect less of themselves. In case conferences, seminars, and many individual supervisions, the focus was often centered on psychopathological aspects of the patients. It would then not seem an unlikely outcome for analysts to fear being exposed and humiliated in front of their peers for the ways in which they failed to meet the standards of mental health. The myth of perfect health and the idea that it could be attained may have created a particular kind of defensiveness and inhibition for the educated of the 20th century.

The content that analysts fear exposing about themselves differs among the analysts. Some analysts focused on concerns that what would be seen about them would lead others to withdraw their affection and regard. Their worry was about disapproval for not measuring up to some standard, rather than the revelation of any particular content. For them, the anxiety about exposure was consciously placed on the concern that revealing themselves, which they might wish to do in order to feel a greater intimacy, might paradoxically lead those to whom they confided to turn away from them once they exposed what they perceived as their flaws.

One of the few statistically significant findings in this survey related to age. The younger analysts were more likely to discuss their self-reflections with colleagues, to seek consultations for themselves, and to return to analysis. As stated earlier, these findings may indicate only that less experienced analysts are more apt to seek help from others. The interviews with the analysts in this study, however, (granted that they are only a small number), suggest that these findings may reflect a change in attitude about self-disclosure among the younger analysts. Candidates often described their pleasure in free and open communication, but they noted that their teachers did not seem as free. They wondered what accounted for the change.

One reason for the difference in attitude between the younger and older analysts may be the transformation in attitudes that occurred in

America during the 1960s and continued into the 1970s. Authority became less revered, often suspect. Similarly, privacy came to be seen as distancing. Egalitarianism, openness, and sharing about oneself became highly valued. The younger analysts in this survey were adolescents or young adults when societal change occurred. It is not surprising that they view self-disclosure differently than do analysts who grew up in an era when privacy was valued. Obviously, as indicated by many of the references to the papers on self-analysis cited at the beginning of this chapter (e.g., Calder, 1980; Gardner, 1983; McLaughlin, 1988, 1991; Silber, in press), many older analysts were also influenced by these cultural forces to feel freer to be self-revealing. Are the sociological conditions so different in the 1990s, or will these analysts become less open as they age?

Psychological Factors

It is not clear that changes in societal attitudes mean that the younger analysts are actually less subject to the experience of shame than the older analysts are. Rather, it may be that the issues about which they experience shame are different. Most of the reluctance to reveal personal struggles likely results from what some of the older analysts described as their fear of public disapproval or private criticism from their professional colleagues. When colleagues make public disclosures of personal issues, their peers may express open disapproval or may experience private discomfort. Most often, however, the discomfort comes because the self-disclosing analyst has presented personal details in a manner that is experienced as affectively discrepant with the emotions expected to accompany the content revealed. In some instances, listeners may judge the disclosure as a counterphobic presentation and view the content of the self-exploratory journey as lacking an affective component. In other cases, the audience responds negatively to revelations that they have experienced as a narcissistic display.

Benefits of Written Self-Revelations

While self-revelatory writing may satisfy a wish for a narcissistic exhibition for some analysts, for others the motives for writing may be quite different. For some analysts, publishing material about private experiences and discoveries provides a more comfortable forum than do other modes of communication: when someone writes rather than speaks to another, the writer is not actually seen. For some analysts, the fear of exposure and sense of shame may stem from *being seen*, as affectively experiencing what one is disclosing; this may be much more anxiety provoking than to expose the same content in writing. It is less threatening if words, the conceptualization of one's affective experience, stand as something between the actual self and the other. Words on a page may move and inspire, or they may distance and repel, but they are less charged than when one is actually speaking them to someone. The authors do not have to see the response they evoke, though they are likely to hear about it. Hearing others' reactions is generally less charged than being present and perceiving how one is seen. Some disadvantages of the lack of immediate feedback are that the analyst does not have the benefit of another's perspective and potential empathy to check perceptions, modify self-criticism, or ease psychic pain.

Because analytic work can become isolating, it is easy for analysts to assume that they are alone with their experiences and difficulties. Methods of bridging this aloneness are needed. When analysts write of personal struggles they encounter in their work, they are potentially providing their colleague/readers this kind of bridge.

Unanswered or Partially Answered Questions about Self-Revelation

Some questions are not answered in these data but deserve consideration. What are the characterological differences between those who wish to share their self-discoveries and process of self-discovery with others and those who prefer to keep these experiences more private? Can any generalizations be made about these different attitudes about self-revelation? Is it possible to characterize more precisely the difference between analysts' presentations of their self-revelations that make many in the audience uneasy or uncomfortable and presentations to which the audience responds with admiration for the analyst's personal courage and is moved by what is said? How much of many analysts' reluctance to share their personal discoveries is a product of earlier training, when they were taught that personal reactions were to be "controlled" and kept outside analytic work? To what extent is "privacy" based on shame, and to what extent is it an independent value? Do we really learn more by sharing, or is this more a need to bridge an existential aloneness, something that analysts may feel more acutely than others since they cannot share with others so much of their life because of the need to maintain patient confidentiality?

At present, there seems to be a frequently expressed need for more personal forms of communication; this need for communication about personal development may be why many people responded openly to this survey.

LEARNING ABOUT ONESELF THROUGH THE PROCESS WITH THE PATIENT

In the first two sections of this chapter, I present analysts' ideas about the self-analytic process. These accounts cover the familiar territory about frequency and method of self-inquiry and begin a broader exploration of the role of "others" in the self-reflective process. An area less well documented is how analysts learn about themselves from their work with patients. While in recent years considerable attention has been given to how recognition of personal difficulties comes about through work with patients (Boesky, 1982; Gill, 1982; Spruiell, 1984; Chused, 1991; Hoffman, 1991; Schwaber, 1992), the way in which the actual work with the patient is related to expanding self-awareness on the part of the analyst is still unexplored. In the previous chapter, I described the *triggers* for recognition of a difficulty that emerged from the patient–analyst interaction. Here I consider the method and the *process* of self-understanding that evolves.

Two examples illustrate two different phases of the process. In the first illustration, analyst 5 discovers the genetic roots of his countertransference response from a sequence beginning with a countertransference reaction, bringing it to peers, and then continuing self-exploration. His account stops at the point of recognition of the personal reasons for his reaction. In the second example, analyst 6 understands only that he is having a powerful reaction to his patient, but not the reason for this reaction. Like the first analyst, he brought his struggle to understand to his peers and engaged in intensive self-exploration. He also consulted his former analyst. Unlike the first analyst, neither step brought further understanding. He then turned to the ongoing work with the patient to further his understanding. Both analysts describe themselves in the midst of a process, and neither would view himself as personally changed despite what he has discovered at this point. Both analysts, however, see their work as changed as a result of their experience with these particular patients.

Analyst 5

> The situation had to do with a patient whom I had thought to be
> eminently analyzable, very bright, involved in her work and
> training, her marriage . . . and to a certain extent because of her

problems was held back and she . . . following the birth of her daughter which was . . . a couple of years ago, . . . began to miss her appointments, was late more often, . . . it seemed very difficult to deal with on the basis of my understanding of the case. I was not being very effective in helping her understand what was going on, that it was a reenactment in many ways from her family situation in childhood . . . so I presented my dilemma to a discussion group. I thought I learned from the group. Some of the people in the group whom I knew better felt that it didn't sound like the work I ordinarily did, and they said, "You're less involved, you're quieter, what's going on anyway?" . . . someone said to me . . . there were three people in the group talking . . . "Isn't it interesting how many firstborn children there are in the group?" And that was the thing that made me realize that I had been missing a dimension as far as my countertransference was concerned . . . complicated because the patient's father's name is the same as mine, and so is her younger brother's This had skewed my listening so that I had not really thought much about my patient's daughter's birth as . . . being a reenactment for me or stirring up conflicts of the birth of my brother until this comment was made. It was following that that I realized . . . something of what I hadn't even really thought about before . . . was holding me back from engaging with the patient as I usually would, and this recognition made a difference. I couldn't say exactly how I'd been different since this; it was just that I have been able to be much more responsive, and interactive. . . . The issues continue as far as her being late and wanting to withdraw from the analysis, but it made a difference as far as my understanding of what was going on between us was concerned.

I guessed it really had to do with being aware that there were feelings that I had about the patient's baby that I hadn't been aware of . . . as being the intruder between us, and her conflict as she was experiencing it consciously was, "I am a mother, I have to spend more time with baby's name," and a lot of reality issues, but I was becoming aware that baby's name was taking her. . . . This little devil . . . taking her away from me. It seemed to make a difference as far as my being able to be more responsive about her, how she used baby's name and the problems of motherhood and her training and so forth . . . to try to remain at some distance from the analysis. I had been distancing her in a way that I just wasn't aware of before the discussion with my peers. I knew about this from my own analysis.

He was not aware of a change in his personal life. Maybe in my professional life. I discovered something I had already known about and had already gone over and over in my analysis . . . and because of all the pulls and the baby there were a lot of other things. . . . These surface things were part of it, and I thought that probably had the intensity of my feelings for the patient, who is a very attractive, smart, younger woman who I really had thought at one point would apply for analytic training, who may still at some point in the future, who would be wonderful at it if she could do it emotionally . . . I thought the birth of [baby's name] came to symbolize, a number of disappointments for me, that I had not been that in touch with regard to my patient. At that time it seemed that probably. . . . I had gotten too distant from the patient for reasons that were rather narcissistic ones.

The patient's father . . . had been very intrusive and invasive in lots and lots of ways, and her mother was very seductive and involving in other ways. . . . Closeness for the patient brings up a whole bag. . . . That's been a whole feature in the analysis really all along, but it really was more pronounced around this. She is very unusual in her intensity and her capacity to grasp things and work with them and her intellectual and emotional capacity, but she is so handicapped by this pulling back. I would say she is exceptional. It is exceptionally disappointing, and in a way it matches, [when name of patient's brother] was born, she was two, and she doesn't remember his birth, but all she remembers is that her life changed dramatically. [Brother's name— same as analyst's] was the only son in the family, and in her life it was a tremendous disappointment between the ages of two and four that the shift was away from her and to him, particularly her father's attention, and she became, not quite, but . . . it was almost as though persona non grata. She is very acquainted with this about herself.

Has he done anything more with what was stirred in relation to this patient? I think the work has been much more engaged since I recognized how it stirred up my memories of my own younger brother's birth . . . but she's now again very much involved in thinking she's going to have to stop, she can't go on like this. . . . The patient thinks her baby is worried . . . about being eaten up. People chasing her and saying to her, "You're so delicious, I could just eat you up." . . . And my patient experiences that I think she wants to be that cute and that devoured or devourable, but it is so frightening that she has to run away, sort of like the gingerbread man or Little Red Riding Hood. Children's stories that she tends to go on and on about.

I was aware of some of the personal connections . . . about how positively I felt about her and how much kind of expectation I had in regard to her, but I suppose not really limited to analytic training but what could be accomplished as a result of the analysis. So that was disappointing. So I was in touch with that but not so much the other thing . . . . it sort of blindsided me, the way this was stirring up my own of being turned away from when my brother was born.

I thought I hadn't pursued it very far but I definitely had that sense . . . that it was not so much a conscious process. I meant I was aware that I was assuming, . . . fairly certain that I got concerned at times about being not just in the transference but really like the intrusive father, my being so engaged with pursuing her in this . . . like the wolf in Little Red Riding Hood or the animal in the gingerbread man and therefore I'd pull back. . . . It becomes more and more clear as we work with it that she wishes for me to do this, . . . if only I would pursue her, indicate that I was frustrated, that I'm angry with her that she's wasting, she's throwing away her opportunities, she should be doing more with this. I think my inclination actually, rather than to be freer with those conscious explanations or things, is to pull back the same way as I had originally, and so in a way we are kind of caught in this, whatever it is that she wants so much for a indication of real interest and love.

I continue to ask myself, What's going on, what's happening, what's so stimulating? With this patient I think there is still a lot to learn about what is going on in me. I assume because it is so intense that what I will learn will change something in me.

In this case, the analyst initially recognized a problem within the treatment. Only when he brought his dilemma to his peers did he see he was behaving unusually. He needed others to point out something that he had not recognized in himself. They described his behavior to him, but they did not offer any speculations about why it was occurring. Stimulated by the observations and comments of his peers, the analyst saw parallels between his patient and himself. He had viewed this patient as analytically gifted; he knew he was consciously disappointed that she was not fulfilling her promise. He realized that he had been experiencing her baby as an intruder, just as he had experienced his younger brother. He felt that the patient's baby had taken the patient away from him as his brother took his mother from him. Memories of his brother's birth and his reactions to it were not new, but this historical material was newly seen as relevant to his reactions to his patient and her withdrawal. He thought he had resisted awareness of his developing countertransference partly by focusing on concrete dissimilarities, such as the patient's baby's being a girl. He became aware of how many positive expectations he had for this patient and how disappointed he felt that she was not fulfilling them.

As he reflected, he began to recognize more similarities between the patient and himself. He saw that he and his patient shared a similar defensive style of withdrawal in the face of disappointment and abandonment. The analyst did not reflect further on this in his interview, but based on his identification with the patient, it seems likely that his disappointment in her has resonated with whatever disappointed aspirations exist for him.

The analyst's response to the patient was not limited to his identification with her. In his countertransference withdrawal, he was also responding to her as his mother and to his patient's baby as the intruder who had taken this valued woman away from him. His feelings about his manner of protecting himself from disappointment were familiar territory. His defensive distancing was overdetermined; it stemmed both from a sensitivity to the meaning that his drawing close could have for the patient and from his own characterological style. It was also a reenactment of his response to his mother when his brother was born.

At the time he reported this case, the work was still in process. A significant shift had already occurred in his work with her. He had become much freer to address the aggression in her withdrawal. The analyst was not sure what he would learn about both the patient and himself. He knew that he was gripped by something that went on between himself and his patient and that something still not understood was being stirred.

Analyst 6

In the second case illustration, the analyst does not describe attaining a historical perspective on his affective reaction. Rather, he turns his attention to the point in the process where the first analyst stopped his reflections in relation to his case. He describes in detail his process of exploration.

> A resourceful, determined, and courageous young woman who had been abused by her family had made notable progress in the first years of her analysis. She had remembered traumatic affect and social unease and had blossomed in her personal life. In the analysis, the transference experience of a kind of asexual but intense idealization began to shift in a more erotic direction. She began to have fantasies about me, and her, us, and was excited to think that she could share them with me, and her experience in the analysis would serve as the basis for her learning about love. Although this seemed exactly what I expected and was trained to help her with, I found myself anxious and awkward in responding to her overtures. Now she was not proposing to have sex with me, merely to talk about it. And I thought this was what I wanted to do. But she picked up (before I did myself) that I became uneasy, circumspect, silent, intellectual—anything but engaged and responsive, which is how she usually found me (and needed me to be).
>
> [The analyst related the patient's romantic, mildly eroticized fantasies of a motor scooter ride. His own thoughts drift to taking such a ride with his wife.] I imagine us bumped off the thing and cut up in their fall. I can't remember exactly what I said to [the patient], but she soon complained (and accurately) that I had responded anxiously, as though I was the one who had a history of abuse. [This kind of interaction repeated itself in different guises over a period of several weeks. It led the analyst to much countertransference soul-searching.]
>
> [The analyst went on to describe how he undertook his self-reflective work and its results:] I have noticed, for instance, that I don't consciously think about her body; I don't find myself aroused in sessions with her. I am more used to having to monitor my countertransference sexual excitement than having to search for it. This is a nubile, loving woman who wants to make beautiful music with me—needs to, actually—and I am in some kind of a panic. I have been discussing this situation with peers and my former analyst at some length, exploring issues of projective identification, my own castration anxiety, oedipal guilt, guilt over my general level of seductiveness, incest prohibitions related to my daughter, etc. I have more than enough formulations to cover the situation, but no single one led to a breakthrough illumination that changed me (or the situation) very much.

The analyst then turned his attention away from these outside self-analytic explorations back to the work with his patient. He recalled a fantasy the patient had at the beginning of this period that involved hurting him. He reminded the patient about this, and they discussed the patient's concerns about harming him. The patient feared being intrusive. She worried that she would confront him with a previously unrecognized inner emptiness that would lead to his affectively experiencing his unacknowledged depression and dissatisfaction with his life. The patient then realized that she was caught between expressing her fantasies, which she believed would harm her analyst, and suppressing them, which she believed would protect him. If she did not pursue her fantasies, her analyst would be safe, but it would prevent her from attaining the freedom and intimacy she desired for herself. While, in the past, she would have opted for protecting him, she could no longer do so.

Clarification of the dilemma the patient was facing enabled the patient and analyst to understand

> the paralysis and paucity of her associations. [The analyst then realized that the patient's constriction] had in fact led me to feel adrift, unengaged, and without much to say—all of which made for a cycle of bad experience and self-criticism on the part of each of us. I think the issue of her being a danger to me is what we are struggling with—though I am not at all sure that her depiction of the terror she holds for me is the accurate one—I think she feels that she needs to make me more honest, and I want to keep my absolute honesty confined to the analytic situation, not have it leak over to my life, my self-assessment, my marriage, etc. (places where a little honesty goes a long way).
>
> I still don't experience her erotically, so perhaps the problem or enactment or whatever is just in abatement but ready to reassert itself when she seeks again to talk about her sexual fantasies.
>
> When I was exploring the countertransference, I hoped for an illuminating breakthrough of the sort analysts like McLaughlin and Ted Jacobs write about—neat, not terribly shameful, something that would "solve" the problem, and maybe make me a better person as a bonus. So far, no such luck. I remet the same themes I spent my analysis (and beyond) thinking about. But I do think that exploring it, trying to find ways to communicate with the patient about what I thought was happening, while neither blaming her nor intruding with all manner of my own concerns, was an exercise that required more from me than usual. In that sense it changed me clinically, slightly. I think this is the way clinical

analysis changes me all the time, demanding yet a little more each time.

I am working, all the time, quite close to the area of counter-transference enactment, and therefore on the edge of new or newly rediscovered self-insight. But when I actually asked myself whether this has produced change in me, I answer both yes and no—yes, I feel it, and I see it in my work with patients, but no, I don't think it's personal change of the sort that shows up in the rest of my life. Perhaps gradually, I become mellower, more accepting, less prone to argue the same lines on and on— but I think my loved ones (and colleagues) might scoff at the idea of a lot of change, currently. My patients are more the beneficiaries because they appreciate it when I work my way out of some box I have been stuck in. But if your use of the word "change" is meant to get at something more profound than the change in one's work, no, I don't deserve to pat myself on the back that much. With patients in clinical work, though, I find the change is real.

In this example, the analyst has worked very hard to attain greater understanding of himself through considerable self-reflection, consultations with his former analyst, and discussion with peers. He tries to be scrupulously honest with himself. He generates many plausible explanations for his difficulty but recognizes that none of them have a deep or lasting impact on him or the process. He is very modest about what he believes all this work has afforded him in terms of any personal or even professional change. Having exhausted all these more familiar channels for a new understanding about himself, he now believes that what he can learn about himself will emerge from his work with the patient, and he believes that it is necessary for him to learn more about himself in order to facilitate his patient's analysis. In other words, as the patient analyzes her fear of hurting him, he recognizes a resonance with this issue that he knows he must explore, or his retreat will stalemate the process. Her specific fantasy of how she would be harmful, the particular content she would be forcing him to face, does not seem to touch him affectively. What he has done, then, up to this point, is essentially say to himself: In terms of what is going on for me, I think you are right that I am afraid that you will hurt me, but the reason you think you will at this point has more to do with something in you than something in me. We have yet to discover why *I* am afraid of your power, but I do think you are right that I am.

The implication is not that the analyst would actually say all this to the patient,[2] though he might well convey the essence of it in what he so succinctly describes as "communicating what I thought was happening while neither blaming nor intruding with all manner of my own concerns." He recognizes the patient's need for him to be committed to being "more honest," and he is trying to be so; simultaneously, he is aware that such "absolute honesty" creates a pressure that he fears will make it difficult to contain this work with just the patient. The content that threatens this analyst is not clear. What is apparent is that he is intensely and intimately involved with this patient and their process.

The patient has already made notable gains from the analytic work. Many analyses stop at the place this patient has reached. This patient–analyst pair is proceeding further because both have the capacity and willingness to do so. The analyst recognizes that in order for the patient to take the next step, he must face something in himself to overcome a fear and that, in all likelihood, based on the work he has already done, this will happen with the patient rather than in any other context. He will be using her perceptions of him, her fantasies and affective reactions to him, to reflect about himself and her. He will match her views about him with his own about himself. He will say to himself what fits and is right and what is off the mark in her perceptions of him, just as the patient takes his reactions, perceptions, and ideas about her and evaluates their relevance and accuracy. Even though the analyst is doing this privately, this is now a process of mutual discovery based on their mutual trust.

The analyst works with great openness both with and about himself and his process. He lets his patient know that she has an impact on him; he acknowledges his retreat. Privately, he knows he is frightened but doesn't know why. It is clear that if he were unable to recognize that she was correct, to try to disconfirm her perception, or even to adhere to a scrupulous neutrality, she would feel too unsafe to proceed. His acknowledgment of his retreat seems, in fact, what makes her feel safe enough to continue to explore her fear of harming him. The acknowledgment means that if he can see it and talk about it, in part at least, he also knows it is a fantasy. As such, this is a disconfirmation of her really being a threat to him. This interchange between patient and analyst means both are open to the impact of the other, and change for both is likely.

---

[2] Ferenczi's attempt at mutual analysis proved sufficiently complicated and unsuccessful that most contemporary analysts do not advocate this route as beneficial to the patient or the analyst (Dupont, 1988).

Although psychological changes occasionally occur without conscious self-exploration, most often for analysts self-reflection is interposed between recognition that some unresolved issue has been stirred and resulting psychological changes. I wish to focus attention on how these two analysts employ such self-scrutiny. Most analysts offering written examples for this survey described either the triggers for self-discovery without a description of process or change or a full account of what they saw, how they worked on it, and what they learned. The illustrations offered by these two analysts are unique in that they present comprehensive overviews of a midphase of analytic and self-analytic work. Going further and deeper for both their patients and themselves requires that they focus actively and carefully on their own psychological processes in the context of their continuing work with their patients.

I also wish to highlight that the intensity of personal engagement and opportunity for personal change occur when there is an interdigitation of conflict, personal characteristics, or both between analyst and patient. The first analyst has come to understand many of the reasons for the acuity of his reaction to his patient in terms of their personal resonance. The second analyst has not yet discovered the overlap between himself and his patient that stirred him so intensely. Further consideration of these vivid accounts is offered to convey how analysts use a self-reflective process to struggle with uncertainity in the face of continuing analytic work.

It is not surprising that at these moments of personal uncertainty, when analysts have employed all their known skills and find they are still struggling to understand—and feeling anxious in their lack of clarity about themselves—they feel vulnerable to the power of a patient who could evoke such a state. Patients certainly feel vulnerable at such times, but they have come to treatment for help with such feelings. At least in part, they expect this state of vulnerability. If the analyst is committed to the patient and their work, only further self-understanding can free the analyst from this position of vulnerability.

In the first example, despite his knowledge of himself, his conflicts, and his defenses, the analyst had been caught unaware by a strong affective response. He responded without being aware that he was in the grip of an unconscious reaction. He needed an outside perspective on himself to recognize that his difficulty reengaging the patient was not a failure in his theory or skill but was rooted in the unconscious revival of early conflict and pain. His familiarity with his psychological struggles then enabled him rapidly to place the problem with the patient's treatment in a personally meaningful context. Given this understanding and his change of manner in working with the patient, why does the analyst not conclude that his difficulties will now dissolve? Why does he clearly state that this is the first phase of a process and assume that what he will learn in the course of the work will result in personal change?

The analyst understands that something emotionally powerful has opened for him in the course of his work with this patient. Recognition of the origins of his reaction enabled him to gain a perspective on what has occurred, but this is not the same as resolving the conflict that has reemerged. The analyst is aware that he has an opportunity now to rework an early painful experience. This experience of early disappointment is not all that is being revisited. The analyst seems to be saying that he recognizes that his reaction to this disappointment is the model for his response to later disappointments, which he seems to suggest he has yet to explore. He is once again confronted by this painful experience and his affective withdrawal from his patient as a reaction to both her withdrawal from him and his disappointment in her. Just as this experience occurred during the course of his own analysis in relation to his analyst, it is now revived with his patient. The analytic process that evolves with this patient then affords the possibility of some transformation of response or feeling for him. The analyst turns his attention to the process with his patient. With his new understanding of his part in the process, he is now more active in trying to engage her. He does not know what will follow, except that he is open to learning about her and, as part of this process, learning about himself.

The second analyst described being caught in the grip of an emotionally intense reaction that he does not yet understand. He understood the benefit of being open to fantasy. For his patient, he appreciated that being open to fantasies about him provided her with an "experience in analysis [that] would serve as the basis for learning about love." Presumably, analysts do not enter analytic work with a need similar to that of the patient. Once, however, we acknowledge that for all analysts there are residual conflicts, the possibility of actively reliving old issues, as this analyst described, is always present.

The extent to which the analyst becomes so personally engaged in the process with patients varies considerably. The particular overlap of issues, affects, defensive and adaptive strategies and similarities of attitudes, values, and beliefs between the patient and analyst are likely to determine the extent of emotional resonance. When resonances are great—and the analyst is not aware of why this is so—it is not surprising that he or she might come to fear the power of a patient who could evoke such strong affects. The meaning of the patient to the analyst is still embedded in an unconscious context. The patient, at that point in the treatment, has the affective importance of a transference figure but cannot be expected to behave with the scruples or consciousness of an analyst. We can see why this analyst, or any analyst, might feel the need to pull back when such a state occurs.

The usual analytic appreciation of how the feelings evoked in the patient and in himself are both about each other and, at the same time, not about each other has temporarily been disrupted. An emotional retreat, while, of course, not the desired ultimate outcome, may be an inevitable temporary state. These times, before the analyst understands what has evoked such powerful emotion, are also the times when enactments are most likely to occur. If the analyst is not as conscious of his or her reactions as this analyst seemed to be, action rather than tense containment of affective reactions may likely result.

The analyst is actively living with uncertainty, knowing something is deeply stirred, and not yet understanding what it is. It is courageous of him to present this uncomfortable, unresolved state. It illustrates an admirable and helpful self-disclosure. It is neither exhibitionistic nor self-flagellating. One has the sense of an analyst who is trying to look squarely at himself, his patient, and their work. He shares his process and the details of his struggle in order to feel less alone with them but also, implicitly, to help others recognize and be more accepting of similar struggles they may encounter in the course of their work.

A number of analysts interviewed stated spontaneously that the psychological changes that evolved in themselves out of their work with patients were an unexpected benefit from doing analytic work. Perhaps because this analysis and this analyst's struggle are active and as yet unresolved, he is less optimistic about what could change for him.

Many analysts may agree that this analyst's more modest view about the extent of personal change is realistic. This analyst has made clear, however, that if we are committed to working intensively and reaching the deeper levels of our patients' pain and difficulties, we must be open to being deeply touched ourselves. If this intense personal engagement occurs, then we must also be open to being changed. This analyst sees that his patient cannot change in the context of their work unless he can change. If he cannot, the work will founder. This does not mean that the patient could not be successful in completing this work with another analyst who was less vulnerable in this area; however, the patient would have to be willing to risk the potential dangers and disappointments of a new analytic relationship. Sometimes a change of analyst is necessary, but it is always painful and disappointing to both the patient and the analyst to accept that they can go no further.

This analyst is far from giving up; he knows from experience that he can, and does, stretch his emotional capacities in the course of his work. He states at the outset that his "basic disposition" is to work "quite close to the areas of countertransference enactment." Being open to this engagement, he expects to be asked to give more than he is accustomed. He is open to pushing himself to do so. If he can, then, just as he said of his patient, "the change is real." While many analysts may feel he has not yet pushed himself to the point of change, others might regard becoming "mellower, more accepting, [and] less prone to argue" as already reflecting considerable personal change.

If one's emotional capacity expands so that what has been feared in intimacy is understood and withstood with the patient, is it possible that this psychological change will be confined to clinical work? Certainly, we may be able to offer the best of ourselves in our work because the requirements of doing analysis are more circumscribed, both in time and quality. Still, it is hard to imagine that a personal change in one area would not have reverberations in another. In the next section, I discuss ideas about change and its assessment more extensively.

PART III

Changes in the Analyst

CHAPTER 5

Similarity of Affect, Conflict, Defense, or Situation

For the sake of the reader who is eager to see the clinical data, the presentation of theoretical ideas on change will temporarily be postponed; they will be taken up again in Chapters 9 and 10. First, however, in the following four chapters I present analysts' descriptions of work with patients that they believe stimulated or facilitated a psychological shift for them. The material is organized in relation to the triggers for recognition of a personal issue, but the focus now turns to exploring the analyst's manner of working on what has been stimulated and his or her assessment of the consequences in terms of personal transformation.

The analyst's recognition of a similarity between himself or herself and a patient means that the affect, conflict, or defense that is perceived in the patient is not so strongly defended against by the analyst that it needs to be disavowed. In order for this characteristic to be so easily recognized as akin to something in the analyst, it must, at least preconsciously, have been known, even if previously not viewed as troublesome. Often the patient may have a more blatant form of something that characterizes the analyst to a lesser degree. The perception of this affect, defense, or conflict in exaggeration may allow the analyst to see more clearly an aspect of himself or herself that is known but not viewed as a particular source of distress. Seeing the patient's struggles and recognizing the consequences of the particular difficulty, the analyst may become more aware of his or her own struggles around the same or a similar area. Formerly unrecognized or unacknowledged consequences in the analyst's life that result from this issue may be seen. Consequently, this previously less focused-on area becomes experienced as less acceptable to the analyst. What formerly was viewed as more syntonic, possibly because it was viewed more as just part of the analyst's character, then becomes experienced as more dystonic as its disruptive aspects are recognized in externalization.

Sometimes the similarities that the analyst perceives between himself or herself and the patient occur in areas that the analyst recognizes as unresolved or still somewhat troublesome. In these instances, the analyst is alert from the outset to the possibility of assuming more similarity than might actually exist and of possible overidentification resulting in "blind spots" for the analyst. The danger here is that the analyst will fail to explore the patient's experience adequately because of an assumption that it is already known and understood because of the similarity. Under these circumstances, the similarity works to the detriment of the growth of both parties. A stalemate of the analytic work is apt to result. A stalemate, at least, is a recognized problem that draws both parties' attention to it and, therefore, is likely to be addressed within the analysis, if it can be, or through consultation with someone else, if it cannot. A worse consequence is a possible collusion in which both patient and analyst feel close in their similarity, but the problematic aspects of the particular characteristics or conflicts remain unrecognized and, therefore, unexamined. This failure to explore and expand the areas in which patient and analyst are similar impedes the growth for both parties. Sometimes such similarities may actually reinforce previously deleterious identifications and, for both parties, may serve to solidify further maladaptive identifications and solutions. Thus, what serves as an opportunity for growth and expansion may turn into a detrimental situation if the analyst does not stay alert to the fact that similar does not mean the same and if the analyst does not continue to question and explore the patient's experience. Usually, when an analyst is referred a patient who is seen as sharing central conflictual issues, the analyst who believes his or her own difficulty is sufficiently troublesome refers the patient to a colleague. If, on the other hand, the analyst believes that he or she has sufficient perspective on these conflicts, he or she may believe that this attunement to these areas may benefit the patient. Under these circumstances, in the course of the analytic work, the analyst as well as the patient may deepen his or her understanding and rework these conflicts and achieve a new integration.

In the following six examples, analysts describe the impact of working with patients whom, in some respect, they perceive as similar to themselves. In the first two examples, the analysts who have identified with their patients around a shared difficulty use the more objective view they maintain in relation to the patients' struggles to achieve a new perspective about themselves. In the third example, a similarity of situation serves as the stimulus for a previously repressed memory to emerge and be reworked. The last three examples illustrate analysts' identifications with their patients in their similarity of life stress, pain, conflict, or any of these, and the reworking of these struggles occurred in the context of the work with the patient.

Analyst 7: A Similar Fear of Loss of Affection and Connection Reopened by a Similar Situation

Identification with his patient's situation and response to it enables the analyst to reopen and rework previously painful experiences and conflict. Recognition of the "unrealistic" aspect of his patient's reactions helps the analyst take a new perspective on his own responses.

> The patient had been to a family gathering where her brother and father got into a terrible argument, and her brother left. . . . The patient was afraid that she was never going to see her brother again due to this altercation. As the patient described this, I felt a sense of loss before the patient was aware of fearing her brother would reject her. I thought the patient's upset was much greater than the situation warranted. . . . The brother and father seemed angry at each other and not at her. I felt my patient was blaming herself for something that was not her fault. . . . I felt guilty in relation to my children because of a divorce. [The analyst then realized that he feared he would lose his children.] I was afraid that my children would not want to have anything more to do with me.
>
> [Later, self-reflection enabled him to place his reaction in its historical context.] As I continued to think about my reactions, I connected my guilt to feelings in relation to my sister. When I was five years old and she was eight months, I had been left to watch her. . . . She had been injured, not permanently, but in a way that had been frightening and very upsetting to me. . . . I knew my being prone to feel too responsible, my concerns about being blamed for things I had not done, and my fear of loss of affection all had their origins in this situation. [The work with his patient offered him a chance to

reopen and rework these issues. The analyst described the manner in which he pursued his self-reflective work.]

Usually if something was troubling me I would attempt to analyze my dreams. In this case, I made a big attempt to spend time lying alone on my couch trying to free-associate [in order] to understand why this situation had had such an effect on me.

Over time, I found that I had much less concern about loss of affection from my children. . . . I felt more secure with them and others, dear to me . . . and I think I became much freer.

The similarities between the patient's situation and the analyst's are that two people in the family (the patient's father and brother; the analyst's wife and himself) have a falling-out with one another. This conflict does not directly relate to, or involve, the analyst's or his patient's feelings about other family members (for the patient, this is herself; for the analyst, these are his children); however, both conclude that the alienation of affection that exists between these family members will be generalized and disrupt both ties of affection and contact within the larger family group. The analyst can, and does, empathize with how his patient feels.

The interdigitation of the patient's reactions with his own reopens these early feelings and fantasies and provides another opportunity to rework this painful childhood event and its vicissitudes. The analyst does not tell us how he reworks these experiences beyond these initial explorations, but over time he believes he becomes less anxious about the loss of affection from his children and from others.

Analyst 8: Recognition of a Maladaptive Personal Characteristic by Perceiving it in a Similar but Exaggerated Form

The analyst is able to see a maladaptive aspect of himself more clearly in its more exaggerated form as presented by the patient. Seeing it so clearly enables the analyst to change his behavior. Once stopped, he believes he can analyze its origin.

The analyst had completed his training analysis before he began to treat the patient about to be described. The patient was a supervised case.

The patient was taking a Ph.D. in theology and was also a farmer. . . . This man felt beleaguered by his mother, a religious fanatic. . . . He resisted her with much rage and self-righteousness. . . . I felt pessimistic about the patient's analyzability. . . . My supervisor thought my reaction represented an identification with the patient and a residue of unanalyzed negativism. He promised me that if the analysis succeeded, I would experience it as a second analysis for myself. [As the analysis proceeded, he thought the patient sounded more and more like him.] My own analysis was focused on oedipal issues, while my patient was engaged in conducting a religious war with his mother as the leader of the Inquisition. This kind of fighting and struggle had not been at the center of my own personal analysis, but in the course of working with this patient, I came to recognize it as more and more similar to my own conflicts.

Two and half years into the analysis, the patient left the analysis and went to work on his farm during the summer and did not return in the fall; nor did the patient drop me a note to explain his absence. My supervisor called me when I did not return to supervision and inquired about what was happening. He wondered whether I should contact the patient. I thought I shouldn't. The patient returned in November. He had been working like a slave. The analysis resumed and was ultimately successful. How did I know the right thing was not to bother him? I thought if I pursued him, the patient would have felt as if he was pursued in the Inquisition.

Putting myself in the patient's place meant that I had seen how the patient and I were the same. Once I saw the similarity, it stood out enlarged. The patient's negativism was like a caricature of my own.

Self-righteousness was a huge issue for the patient, and I saw that it was for me as well. Seeing an issue so clearly made it more pathological. It became like looking in a mirror that enlarged the image and made it look more ridiculous. Then one stops it . . . one changes one's behavior first and then gains insight after. Only after it stops does one become clear about what function it served. . . . One doesn't change overnight. I can still get self-righteous but now with some embarrassment.

Having become aware of my vulnerability to engage in struggles, I turned my back on situations that were likely to get me caught in struggles. . . . It would be misleading to attribute the change all to this one negativistic patient. There were many other experiences. . . . So there were always reminders of my impulse to struggle. . . . I found I was increasingly successful in dealing with patients' negativism over time. . . . I stopped fighting and started doing my own work. It took a long time. . . . Gradually as this tendency to oppose others turned into an eagerness to think for myself, it became easier not to accept the projective identification where I was the inquisitor. . . .

Over time, I became able to respond to patients' provocations with more and more humor, joking with them that they expected me to be a sucker, to fight with them like their parents did. . . . I would make it clear that I experienced the provocation, but it became easier to deal with it. . . .

I don't think negativism has played much of a role in my personal life as an adult after my analysis, but it did creep into my dealing with professional organizations. In this arena, I feel I was still vulnerable to be drawn into struggle and to demonstrate intolerance. . . . I tried not to be involved because I knew my tendency. My solution was to stay away from trying to be in positions of power and instead to have and express my opinions, however maverick they might seem. Over the years, I believe I have become less judgmental.

This analyst believes that a cognitive recognition of personal difficulty is the first step in the process of change. Following his perceiving his negativism, he resolved not to engage in this behavior and avoided those situations that stimulated this tendency in himself. He believes his tendency to be negativistic gradually was transformed into his holding his own point of view. He does not report the process by which this transformation occurred. Nor does he explain why or how he became less judgmental. Unlike most accounts in the psychoanalytic literature and many of the examples offered by the analysts in this survey, this analyst's view of psychological change is that behavioral changes precede, rather than follow, insight and working through. Recognition, stopping the recognized behavior, and then some unspecified method for reaching an understanding of the development of the characteristic and the function it served are the steps that this analyst describes in the process of transforming a maladaptive quality into an adaptive one. He makes it explicit that the transformation in himself did not occur based on one experience. Rather, it was achieved slowly over time and remained a tendency he had both to struggle with and keep in his awareness.

Analyst 9: Recovery of Repressed Memories Evoked by Similarities of Anxiety Around Separation and Loss

Through the exploration of her patient's similar situation, the analyst reports recovering a repressed memory and reworking painful affect from an early childhood experience. Long-standing symptoms were newly understood and alleviated.

The patient, a woman in her mid-30s, had developed severe anxiety, which had never occurred before in her conscious memory. In her anxiety, she found herself in a frenzy, going several times a day from her own house to her mother's house, which was a couple of blocks away, to her sister's house which was a couple of blocks away in the other direction. She had no conscious idea what she was looking for or why she suddenly felt the urge to do this. The only thing I knew about her in terms of her childhood history was that during her latency, [the patient's] parents' marriage had dissolved, and her father had left. As I listened to the patient struggling with anxiety, I had a wave of memories of my own that had to do with my having been taken from my own mother when I was 26 months old. My mother had been very ill. . . . At 4:30 in the morning, my father had taken me to my maternal grandparents because my mother's illness was considered very contagious.
[As the analyst began thinking about this incident, which was not a new memory, a new memory came to her.] I remembered going outside my grandparents house and going up and down the street looking for my father and mother's house which was really not close, but I didn't know how far it was, and feeling in a kind of frenzy. I then spontaneously said to my patient, "You're trying to find your father."
The patient had not seen her father since he disappeared, although the mother had some contact. The patient began to cry, which had not been something she had done about this experience. She then told me that her anxiety was just sort of ebbing away, and she said, "now I remember. . . . I was in kindergarten, and I came home from school one day, and I found that my father wasn't there, and I thought that I'd never see him again. Where did he go?" . . . She ran all over the neighborhood looking for her father. . . . This is what it was feeling like to her, this activity that was going on in her life recently. . . . This is exactly how it felt. And after that session, this behavior stopped, and we got on to other things that had to do with her father's disappearance.
[Following this hour, the analyst began to rework her own childhood experience.] I began to dream about my early separation experience again. I also began to understand the anxiety I would experience waking at night. . . . The memory revived in

relation to my patient brought together a number of other memories that I had about that particular situation. . . . It also explained some of the anxiety that I found I had in certain circumstances. . . . Very often I would wake up at 4:30 or 5:00 in the morning—which was the time that I had been taken away—with this kind of anxiety. . . . I began to dream about this experience again. I was in analysis at that time and was working on this whole issue. I had a new memory in my own analysis of waking up in the early morning of the day that my father took me and having gone into my mother's room to get a doll because I knew that I was going to be taken away . . . and seeing my mother looking very dead. [The analyst then thought she understood the reason for her nighttime awakening.] It occurred in order for me to be sure that I was alive, . . . to counter an identification [I had made] with [my perception of my] mother at the moment when I was taken away from her. The experience with my patient had triggered a whole series of psychic events for me that caused a lot of memories and new understanding of some of the symptoms that I had had in my adult life.

   I also found that my previously defended-against empathic abilities were now enhanced when dealing with certain aspects of pathology in patients for whom separation was an issue.

A patient's intense, but not yet comprehended, anxiety around separation and loss mobilized similar memories of early anxiety about separation in the analyst. The similarity of situation and affect stirred brought these new memories of the analyst to her consciousness. Whether or not what the analyst calls a memory is the recollection of an actual event is, of course, not clear. It may well be a useful constructive blend of her past experience and her patient's experience. In any case, the analyst's uses her "memories" as a guide to understand the reasons for the patient's anxious state. She uses these thoughts as a bridge to the patient's similar experience and thereby reconstructs the reasons for the patient's panic. The patient's calming and her further associations seemed confirmatory of the analyst's hypothesis.

   The experience of exploring her patient's panic and its resonance with the analyst's own early separation and experience of panic reopens the analyst's previously explored, but never quite calmed, feelings of anxiety around separation. The patient's image of herself frantically searching is matched by the analyst's previously repressed memory of her own frantic search for her mother when she was separated from her. Reopening anxiety-laden memories from early childhood and linking them to her symptom of anxious night waking begin a process of her reworking this traumatic period in her dreams. Her new understanding had a calming effect on her. She states, but does not elaborate in a manner that the reader can grasp, that her capacity for empathy with some defensive adaptations to separation issues increased.

Analyst 10: Similarity of Attitudes, Values, and Approach in Relation to a Similar Frightening Life Event

Working with a patient who had a similar character structure affords the analyst an opportunity to rework and better integrate a frightening life event. The analyst had had breast cancer at a relatively young age. It had been detected very early in its onset and treated successfully.

> As time went on, the memory of it fade[d]; I never repress[ed] it, but the affective intensity diminished. Nevertheless, my fears could be reawakened and stirred up very rapidly again when others in my personal and professional community who knew of my experience with dealing with cancer came to talk with me when they found themselves diagnosed with this illness. I made the decision not to treat others who had cancer, thinking this would be too frightening to me. I thought I would not be able to attend to their concerns, that it would be awful for me and not useful for them, and I didn't need to do that to either of us so I turned away those referrals.
>
> Quite a number of years later, a beloved supervisor of mine—someone very important to me—who had retired, referred to me a patient whom he had previously analyzed. He didn't ask me if I wanted to see her; he just said, in essence, you are going to see her.
>
> [The former supervisor said he thought they would be "a good match."] I felt I could not have done it earlier, but based on my feelings of admiration and affection for him and because of his confidence in me, I wanted to try it. . . . The patient came to see me in a state of panic. I understood that the cancer we had each faced was very different. While my own prognosis had been positive, and the postsurgery treatment had been short-term and not intensive, though still very frightening, the patient had been diagnosed with a severe form of cancer, likely to be fatal, and had intensive postsurgery chemotherapy. In spite of these very real and signifi-

cant differences, I felt that in helping this patient . . . in knowing firsthand and reliving as the patient talked of some of her experiences, . . . although some of the experiences were very different because of the differences in the cancer, . . . that something inside of me got worked through in relation to my own previous traumatic experience with cancer. . . . As I talked with my patient about her terror of dying, I had to confront my own terror again . . . as I did this, I found something shifted inside of me that had to do with gaining control of certain fears but also feeling more at ease with the notion of dying. . . .

The patient was seen in an obviously supportive psychotherapy. However, the patient made use of her previous analysis, . . . worked on dreams and easily brought in previously attained self-awareness, which she could now employ to see the ways in which she reacted maladaptively. I found it easy to follow her lead . . . to be helpful to this patient, whom I greatly admired.

The patient handled her illness with a wonderful courage and a witty sense of humor, which she used in her best interest. I felt that my admiration of her coupled with my ability to help her when she was falling apart was extremely useful to me personally. . . . I could identify with my patient's courage and could feel very good about myself because I felt I was so useful to her in helping her face what she had to face and making it go better for her.

The patient was very grateful for my insights . . . it gave her control over her fear and in fact a lot of control over situations and doctors and helping her husband. . . . There were clear, quick, observable results. . . . I felt identified with the patient and was very admiring of her capacity for adaptation and mastery. . . . In the background was my beloved supervisor, who had been this patient's beloved analyst. The patient felt he had been of enormous help to my patient . . . she had been very grateful to him. My patient saw me as an extension of him and came to trust me. . . . For me, my mentor's belief in me and my capacities felt like an endorsement. . . . I also think our being women together was very useful to both of us in our shared working through of terror of cancer.

[The work with the patient felt "very circular" to the analyst; helping the patient master her fears helped her master her own.] I could borrow her [the patient's] courage and . . . use some of my own thinking in a way I had not done before. [As a result of this very powerful and initially dreaded experience, the analyst came to feel less afraid of having a recurrence of cancer.] I feel less scared of my own fear, and more grown up.

[The analyst was clear that it was not just that she had worked with a patient who had cancer that had helped her master her fear but that she had worked with someone with whom she was very positively identified.] This patient was someone whose characterological adaptation to this illness was one I admired. . . . I wished to identify with her. [Later, she treated another patient who had cancer and toward whom her feelings were the opposite.] This other patient with cancer used her illness in a manipulative way, in line with a previously hypochondriacal style that I did not admire and wished to distance myself from. . . . The first patient was a fighter as I wished, and wish, to be; the second patient was not and presented countertransference difficulties for me. . . . I had to fight against my feelings of disapproval of her coping strategies.

The analyst concluded that the psychological change effected in her by working with the first patient with cancer had as much to do with their being a good match in terms of character as their sharing the experience of an illness.

All the qualities the analyst admired in her patient the analyst herself seems to have. The similarity of experience and character enabled this patient–therapist pair to explore the impact of their terrifying illness in the context of mutual respect and admiration. The patient, in these respects, served as a good parent or supervisor in relation to the illness. The mutual tie to, and admiration for, the analyst's supervisor and patient's analyst, still further strengthened their emotional bond. He seems to have provided support as a mentor or guide to both patient and analyst, at least in their fantasies. The analyst reported that the treatment did not involve the analyst's self-disclosure about her illness and reactions to it, though, at times and in minor ways, this may have occurred. The focus was the patient's experience, and there are no indications that any mutual analysis took place, but the treatment provided support and promoted mastery for both participants. A perspective was also gained through the passage of time since the analyst's original illness and the comparison of the analyst's situation with the patient's. The psychological shifts seem less related to insight than a reopening and reworking of early pain and fear in the context of mutual respect and regard.

Analyst 11: Similarity in the Use of Work to Master Early Life Trauma and Similar Depressive Pain

Identification with a patient's use of his work both to master and to reexperience painful experiences from the past facilitated an analyst's deeper exploration and reworking of his own residual pain.

> One of my control cases was a social worker who worked with disturbed children. He was very good at what he did and amazed other people and me with his tolerance and his patience and his ability to deal with particularly very disturbed adolescent boys. . . . He was kind of a nice, gentle man to begin with. . . . One of the reasons he went into analysis was that in other areas aside from his work he was rather inhibited in relation to other people and rather chronically depressed for reasons that weren't clear. He was married. He also tended to drink a fair amount, which was a part of his depression. The thing that . . . activated my self-reflective process was the recognition that his work with these disturbed adolescent boys had a lot to do with his early childhood experiences with a younger brother who was a very disturbed kid who later ended up in a state prison and was a chronic criminal. He [the patient] was very good at his work but . . . one of the problems connected with it—was that it also reminded him of his childhood experiences with this brother and how painful it had been, . . . particularly later when he had to visit him in juvenile detention homes and in the course of going through this with him. I began to be aware of how I had been affected by my rather depressed mother as a child and how involved I had been with her in trying to bring her out of her depression or deal with this and how I sort of became her therapist. It was something I was aware of before. . . . It was sort of a mixed blessing. It led me into the profession I am in, and I think I also have a capacity to be pretty good at this work, but at the same time there was a depressing quality to it. That was the thing that I learned from this patient, how what he did and what he was so good, at the same time, reminded him of some very painful and depressing childhood memories that I had thought I sort of worked out in my own analysis a fair amount. This all occurred postanalysis for me. It gave me a chance to . . . rework all that and to understand myself better . . . why I still had a tendency to get depressed at times when I didn't, couldn't, see anything else that I was going through except that I was engaged in working with some rather

depressed patients at the time. Their depression would sort of activate something in me. . . . The interaction with this patient in a sense was therapeutic for me. Over a period of time it led to greater self-understanding and ability to . . . not be so affected, as I tended to be, particularly working with depressed patients. . . .

It was mainly self-analytic work. I did talk to a couple of colleagues who I found out had had kind of similar experiences in early life. They had been involved with a rather disturbed parent, and we were able to compare notes and talk a bit about our experiences and what led us to becoming analysts and how there was a kind of revival of some of the old childhood traumas at times involved in our work. But it was mainly . . . a self-examination and kind of identifying, a bit of empathizing with this patient, . . . one of the problems I became aware of with him [the patient] was of being careful sometimes not to confuse what [my patient] was telling me, what my patient's experiences had been, and what my own had been. So I had to watch that. . . . It was a supervised case, and the supervisor, who was an experienced analyst, was rather helpful to me about this. . . . I told the supervisor a bit about myself and why this was a problem so there was a fair amount of discussion about it. . . . I would begin a process of reflection when I noticed a mood alteration, particularly a depressive mood when I couldn't really hook it up with a life experience, anything that was going on that was bad, or having trouble with anyone. Something was getting activated, and then I would start thinking about it, and often it would lead back to some clinical work I had been doing with some patient, often a depressed one that was affecting me in ways that I had not been too aware of at the time, or thought much about, and I just began to become aware of this kind of potential . . . which hasn't entirely gone away completely after. . . . I still have down moods that get set off by going to see certain kinds of movies where I get caught up with one of the characters and what they are going through, and I notice it will affect me for two or three days. Then I start thinking about what that is all about and will refer it back to the movie and what was going on there. . . . At least I have a much greater awareness of this and less vulnerability to getting depressed moods than I used to several years ago, and I'm able to pull out of it more rapidly. . . .

In addition to a depressed mother I also had a somewhat alcoholic father, and they were sort of connected. That's one of the reasons that she was so depressed, because he had a rather severe drinking problem . . . that used to cause when I was growing up a fair amount of distress, and I used to get pretty angry at him about it. . . . There are times that specific . . . marital conflicts that I hear about will remind me of that. I don't like to hear people argue . . . even in the movies . . . I get distressed at that kind of marital battle going on, and yet, interestingly enough, I have done marital therapy for about 25 years. I consider myself rather good at it, too, but it still bothers me . . . and it isn't so bad when they talk about their battles, but when they do it right in front of me, then I don't enjoy it very much. . . .

One of the problems that I had particularly as I got older and got into adolescence was feeling a great sense of responsibility for these fights. I was an only child. It was my responsibility to solve their problems, and yet I'd gotten pretty upset and angry at them for having these fights. I think that over a period of time I've been able to be a bit more empathic with myself as I was back then and not be so self-judgmental, and also it helped me in my clinical work over the years. I used to have a real problem about feeling too responsible for what happened. Like it was . . . up to me to solve the problem, and if I didn't, if things didn't go well, I was a major failure. I still take my work very seriously and try to do a good job, but it doesn't get to me nearly as much as it used to.

My analysis . . . allowed me to feel much more comfortable with myself and much less prone to getting into really deep depressions, but in terms of percentages I think there are still some residual issues.

A difference now is that I sort of have an ability to be empathically involved but still at the same time removed . . . not get caught up so much or have my own emotions get caught up so much, to be a bit more objective if you want to call it that. . . . It used to be a greater problem than it is now. Not that I'm indifferent or don't care what happens to people or that I'm not often affected by what happens to them, but I think I'm much better able to deal with its really getting to me or causing me personal difficulty or grief or getting particularly depressed.

I think . . . it is . . . the ability of greater understanding over a period of time about why people get depressed, and maybe I am even less wholly committed to the idea that it is just life experiences, that some people are prone to it, that it is based on some kind of genetic or biochemical propensity or vulnerability. . . . I no longer just ascribe it entirely to unempathic or poor parenting or life experience alone but maybe that they just had a . . . vulnerability to begin with. I think being a parent and grandparent, I've developed a greater empathy . . . understanding of parents and the parenting process and how difficult it is . . . I think I have been able to go back and . . . be more forgiving and accepting of my parents and less critical of them than I had been, or once was, which made me feel rather guilty because I was rather critical. . .

It is not so much going back and finding fault, particularly with my parents. I no longer think that they shouldn't have done this or that . . . I have a greater appreciation of how difficult it is for people to be parents who are suffering themselves as my own parents were and as many people are . . . how difficult it is to come from backgrounds where they have not had ideal family circumstances that were caused by the difficulty that their own parents went through. . . . A roundabout way of saying that I am more accepting of human frailties and shortcomings than I was 20, or 25, years ago, including my own. . .

When my own grandson, who had been sick from birth, died at six months, my tendency to be depressed beyond the understandable grief returned. . . .

I was really glad I was able to regain my balance and be helpful to my daughter with her grief in a way in which I felt very proud. I feel that I have been happier and less prone to depression in the last 20 years.

The analyst's work with this patient facilitated his recognition of the pain that is reevoked by his working with patients whose depressive issues mirror some of his own affective experiences. His acknowledgment of feelings that he implies were previously at least partially denied or isolated enabled him to rework and reintegrate his pain.

Sharing with colleagues experiences of similarly determined needs, overlapping experiences of affect, and an awareness of their influence on their selecting a career, the analyst broadened and deepened his appreciation of the role that depression and the struggle to master it plays in people's lives. This increased exposure to others' similar experiences served both to protect his treatment with his patients from the intrusions of assumptions of unwarranted similarities and to expand his appreciation of the nature of depressive feelings and dealing with a depressed family member. From what he describes, it is clear that this analyst always had the capacity to be helpful to others. The psychological change he describes is not in his empathic, caretaking ability but rather in the extent to which he is able to gain some distance from his own depressive tendencies and experience more pleasure and happiness in his life. His awareness of the role of depression is brought more sharply into focus by his work with the patient described. But he makes it clear that his reworking and reintegrating his issues take place gradually over time and are facilitated by multiple life experiences.

Analyst 12: Similarity of Struggle Around Identification as the Victim or Victimizer

An identification with a patient in her terror and her wish to distance herself from it leads an analyst subtly to enact the experience of terrorizing and being terrified in the transference–countertransference interaction. The enactment reopens his early-life frightening experience, which was further reworked in his self-exploration.

> A married woman patient, mother of two children, dreamed of a little girl for whom she felt maternal responsibility. In the dream, the girl was in danger of being raped, and the patient rescued her. I recalled and reminded the patient that she had told me that she had been raped at knife-point as an adolescent. My memories then went to being in the basement as a child, where my mother would kill fowl by slicing their throats with a knife. In later years, I realized that I was terrified of my mother. . . . And I remembered that I had felt discomfort when my patient told me that she wanted to slice the balls off the rapist. . . . I told the patient that her dream might be a reliving of her rape. She became angry and accused me of forcing her to recall this experience. She called me the rapist. . . . We had each played out and experienced being the aggressor and the victim at the same time. . . . The patient reexperienced the rape, and I reexperienced my fear of my mother as the attacker. I felt attacked by the patient, and she felt I had attacked her. . . . After the session I worked on the notion of my fear of my mother and my fear of my guilt. . . . I felt a sense of well-being and thought that I was probably in the process of mastering residual sadomasochistic aspects of myself. . . . I recalled as a child I had engaged in sadistic acts toward animals, like toads,—not for food as my mother had. These were known memories . . . over the last few years in my work with a borderline patient [a different patient, I had become more experientially aware of my latent aggression. . . . This regressed woman had put greater pressure on me with her demands. . . . I felt that I had given inordinately but it had never been enough for the patient. [In my work with

this borderline patient the content [that I explored in relation to myself was not new, but the extent of awareness and experience of my anger and its mobilization was greater. I had to struggle to make aggression more syntonic. . . . I get angry and then feel guilty about my anger. . . . Gradually, it got less extreme, more ordinary. I became more knowing of my own rage. . . . With the first woman patient the woman who had been raped, I had a more abstract awareness of her aggression. My response to her was the resurrection of shopworn memories and an awareness of an identification with the patient as both aggressor and victim. With the borderline patient, the affects stirred had been more intense . . . a lot of *Sturm und Drang* . . . endless phone calls, followed by suicide threats, leading me to feel frustrated, angry, irritable, and at times unable to sleep. The current affective distress and sleepiness brought up memories of difficulty sleeping as a child and my fury with my mother. As I went over these memories in conjunction with each incident with the patient, my memories became fresher, more filled with affect. I felt less need to apply reaction formation to my feelings . . . more acceptance of myself and more pleasure in knowing myself and my feelings than in my previously experienced sense that I needed to meet someone else's standards . . . my increased acceptance of my anger allows me to use it more creatively in my work. Personally, I came to have less doubt about myself, more acceptance of mortality, fewer narcissistic defenses, and more participation in the world both joyously and sadly.

Although the analyst does not spell it out, he refers to his reaction formation against his aggression, his way of distancing himself from his early terror, and seems to suggest that he achieved this mastery by turning passive into active, an identification with the aggressor, and then a reaction formation to that aggression. His patient in her dream, through becoming the rescuer of the victim, seemed to be trying to master the terror of her rape by turning passive into active. In the dream, the patient then successfully avoids reexperiencing the terror of the memory of the rape, just as the analyst did when he successfully employed, reaction formation against his sadistic impulses or even when he was in the position of the attacker. His countertransference was to his patient as his mother, who forced on him a scene that was frightening.

The analyst describes his enactment of forcing his patient to reexperience the rape and so leading her to feel him as the rapist; this enactment is his response to feeling he was made a victim by her; her memories of her terror have evoked his memories of his own terror. While this seems to reflect what had occurred, it bypasses a first step in which he seems to have responded to her defensive avoidance of terror by an unconscious sadistic wish to disrupt her relatively effective strategy. The analyst relates that work with another patient had led him to experience and face previously unknown depths and intensity of his own anger. It is as if the analyst, having had to face and experience the pain and shame of owning such powerful aggression and having had his effective defensive strategy disrupted by the aggression, mobilizes himself in reaction to the previous patient's aggression. In retaliation for his facing his aggression, he then becomes impelled to dislodge this patient's relatively comfortable distance from her aggression. If he has to experience his aggression, she has to experience hers. It seems that because he was no longer so defended against his aggression, he comes closer to the experience of the original terror that led to his aggressive reaction. Since the patient's dream stimulated memories of terror and, presumably, affects of terror for him, unconsciously he felt justified in "terrifying" her in response to her having terrified him. His conceptualizing the interactions with his patient as a continued reworking of his own sadomasochistic issues seems supported by this account.

As we have seen, the recognition by the analyst of a similarity between a patient and himself or herself has the potential for expanding the analyst's self-knowledge and shifting some aspect of the analyst's psychological organization. The nature and extent of this shift depend on the particular overlap of issues, character, and situation as well as the analyst's openness to undertaking self-exploratory work at this particular time. I now return to these examples with a focus on the analyst's process. Each analyst undertakes this personal analytic work in a slightly different manner, although it is apparent that all these analysts subscribe to a similar theoretical perspective.

A new perspective can be gained when an analyst views a patient's struggling with conflicts similar to his own and is able to recognize the power and difficulty of relinquishing irrational beliefs. When analyst 7, who continued to fear loss of affection and felt "too responsible," sees that his patient's similar feelings are unwarranted by the reality of her situation, the comparison made him more aware of the irrational nature of his own feelings.

It may be precisely because he recognized that his patient's feelings were not rational, based on the situation, that his response caught his attention. If he were to respond as he did in relation to a situation in which his patient's fears of lost affection and contact seemed a likely outcome, he might have thought his reaction a rational, understandable empathy with his patient. Since he saw her response as irrational and, nonetheless, empathically joined her, he needed to reflect on what was being stirred in him. Recognizing the resonance, he compared his patient's feelings and the situation that evoked her response with his own feelings and situation. The fact that he saw that his patient's fears were not warranted by the circumstances could then be used as a new way of considering his own situation: his fears in relation to his children might be equally as irrational as his patient's fears with respect to her brother. The comparison helped him achieve more distance from his affective response.

Returning to thoughts of his own history, he made understandable to himself why these "irrational" beliefs and fears developed. In other words, he did with himself something analysts do with their patients; he elaborated the factors that contributed to his current feeling and thinking. The analyst explored why he was prone to respond with the expectation that he would be blamed and ostracized by his family. His self-reflection connects his current sense of guilt with a childhood experience of guilt. As an adult, he could understand that a five-year-old child was too young to be given this much responsibility, that her accident had not been his fault. He seems to imply, though he does not make it explicit, that it was also irrational to anticipate he would lose parental affection because of this occurrence. His vulnerability to feeling overly responsible, self-blaming, and anxious about losing the affection of others was then reevaluated in this context. He then was better able to understand how these earlier constructions are being "irrationally" applied currently.

Undoubtedly, this analyst had done this reconstructive work in his own analysis; however, the analyst is at a different stage of life. His analysis took place prior to his divorce and remarriage. Changes in the analyst's life necessitate reworking old conflicts in the context of the current situation. In this present context, seeing his patient experience a reaction similar to his own brings home the "irrationality" of his reaction with a new force. Using his recognition of his similarity to his patient created a greater perspective on his own reaction and helped him better separate the past from the present.

For this analyst, the psychological shifts are subjective. There is no indication that he believes anyone other than himself would detect his internal shift. Nonetheless, for himself, the shift in his sense of security in his relationships means a concomitant decrease in anxiety and inhibition and thus a greater sense of well-being.

Characterological traits may come to be experienced as dystonic when the analyst sees an objectionable character trait in a patient that is perceived as similar to a trait in himself or herself. Discerning the similarity permits the analyst to view it more objectively. This changed view creates a shift in perspective that presumably leads to behavioral changes that are potentially observable, not only a changed internal experience. The existence of an analyst's character trait in the patient in exaggerated form enables the analyst to gain a greater sense of its maladaptive quality. The analyst who perceived his patient's self-righteousness and negativism as exaggerations of his own character traits used this recognition to stop his similar behavior. By seeing the self-defeating effect of his patient's behavior, he realized the undesirability of his own similar tendencies. He then proceeded to explore and ultimately to understand the factors contributing to the development and function of these traits in himself. Having interrupted the current expression of these traits, gradually over time, he was able to transform a maladaptive negativism into a creative independence of thought and become more tolerant of others.

Similarities of situation often create similarities of conflict and of affective responses. Under these circumstances, previously repressed memories may be reawakened and brought into consciousness for the analyst. Separation anxiety was a known problem for analyst 9, who was affectively stirred by her patient's "frenzy" to be with her family. Working with the patient to try to understand the reasons for her panic, the analyst found not only an affective resonance in herself but the emergence of new "memories." She used this new memory both for the benefit of the patient, by linking them to a parallel instance in the patient's life, and for a deepening understanding of herself and her symptomatology.

This analyst has made a reconstruction through the retrieval of a memory. She believes that the increased insight about the reason for her night waking diminished this symptom and freed her previously defended empathy for some patients suffering from separation anxiety whose solutions she had viewed as maladaptive.

The three analysts just described used recognition of the similarity with their patients to achieve greater perspective on themselves and their residual difficulties. From their descriptions, they learned more about themselves from what they saw in their patients, but the actual work they did on their personal issues was primarily self-reflective and occurred apart from their work with the patients. The other three analysts who offered illustrations of the impact of seeing similarities between themselves and their patients describe the reverberating effect on their patients and themselves of working on issues that they knew to be similar to their own.

Analyst 10 specifically related to her actual work the therapeutic benefit from treating a patient who is struggling with difficulties similar to those of the analyst. Her fears of dying were revived by working with a patient who had an illness that she had previously had. By reconfronting her fear and terror as she tried to help her patient master her own acute and more reality-based fears and terror of dying, the analyst increased her sense of control over her affects and lessened her fear. She described the work as circular: helping her patient master her fear helped her master her own fear, which, in turn, helped the patient.

Part of the facilitation of the analyst's mastery of her terror derived from her admiration of her patient's coping style—her "courage," "witty sense of humor," and being a "fighter." This, however, is not an example of a patient who was ahead of the analyst and helped the analyst to master something the analyst had not mastered. In this instance, the analyst and patient both had these qualities, and this was the likely reason the analyst's former supervisor had thought they would be a "good match." The similarity of their characterological approach and their attitudes and outlook on life was apparent in their work together and provided a mutual support in which fears could be experienced with increasing fullness. The patient explored this experience with the analyst. The analyst experienced her affect with the patient and reflected on, and explored, her experience outside the context of the treatment. She shared the feelings stirred and insights gained primarily with her husband.

The mechanisms by which we change are complicated and complex. In addition to their shared illness and the characterological similarity of this patient and this analyst, in her countertransference, the analyst may have experienced and represented the patient as a good parent or supervisor whom she internalized. From the analyst's description, it seems likely that the patient experienced her in the same way. While, in one sense, the analyst always remained the therapist, in another, the characterological similarity and their admiration and support for one another created a mutuality that went far beyond the similarity of their illness.

Analyst 11, who was aware of his unresolved issues around depression, found a greater expansion of feeling stimulated in himself in the course of treating a depressed therapist. He used his work with the patient to gain a greater appreciation of his own mood alterations as they emerged in reaction to affect-laden material in the treatment. He described an oscillation of reflection between memories from his history and thoughts about his current work with depressed patients. Each informed and stimulated the other in a reverberating fashion. With this patient and other depressed patients, he explored the development of their depression, which he compared and contrasted with his own. Over time, as he also explored these issues with some colleagues, he gained a greater appreciation for why people become depressed and no longer assumed it all derived from parenting. His own experiences as a parent and grandparent further contributed to his changed view. Blaming his parents less; he felt less angry, more forgiving and understanding, and consequently less guilty. These changes in his feelings occurred gradually over time.

This analyst still resonates with depressive affects in his patients, but the work he has done around these issues has resulted in a stronger sense of himself as more separate from their affective pull. The affective charge has diminished for him as a result of the repeated reworking. He is better able to separate the past from current reality. While he and these patients share aspects of affective history, he also now appreciates the difference in their stance and perspective on this emotional history, and the revival of his own depressive reactions is not as intense.

The mutual benefit to patient and analyst that can occur when overlapping issues are actively explored in analytic work is also illustrated by the analyst whose terror and sadism are revived and reworked in the context of his patient's terror and sadism. What the analyst described might accurately be characterized as a transference–countertransference interaction in which analyst and patient alternate in the experience and understanding of being both the victim and victimizer; however, since the analyst was conscious from the outset that he and the patient were both struggling with both roles, he identified and experienced that in this work was a similarity of conflict. He recognized that he and the patient were both reliving and reworking sadomasochistic aspects of themselves and described the reverberating manner in which each side of this struggle was experienced and explored. Initially, the analyst experienced terror when the patient disowned this experience and viewed herself only in the role of the rescuer. The analyst fought against staying in the victim role by reversing their positions. His reversal may not have been only an escape from the victim role; it may also have reflected the expression of anger that his patient was not owning the aggressive aspect of herself that he painfully had come to acknowledge as part of himself. The previous identification as rescuer or helper was a far more comfortable self-representation. The analyst lost his ability at that moment empathically to contain and shape his intervention, since he had not yet firmly enough extricated himself from these conflicts.

The analyst saw the enactment of this conflict as evidence that he was actively reworking this aggressive aspect of himself. None of the material mobilized was new. In fact, the work with the former borderline patient he described was much more affectively charged and, in some ways, better illustrates a changed level of self-awareness emerging from work with a patient. What the analyst seems to be illustrating, however, is that this much milder experience of aggression, expressed in the transference–countertransference engagement in which patient and analyst alternate as to who is the mother and who is the child, each scaring the other, demonstrates a continuing working through of this conflict within himself.

This analyst would maintain that the work he and his patient did ran in parallel. This is not the same as believing they were engaged in doing mutual analysis (Ferenczi, in Dupont, 1988.) Mutual analysis entails a mutuality of expression in the process. This analyst, like almost all the analysts offering illustrations for this study, did not share his reflections and explorations about himself with his patient. Though these thoughts ran in parallel to material from the patient, they remained a privately worked-on process for the analyst, while the work on the patient's material was actively shared between them. In terms of the patient's process, the analyst used his self-understanding, gained in relation to the parallels between them, only to help inform himself about the patient—not as a subject for their mutual engagement and work. While a preconscious assimilation may likely have occurred in the actual work with the patient, the conscious, active reworking of the analysts' conflicts occurs outside the patient's sessions.

Admiration for Qualities or Characteristics of Patients

Many analysts believe they learn something new from specific characteristics of patients, especially when these are admired qualities. From the analysts' interviews it can be seen that the analyst's recognition of an attribute that he or she experiences as a desirable trait—a personal value, attitude, belief, or coping strategy—is given support if it is perceived as characteristic of a patient. The patient, in these cases, has a quality or characteristic that the analyst consciously admires. The analyst may use the perception of the patient's greater access to an admired characteristic as encouragement to develop further this aspect of his or her own character.

Sometimes the analyst feels deficient in this attribute, admires the patient, and recognizes a longing to be like him or her; sometimes the analyst believes that he or she has this characteristic but that the patient has developed the quality to a greater degree; sometimes this attribute of the patient changes the analyst's view or leads the analyst to modify some previously held belief.

The meaning and function of this characteristic may be similar for the patient but also may be very different. Admired characteristics are often desired because of their adaptive aspects; however, the same characteristics most often have defensive uses as well. In addition, while the analyst may consciously admire and wish to emulate a patient's adaptive behaviors, feelings of envy and competition may also, especially unconsciously, play a role.

When the aspect of the patient that is esteemed is one of attitude or adherence to a set of values, the analyst's conscious emulation leads to changes that often seem conscious and volitional. Changes in attitude or belief that emerge from working with a patient who expands the analyst's perspective seem to stem from these more conscious and volitional processes. In contrast, when the aspect of a patient that is admired is a quality of character, and the analyst comes to develop or expand this characteristic, the process by which this occurs seems far less cerebral. In these instances, we need to consider whether a process of identification with the patient has occurred, a process that, at least in part, is unconscious.

In the examples that follow, analysts describe experiences in which they believe, as a result of the work, they were able to make some admired aspect of the patient part of themselves. Sometimes the analysts explore the psychological reasons that this particular characteristic is important to them, but other times, particularly when the attribute is an attitude, they do not. As a consequence, these examples are explored in varying degrees of depth.

Analyst 13: An Interest in Fashionable Dress as the Manifestation of Identification with the Father

A patient's positive identification with an aspect of his father provides an analyst an opportunity to rediscover and ultimately recover a positive identification with that same aspect of his own father that he had previously repudiated.

> I had a patient who was very interested in clothes. The origins of this interest became clear to both of us during the course of his analysis—an ongoing attachment to a lost father who dressed well and valued material possessions. It was for the patient a search for the man within himself that made temporary appearances in stylish dress, which were often a front for a little boy who didn't feel strong or able. He would spend a lot of time in treatment talking about shopping, about designer suits he loved, about encounters with shoes, ties, shirts. . . . The way he dressed was connected with particular needs that had to do with a wish to be admired both by women as he felt his father had been and by his mother, clearly in terms of his oedipal feelings but also with a

search for a father, whom he had lost when he was fairly young. . . . Wearing fine clothes put him in contact with the father he had lost in his imagination, so it was very important. The patient would comment on my clothes. I didn't dress badly, but it was a little bit conservative, kind of drab. . . . At first I felt put off by what seemed the patient's excessive materialism. . . . I noted, after I had been working with the patient for a while, that I began to study men's fashion sections in the newspaper more closely. I began to pick more fashionable shoes and ties, much to the delight of my wife, who had complained that I dressed too conservatively. I also found myself vicariously enjoying the freedom this patient allowed himself in his dress and his open admiration for style. . . . It got me curious about why this . . . out of all the things the man said about himself and me, was what had become the focus of attention for me. . . . That started a kind of self-analysis, which brought me back to memories of my own parents, the way they dressed. I realized I had an identification with my patient . . . I had some feelings about my father that the patient had about his. I felt some disappointments in my parents, kind of deidealization that I had turned against some aspects of their dress, their materialism. It was a way I had distanced myself from them. . . .

[The analyst began to reflect on his parents' interest in clothes.] Despite their communist leanings, it had been considerable. My father had had his suits tailor-made, and my mother bought and enjoyed wearing very expensive jewelry. I recalled how at one time my parents had seemed like gods to me with their fine clothes and high style. . . . But then my inevitable disappointment with who they were—their lack of omnipotence and omniscience—turned me against their wardrobes and associated exhibitionism. . . . My reaction to my patient, my observation of my responses, and my reflections about my own history in relation to clothes made me think about reaction formation . . . and my defenses of constriction against what was once most desired and admired. . . . My patient simultaneously struggled to be like his parents and to be free from them. It was unclear whether his clothes conveyed something about himself or whether they were borrowed from grown-ups.

[The analyst then more fully understood his reactions to his patient. The ways the patient and the analyst had handled these conflicts were different, but there was also a similarity.] My reaction to my patient reopened an area I had shut off in myself. The patient noted that I had a slight change in dress and attributed it to a general increase in flexibility and to his sartorial influence. I believed that he was not far from the mark.

The analyst had first felt "put off" and "distanced" by the patient's emphasis on materialism, but he then realized that he was envious. This first response was a mild, but clear, negative countertransference. Self-exploration, however, led the analyst to recognize a similarity between the patient and himself. He identified with the patient's search for the father with fine clothes. The analyst's self-analysis revealed that to him in his deidealization of his parents. He saw that his subtle judgment of his patient's materialism was linked to this earlier judgment of his parents' values. These judgments also served to conceal a certain envy of their exhibitionism and freedom.

In the course of the analysis of his patient, the analyst explored his initial negative reaction to his patient's interest in clothes and high style and discovered he had identified his patient with an aspect of his parents that he had repudiated earlier in his life. Further reflection allowed him to acknowledge his own hidden wishes for display and the envy of his patient and his parents for the pleasure they took in exhibiting themselves and for the freedom that it expressed.

One price of repudiating his father in the way the analyst had was a constriction in himself. The analyst recognized his defense against his wishes for self-display and by implication his defense against his longings to be like, and close to, his parents. Something that previously had been devalued was now valued—not the materialism itself but the pleasure of displaying himself. His conscious decision to dress more fashionably was, therefore, not merely a superficial change of style of attire. If the analyst has relinquished his old reaction formation in relation to this facet of his parents, why did this occur? The analyst suggests that he has transformed an aspect of a negative identification into a positive identification. If this is so, it reflects a shift of an internal representation of an aspect of both his parents and himself. In addition, he thinks a constriction in his behavior became somewhat looser. For such profound internal changes as an increased flexibility and a modification of his self and object representations to occur, it could be speculated that the analyst may have had a transference to his patient.

Analyst 14: Tolerance of Disappointment of Ambition

The analyst describes how his patient's development of the ability to tolerate disappointment aids him to face disappointment more easily himself.

The patient was a writer who was highly regarded by his peers who were writers, but his novels never received the commercial success he expected. Each year he expected a breakthrough novel. A seemingly less talented writing peer, whom [the] patient had not viewed as someone who would write a notable novel, made this breakthrough with his next novel, while [the] patient's novel received mediocre reviews. One day shortly after this, the patient came in wearing a T-shirt saying, "minor regional writer." The patient had dealt with his relative lack of success by using humor. He had begun to come to terms with his situation. I also had aspirations to be a writer. [Earlier in his life the analyst's ambitions had taken a different form.] Until puberty I had considerable success as a leader, but developing later than my peers, I found myself moved from center stage. My ambitions shifted from wishes for peers as my audience to wishes for success as a writer with authors as my audience. . . . I actually was given recognition for my skill in writing but not at the level I had hoped. The line on the patient's shirt stirred a feeling in me about my own unfulfilled aspirations that helped me accept that I, too, was not Prince Hamlet and not meant to be, a recognition that I was unable to attain all I had aspired to. . . . My patient's attitude of humorous acceptance of his limitations expressed in the line on the shirt was the culmination of long and painful work. . . .

The patient's letting go of his painful insistence that he be a star preceded my ability to modify my ambitious expectations. . . . Seeing my patient's ability finally to acquire a perspective of humor helped me to feel less caught up in frustration and disappointment about being unable to achieve what I had wished. [Following this shift in perspective, the analyst found his feelings were also changed.] I was better able to take pleasure in my own standards of what was good writing and to be less caught up with the assessment of my peers.

The analyst's adult adaptation is different from his adolescent one. The analyst had turned away from seeking a leadership role with his peers to looking for recognition of his literary talent. Although he did not receive the notice he wished, he did not abandon writing. What shifted for the analyst was that this time he does not turn away from his ambition but instead changes how he feels about his accomplishments.

The analyst's change of perspective comes from listening and watching his patient doing analytic work that results in an outlook that the analyst sees as more adaptive than his own. Over the course of their work, he both listened to, and assisted, his patient in exploring his feelings of disappointment and anger about the limited recognition he had attained. The analyst resonated with these affective experiences. He not only identified with his patient but also admired him—for his ability as a writer, for his perseverance, and for his capacity to release himself from his sense of disappointment through humor and perspective. It may be that in his admiration and respect for his patient the analyst creates a new peer group for himself. It may also be that he uses the patient both consciously and unconsciously to modify his ego ideal. Uniting himself with someone he esteems, he can better accept not receiving the extent of external recognition he has wished from the world. In this identification with his patient, he can also view himself as admirable and expect that others will share this view—possibly not for his writing but perhaps for adopting a similar attitude of humorous acceptance. The admired qualities that he wished would elicit external recognition and acclaim have been shifted from his writerly skills to his perspective on the need for public recognition.

The fate of this analyst's competitive and envious feelings is not addressed in his account. This omission is not unique to this analyst but rather is characteristic of most of the examples analysts provided in describing the effect of admired characteristics of patients on themselves. A discussion of this recurrent, more conflict-laden side of the analyst's feelings is presented later. It is necessary to note here only that the possible "darker" side of the analyst's feelings, his unacknowledged envy, has not been overlooked.

Analyst 15: Freedom of Self-Assertion in Relationships

The analyst reports, this time in a written response, how her patient's increased freedom of self-assertion develops in concert with her comfort with her aggression. These shifts in her patient facilitate the analyst's changes in her own ease, availability, and management of aggression.

> During the course of her analysis, a patient with a very intrusive mother became able to challenge her mother over boundaries. In her transference to me, she was enviously attacking, although at the same time she maintained an excellent rapport with me. As the patient's courage in dealing with her mother grew, I saw that my own ability to deal with boundaries in my personal life also increased. Many of the affects that the patient explored resonated

with my affects, some of which I was then able to experience and explore for the first time in my life.

The analyst is aware that the problem areas the patient is confronting are similar to her own. Not being caught in the intense emotional reactions that the particularity of the specific details from her own history in these areas potentially stirs, she is able to attain greater perspective. Her patient's exploration of these areas aids her in being better able to tolerate her own similar struggles. This example illustrates the insights and internal shifts that can occur when working on personal issues in displacement.

The analyst does not detail this exploration but rather presents us with a summary of the outcome. We assume it went something like this: seeing the patient's positive feelings coexist with the aggression and envy expressed toward her, the analyst appreciates that these intense feelings do not destroy the bond between them. Seeing that the patient can be effectively assertive with her mother without losing that relationship, the analyst realizes the need to confront her own fears of being self-assertive, of limiting others' intrusions (my inference that the analyst has felt intruded on) and the anticipated punishment for setting such boundaries. If her patient can be so effective with her help, why can she not do the same for herself? This question to herself reflects the motivating effect of the patient's mastery of her fear of aggression. As in the previous example, the analyst's account does not address any competitive or envious feelings in relation to the patient and her achievements.

Analyst 16: Freedom of Self-Assertion and Flexibility in Work

The analyst finds greater freedom for self-assertion in the area of work as a consequence of working with a patient who enters analysis already possessing this quality.

> The patient was a young psychiatrist who was much more aggressive in the management of his own practice than I was. . . . He worked more hours, earned more income, and entered into many more diverse professional activities. . . . His enthusiasm and optimism about his work [at this time] were in marked contrast to the attitude of my analytic colleagues and myself. . . . I was focused on doing analysis, discouraged and frustrated by short-term work, and uninterested in doing psychopharmacology. My colleagues said that if you wanted to see more analytic

patients, you can see them, but you had to earn less and less money. . . . My interest in analysis was very strong, but I just couldn't reconcile myself to earning so little. Even my senior colleagues expressed discouragement about referrals and pessimism about the future. My own training analyst had stopped practicing at an early age. . . . I was surprised that someone trained as a psychiatrist could have such a different attitude and become as financially successful as my patient was. I was impressed and admiring of his energy and activity and the pleasure, ease, and comfort that he took in being a psychiatrist. [Working with the patient, the analyst felt a change in his attitude.] I regained an aspect of myself that I had put away during the course of my analytic training. . . . I identified with my patient in his early struggles in professional development. The patient had an ongoing conflict about whether he should train as an analyst as well as conflicts about analysis as a method of treatment. He was steeped in many other types of approaches to conflict resolution. Yet he remained an extremely involved analytic patient and was very successful in analysis, getting a great deal of help out of being in treatment. I was someone who also had an awareness and appreciation of the unconscious and the conflicts arising from it. . . . My patient not only employed other treatment modalities happily and successfully but also did a lot of writing . . . something I wished to do. . . . My consciousness grew out of my own wish to be busier and earn more money. [Over time, he found that as he worked with this patient, these feelings increased. Eventually, he did effect these changes in his own work.] I still wish to do more analysis and have the residual feeling that if I were really good at analytic work, I would be referred analytic patients; but this no longer stopped me from undertaking other kinds of treatment with patients, enjoying my work, and my sense of being financially successful. I think I was able to identify with a part in my patient that was freer and more optimistic than I felt. [Perceiving these qualities in his patient as something he wished for himself enabled him to re-evoke an earlier, abandoned aspect of himself and develop these qualities by using his patient as a model. The analyst wondered if his own analyst's leaving the field also contributed to his relinquishing a focus on doing only analysis.] Yet I believe I am very different from my former analyst, who had removed himself entirely from both his work and colleagues. I am very invested in my work and take great pleasure in my contact and sharing with colleagues.

The analyst is able to use an awareness of a difference between the patient and himself to reconsider his own values and choices. Finding that his more recently acquired attitudes and goals had not turned out to be as fulfilling as he had hoped, he was able to reidentify with earlier held attitudes. This reclaimed identification was especially easy to renew since he saw that these attitudes kept his patient from the discouragement that the analyst and his colleagues felt. The analyst is able to shift his identification with his peers to align with his patient both because it resonates with a former, temporarily abandoned part of himself and because he views his patient as an admirable person who is able to find more satisfaction professionally than the analyst.

The loss of the analyst's own analyst as a model for identification due to his abrupt and total departure from the field of analysis may have added to the analyst's relative ease in shifting his model for identification. To the extent that he emulated his analyst, his analyst's identity as an analyst may have also been revered. When his analyst gave up this role, this analyst in his continuing identification with his former analyst may have experienced being an analyst as a less desirable role. In this context, the analyst became more open to considering others as models for identification who seem to be more committed to, and satisfied in, their work. The analyst makes clear that, unlike his former analyst, he has not left the field of psychoanalysis but rather just broadened his sources of satisfaction.

The analyst's focus in this account is on the effect the patient has had upon him and not the treatment process for his patient; however, the complex and reverberating nature of the analytic work needs to be kept in mind. The patient's views about psychoanalysis and his positive feelings, as well as his reservations are likely to have transferential meanings as well as reality-based ones. Is there some denial of a discouragement he may sense in the analyst about analysis? Is the patient's enthusiastic embrace of alternative methods of treatment in part a response to an unconscious registering of the analyst's discouragement? If either is so, what effect do these less conscious and nonarticulated responses of the patient have on the analyst and his perception of the patient's perspective?

Analyst 17: The Ability to Laugh at Oneself

An analyst who viewed herself as a serious and self-critical person admires her patient's ability to laugh at herself. Sometime after the patient terminates, the analyst discovers that she has acquired this desired characteristic.

I am a serious person who was in analysis with a serious analyst; one of my first analytic patients had a remarkable ability to laugh at herself. Though the patient had had many difficulties in her life and in the analysis, she did not feel sorry for herself; rather, when she saw herself once again resort to some self-defeating behavior, she would be able to step back with a bemused attitude of "There I go again!" I envied the patient's ability not to sink into self-recriminations as I tended to do. My usual style was to relate with pain and then more pain. I saw this as an undesirable quality in myself but could not stop it. I knew my way only prolonged my own misery. . . . By keeping myself focused on self-blame instead of working on my conflicts, I slowed the process. . . . I was still in my own analysis after my patient had terminated. About two months after my patient ended analysis, I was reflecting on my response to an event where I laughed at myself for some defensive maneuver I had employed. . . . My analyst noted at once that this reflected a different and much more lighthearted attitude than I had ever expressed before. I thought of my former patient . . . I had so admired her for her capacity to laugh at herself. . . . This moment of first being able to laugh at myself was a turning point in my own treatment. . . . After this I felt I was different, . . no longer got buried in more pain when I related something painful. . . . I wonder whether unknowingly I had identified with my patient and taken on this quality as an aspect of myself through the course of our work. . . . My work with this patient had been very powerful. The patient had loved and hated me intensely . . . and had moved and changed in the course of the work. . . . I found her very gratifying to work with. . . . I felt my own training analysis had been much more distanced and cool. . . . I attributed this contrast more to a difference between my patient and myself than to something between my training analyst and myself. I had not identified with my patient. In retrospect, I see we had some similar conflict areas, but my patient's defensive structure was very different. My patient freely identified with the aggressor and was open with her anger in ways it took me years to achieve. [Nonetheless, even at this much earlier time, she saw how her work with the patient had led to a transformation in herself.] I have come to wonder if this unconscious shift had occurred in relation to the patient's termination. I greatly valued this patient both for her attributes and for her importance as an early training case. I may have internalized this admired quality of my patient as a way of dealing with our separation.

In this example, the analyst sees her patient's adaptation as preferable to her own in several crucial ways. She admires her patient's freedom to experience and express her anger, her ability to keep from getting caught in pain and self-blame, and her capacity to use humor to attain a perspective on herself. These dissimilarities between the analyst and the patient take on even greater importance as qualities to emulate when, retrospectively, the analyst realizes that she and the patient have some similar conflict areas. The recognition of this similarity means that the characteristics of the patient that the analyst admires are relatively successful modes of adaptation for conflicts with which the analyst had not yet found a successful means of coping . While the analyst believes that the patient gained a great deal from her analysis, these gains were in different areas, ones where the analyst's own difficulties did not impinge.

Since the patient did not have a particular problem in the area in which this analyst as a beginning candidate had not yet resolved her conflicts, the analyst's limitation in this area did not adversely affect her. The analyst, however, had the good fortune at this particular time in her professional development to have a patient whose adaptive strengths were in areas in which she still had issues. This circumstance was especially fortuitous since the analyst's own training analyst was less well matched to her needs in this respect. The intensity of emotional involvement of this analyst and her patient with each other in the analytic work and their mutual respect and admiration allowed them both to learn beneficially from, and identify with, each other in the areas in which each of their particular strengths complemented a need in the other.

Analyst 18: Affirmation as an Attitude and a Behavior

Another, more conscious use of a patient's strength is illustrated by an analyst who employed a patient's specific strength to support a burgeoning conviction of her own.

> The patient was a particularly gifted psychotherapist . . . who had a remarkable ability to see the positive and comment upon it. She was very successful in helping her patients. While the patient did have a problem about being overly anxious to please, I thought that her valuing the positive aspects of people was not based primarily on reaction formation; I believed the patient was a genuinely nice person. . . .

I see myself as a positive and confirming kind of person despite the absence of much spontaneous affirmation in my own family of origin. This lack of a positive, affirming attitude was repeated in both my personal analysis and my analytic training. . . . I believed that psychoanalysis had been deficient in not offering positive appraisal to patients . . . in fact . . . it made you feel if you were positive, as if you were doing something wrong. . . . In my training there was a tendency to make you feel that it was OK to be positive with your psychotherapy patients but not with your analytic patients. . . . I have come to believe that communicating positive appraisal to a patient is as much an interpretation of reality . . . as making a patient aware of an interfering characteristic. . . . My patient's use of positive appraisal was sort of a reinforcement or confirmation of a position I had already come to. Treating this patient expanded my awareness of an aspect of my personality. . . . I had already been thinking that offering positive views to patients about themselves was something that I saw as valuable and important to do and facilitating to the treatment. . . . Being more expressive about positive features of patients was a character style that I admired. . . . I think that I have that quality, but my patient had it much more . . . and was much more inclined to be verbal about it. . . . My character style was in this direction, but my patient was someone whom I saw as being more developed in her free expression of what was positive about others.

[The analyst believed that treating this patient, who was more positively expressive than she, expanded her awareness of a capacity in herself.] It reminded me of the importance of commenting on positive qualities to reinforce natural skills and enhance people's confidence and self-esteem. . . . Seeing how successfully the patient did this with her own patients and in her life in general led me to become more positively expressive.

The analyst's identification with her patient was conscious. She used a characteristic of her patient to bolster actively something she already believed. She sought this support for her belief, it would seem, because it ran counter to both her experience in her own family and the stance she had been taught, both formally in classes and supervision and in her own analysis. In this respect, the patient was an antidote for the analyst's own earlier experiences. Since the patient was very skillful in her manner of conveying others' strengths, the analyst could also consciously model herself on her patient's style and thereby increase her own sense of skill and effectiveness in this kind of communication. As in the examples previously described, the analyst's competitive or envious feelings or both, if they exist and if they are conscious, are not addressed in this account.

Generally, analysts assume that admiration and envy are related. Therefore, it is noteworthy that in these accounts few of these analysts addressed feelings of competition and envy in relation to their patients' admired adaptive capacities. It is possible that the analysts were conscious of these more conflicted feelings and did not mention them. They might well have been willing to do so. They probably did not because it would have caused them to stray from the main point of their reply to my question. The analysts were attending primarily to how the patient had positively affected them and, therefore, may have focused exclusively on the beneficial identifications with their patients. It is also possible that to the extent that the patient came to serve as an ego ideal in particular areas, the analyst's competitive and envious feelings toward him or her were denied and remained unconscious. If we postulate that such feelings in relation to these patients did exist, then their effects need to be considered. For example, would these more negatively tinged, conflicted feelings influence the stability or duration of the new identification? Would the vicissitudes of this unrecognized aspect be worked out in relation to other patients or other persons in the analyst's life, or would its lack of acknowledgment create some interference with these relationships? We do not have the data to answer these questions.

While feelings of admiration are often linked to envy, at least unconsciously, we need to question whether the two are inextricably linked. Envy is most intense and persistent when people do not believe they can have for themselves what the others have. Probably analysts who admire characteristics of their patients and feel themselves unable to use this admiration to further their own development are more conscious of their envy. Perhaps if some of the analysts in this study had recounted these examples before experiencing these changes in themselves, they would have included a recognition of envy in their accounts. Most of the examples offered by these analysts describe admiration that eventuated in their acquiring the characteristic that was admired. The analysts focused on what they gained from their patients, not what they lacked in comparison. Once a person has acquired the desired quality, there is no longer a reason to feel envious. If it is possible to have for oneself an attribute or adaptation or, in other instances, a possession that one admires in another, then envy may be only fleeting or possibly not operative. The admired characteristic has served primarily as a motivating function. In addition, it is also possible that if people are relatively content with their own characteristics and attainments, they may be less inclined to experience envy in any particularly troubling way. Feeling good enough about themselves, even when they admire a characteristic or attainment that they themselves lack, they may be able to retain a perspective that personal assets differ, and no one has them all.

The patients discussed possessed or developed some quality that their analysts admired. In most instances, this characteristic was reflected in the patients' coping strategies. For some analysts, the admired attribute was a quality they felt lacking in themselves and longed to acquire. Such a situation existed for the analyst whose writer patient came to terms with his disappointed ambitions through the use of humor. It also characterized the analyst whose patient maintained her sense of perspective and optimism by laughing at herself, and the analyst whose patient developed courage to set appropriate boundaries on her intrusive mother.

Other analysts perceived themselves as having the quality they admired in their patients but viewed their patients as having more of this desirable characteristic. Both the analyst whose psychotherapist patient helped herself and her patients by her positive and confirming attitude and the analyst whose psychiatrist patient expressed enthusiasm and optimism in his assertive management of his successful professional activities illustrate this situation. To a certain extent this also characterizes the analyst whose patient took pleasure in his exhibitionism and material possessions and, in living out these interests, made an identification and connection with his father. This last example differs from the others in that the analyst describes reworking an unconscious conflict once he realized that he liked smart clothes and had been dressing more drably in order to avoid being like his parents.

Most of the analysts believed they learned better means of adapting to difficulties from their patients than they had found for themselves. For the patients, of course, these coping strategies also had defensive meanings with respect to the patients' own struggles. In the instance of the patient with the interest in clothes, the solution was not necessarily better than, only different from, the analyst's.

The patients' compromise formations seem especially adaptive to the analysts because they offer a model of different and what appear to be more adaptive, solutions for manifestly, though not necessarily dynamically, similar difficulties. For example, the patient who took pleasure in clothes as positive identification and connection with his father needed to analyze his own lost manhood expressed through the clothes. Wearing clothes that he believed displayed his manliness both concealed his feelings of inadequacy about his manliness and expressed his positive link to his father's manliness. For the analyst, the patient's particular solution stirred up memories and conflicts related to issues of identification with his parents. The analyst then reworked these conflicts, at first unconsciously using the patient's compromise formation as a way to identify more positively with his own family. Later, the analyst had a conscious understanding about both his internalization of this aspect of his patient and his responses to the patient as an expression of a particular kind of countertransference.

Most of these patients had problems in areas that did not overlap greatly with their analysts' conflicts. In those areas in which their patients were troubled, the analysts helped them, but in the areas currently considered, the patients inadvertently helped their analysts. Two exceptions where central problem areas were shared are the writer patient and the patient with the intrusive mother, neither of whom entered treatment with adaptive skills for dealing in these areas of difficulties; they developed more effective ways of managing their distress in the course of their analyses. They developed these capacities, even though the analysts themselves did not yet possess these capacities for coping as effectively.

This phenomenon suggests a need to rethink Freud's (1912) statement that analysts cannot help a patient go further than they themselves have been able to go in resolving their difficulties. Freud's idea at that time may have been based on an assumption that psychological change resulted from insight alone. The statement was made in an era prior to his discovery of ego psychology, long before Freud actively considered character issues. Since no two people are psychologically organized in exactly the same manner, even when areas of conflict overlap, it does not necessarily mean the analyst cannot help the patient. When, however, the analyst is too defended or too threatened to be able to pursue material or becomes caught in unanalyzed enactments in joint areas of conflict, the analyst's unresolved difficulties impede the patient's treatment. In the examples of the writer and the patient with an intrusive mother, the patient's' psychological change preceded the analysts', who, in fact, then learned from their patients' examples. This learning took place as they worked on mutual issues with the patients' histories, affects, defenses, conflicts, and fantasies as the data through which these mutual issues were explored.

For the analyst with the patient who had an intrusive mother, her personal work ran silently in parallel to her patient's work. The result was that both patient and analyst shifted in similar ways—the analyst first helping to free the patient and the patient's increased freedom serving further to free the analyst. This process of mutual freeing seems to be possible because, while both patient and analyst were inhibited in a similar area, neither was "blind" to this problem. Neither patient nor analyst was so inhibited that they were blocked in their attempts to free themselves when the problem was addressed, and adequate safety existed in the context of their relationship. Under these circumstances, their similarity of conflict served to facilitate the treatment, since both patient and analyst were motivated to push beyond their current solutions. Their resonance provided a framework for mutual work and growth.

Psychological shifts for the analysts emerged directly out of work with their patients: the analyst who changed his attitude toward fashionable attire felt freer and more flexible; the analyst who became less dependent on the assessments of others found value and pleasure in his own writing; and the analyst who became more assertive in setting limits on others' intrusions felt freer and more effective.

The analyst whose patient was fashionably attired is most detailed and specific about the process of work that facilitates these shifts. He describes the manner in which he reflected on his patient and how he juxtaposed these thoughts with reflections about himself. He illustrates the reverberation between self-and other-reflections and shows how thoughts about similarities and differences between himself and his patient served to deepen his self-understanding.

This analyst takes us step by step in showing how he works with patient material to learn more about both the patient and himself. There is a conscious and volitional aspect in his approach and the insights he accrued. His psychological shift, however, does not seem entirely cerebral. The process of working through these insights is deeply rooted in an affective, relational context. The nature of the relationship, both interpersonal and intrapsychic, is crucial to the therapeutic impact that the psychological work has on both the patient and the analyst.

For many of the analysts described in this section, their patients may have come to stand for ego ideals in certain areas. The two analysts with psychotherapist patients who held different stances in relation to their work describe consciously embracing characteristics they revered in their patients. Both these analysts believe they had the same trait they valued in their patient but saw the patient having a more developed aspect of this quality.

Both these analysts describe a process that was conscious and volitional. These patients brought these particularly valued characteristics and attitudes with them when they entered treatment. Their analysts were ripe to be responsive to these dimensions and enthusiastically tried to model themselves on these characteristics of their patients. An unconscious assimilation of aspects of these qualities may also have taken place in the course of their work with these patients. These two analysts, however, reported a more conscious process of learning from their patients than did other analysts in this study.

In contrast, analyst 17, who attained the ability to laugh at herself, is specific that this change in outlook, this new capacity for lightening of her psychological pain, did not emerge out of any active self-reflective work. She had not consciously employed self-observation or actively considered the reasons her patient had the capacity to employ humor to gain perspective, and she did not. She knew only that she admired this characteristic of the patient and that she wished to have it herself. When she found that she actually possessed it, it had come unbidden, though certainly desired and welcomed by her.

The analyst was able to use her patient's humor to help her gain perspective on her self-blame and self-pity, something that her analyst's seriousness had not helped. The analyst and her training analyst were taken by surprise; both had been unaware that such a psychological shift had taken place within her until it became apparent in her reaction. Given the lack of conscious self-reflection in relation to this characteristic, it is likely that this psychological change was primarily the result of an unconscious process. The analyst seems to have made an unconscious identification with her patient, an identification that may have been facilitated by the patient's ending treatment, a way of keeping this admired patient with her after she was gone. Since her analyst also was aware that she demonstrated a quality that had not previously been apparent and that was not an area they had explored in their work, this shift seems to represent a psychological change that emerged from her work with her patient and not from her personal analysis. While the analyst does not explicitly state a complaint, she seems to convey that she got something from her patient that she did not get from her analyst.

Whether the process was primarily conscious or unconscious, all these analysts describe how their emulation of some quality of a patient led to their acquiring this admired characteristic. The fact that a patient may be ahead of the analyst in some respects and may serve as an ego ideal in these dimensions should not be surprising. Many patients, while seeking help in some aspect of their lives, may be very effectively adapted in other areas. The relationship between patients and analysts can be very intense at times; patients can take on important emotional meanings for their analysts. When affectively intense engagements between patients and analysts occur, then particular characteristics that have value for the analyst, for whatever personal, historical reasons, may become intensely invested. We know this kind of investment takes place for patients in relation to their analysts and count on it as part of the impetus that leads to patients' psychological changes. Here I suggest that the same process can, and does at times, take place for the analyst in relation to the patient.

CHAPTER 7

Patients' Interpretations
of the Analyst

It is now commonly accepted that patients' perceptions about their analysts, while introduced in the context of the particular transference meaning that they have for the patient, may often reflect accurate characterizations of the analyst or the analyst's behavior. The "trigger" for the patient's reaction comes from the analyst, while the meaning the patient attaches to what she or he has perceived resides in the patient's own psychological history and struggles (Gill, 1982; Hoffman, 1983). In other words, what the patient says about the analyst is simultaneously about the analyst and not about the analyst. Many analysts realize, and now most analysts have come to acknowledge, that they are active participants in the analytic work, that their subjectivity is inevitable (Renik, 1993), as are their enactments of conflicts (Boesky, 1982; Chused, 1991; McLaughlin, 1991). Once analysts accept that their personal characteristics are revealed as part of the process, whether in a role-responsive way (Sandler, 1976) or in more subtle characterological forms (Baudry, 1991; Kantrowitz, 1993, 1995), they are able to make productive use of their patient's observations to deepen the patient's analytic work but also potentially to learn something about themselves. Their patients' interpretations of their charac-

ter and behavior then become a source of data for them about themselves.

The patient's observation about the analyst may be viewed as an
interpretation to the analyst, similar in impact to the analyst's interpretation to the patient. There are, of course, differences. One difference,
referred to in the discussion of triggers for self-reflection, is in motivation. The analyst's conscious intent is to make an interpretation with
the patient's interests in mind. The patient's motivation is understand-
ably much more self-focused and often motivated by something self-
protective. Patients do not have historical or associational data about
the analyst in which to embed their perceptions. In most instances,
what the patient knows about the analyst is known only in the context
of the analyst's behavior with him or her. What goes on between the
patient and analyst, however, has an affective immediacy that can be
very powerful and revealing. The observations derived from this interaction have a freshness and vividness that, if the analyst is open to
them, can be very informative. To have the patient's perceptions make
an impact on the analyst, the analyst must, of course, be open to this
process. The extent to which the analyst respects the patient and his or
her views, the nature of their current alliance, the kind of transference
at the time, the patient's tact and timing, and the emotionally important
factors at this time in the analyst's life—all undoubtedly influence how
open and receptive the analyst will be to taking in, reflecting upon, and
trying to make the patient's view personally relevant and meaningful.

When analysts are open to their patients' interpretations, the impact
they can have works similarly to the impact of the analyst's interpretations to their patients. The psychological work and the process that are
stimulated are also parallel.

Analyst 19: Confrontation with Lack of Curiosity Reflecting Avoidance and Denial

The patient confronts the analyst with a behavior that was uncharacteristic. In response, the analyst faces a conflict that had been denied.

> The patient had been in analysis for five years at the point she
> began to complain about headaches, night sweats and general
> being out of sorts. I explored dynamic factors that might be
> related to these complaints. A friend of the patient's raised the
> question whether these were menopausal symptoms. A visit with
> her doctor confirmed this diagnosis. The patient confronted me

and complained very angrily that I had not recognized the symptoms of menopause as a possible cause for her distress. She wondered why I had not thought of this and also wondered what it was that prevented me from thinking about her. The patient was turning the tables, saying, I have come to know you as someone who is usually so interested and curious, . . . as somebody who was patient and thorough . . . as if she had asked me, "Why aren't you interested in me?" . . . I became aware that I was experiencing some resistance to acknowledging some of my own menopausal symptoms, which were more advanced than my patient's. . . . It revived in me some competitive feelings I had toward my sister, some feelings of wanting to do this better than the patient and secondarily . . . some opinions about specific ways in which . . . I had some disagreement with the patient's way of approaching menopause. . . . My feeling that I wanted to deal with my own menopause differently from the way my patient was dealing with hers became clear to me . . . I became aware of a compact of silence we had entered into about menopause and how it was dealt with that prevented . . . her curiosity about menopause and held me back from listening in the way I ordinarily did. . . . I had to consider whether I was transferring competitive feelings from an earlier situation in my life to the current situation with my patient. . . . Thinking about it carefully, I thought I was. My sibling rivalry in relation to my sister was playing itself out with the patient.

[Stimulated by her patient's "confrontation," the analyst's self-reflective work increased.] I saw I had had an uncharacteristic lack of curiosity about my patient's symptoms and recognized previously unexplored competitive feelings that had their root in sibling rivalry with my sister. . . . I realized I had not explored these feelings in this way in my analysis. I also recognized my characterological tendency to muscle my way through issues. [Both these realizations led to changes for the analyst.] I had a renewed ability to work with the patient on the issue of her menopause . . . and my patient's experience with me in my failure to have actively addressed it. . . . It also opened up my self-inquiry around the topic of my own menopause and around my rivalry with my sister . . . then I explored and understood it more fully.

We cannot tell from this example if the psychological shifts that result from this patient's confrontation of her analyst with her denial and unusual lack of curiosity lead to any permanent modification in the analyst's style of trying to "muscle" through hard times or change the nature of her relationship with her sister or other women with whom rivalrous feelings arise. The shifts we can observe are in her short-term behaviors and attitude. The confrontation led her to stop her denial of her menopause, increase her ability to focus on her patient's menopause and distress, take responsibility for her behavior, and explore the origins of feelings of competitive rivalry. She seems to have gained some insight into the source of both her denial and rivalry, but we cannot tell what, if any, reverberations there will be as a result of new understanding. We can say, however, that the patient's observation and confrontation of the analyst with what she saw led to the analyst's becoming more aware and self-reflective in areas she had previously avoided exploring.

Analyst 20: Confrontation with Hesitancy Expressing Identification with, and Anxiety in Relation to, Authority Figures

The patient confronts the analyst with an observation about a habitual, characteristic way the analyst behaves. The analyst is able to use the patient's perception to focus his attention more sharply on his behavior, more fully reflect on its origin, and slightly modify his reactions.

> The patient was someone who had a real gift for intuitively understanding people's strengths and foibles. On one occasion when I was hesitant in the manner in which I made my intervention, the patient said, "Don't worry. You can say what you really think. Daddy's not looking over your shoulder." The patient's confrontation with this perception of me evoked a whole series of memories and feelings. . . . I recalled my analyst, who actually looked over my shoulder, my teachers and supervisors, who had many strictures about psychoanalytic technique, and . . . behind that some memories about my father and his silences and his strictness. My father was very careful about what he revealed to other people and always ashamed about himself, as though he couldn't allow very much personal about him to be revealed. I had taken over some of those attitudes from these authority figures and felt that they were operating to restrict me in my work with my patient and with other patients. That night I had a dream in which a man was lying on a bed. It was really a corpse, dead, but [it rose] from the place he was lying and put his fingers to his lips and motioned me to be silent and not to speak, and again . . .

I thought of my own analyst, who had died within the preceding year, and of my father, who was such a silent man. It made me realize how my own personality had taken over some of those traits, an identification of being silent. I knew that this identification with being more silent and cautious was partly a defensive identification. . . . It had become part of my operating style as an analyst, subconscious identifications that were partly defensive because I didn't always really agree, but [also] didn't want to make too much of a fight with either my analyst or my father.

[The patient's focus on this aspect of the analyst then restimulated the analyst to confront this aspect of himself and work it through to a new level.] It was the impetus for renewing the process of working through this conflicted identification. I was able to reengage with some of these issues that had become automatic. . . . It led to a whole series of reflections and memories and memories of my own analysis . . . and . . . to renew a process of working through issues that I had begun but hadn't finished at all in my analytic work.

[The analyst believes that the work he did resulted in some shifts in his way of working.] I was able to be looser and more responsive with this patient and other patients who needed this in order to feel safer. . . . I saw how my being on guard had made these patients be more on guard themselves. . . . My being stiff and hesitant, made it harder for them to be open. . . . I had already been alert to considering that a loosening of my technique might benefit some patients. My patient's commenting on my perception of him "sharpened" my awareness of this quality and stimulated my grappling with it more consciously and actively. [The analyst was not sure whether the changes in his work had reverberations in his personal relationships.]

The confrontation by his patient does not provide him with new information about himself; rather, his patient's perception presents the analyst with the fact that a characteristic of his that he consciously wishes were different is still active and apparent. The impact of the patient's words is forcefully to draw his attention to this particular aspect of his character and behavior and to increase his motivation to try to change this quality in himself that he does not like.

Private self-reflection, use of dreams, and, to a lesser extent, sharing his discoveries with a few colleagues and his wife[1] are the primary

---

[1] This information is based on part of the interview not reported here.

methods this analyst describes for integrating and reworking mobilized issues. The analyst does not refer to the process of working through. I speculate, however, that working through, even if not conscious on his part, has primarily taken place in his work with the patient. There is some suggestion that the analyst had a father transference to his patient. He may have experienced his patient as more benign and permissive than his own father and the later father figures to whom he refers. In this respect, his work with this patient may have provided a corrective to his earlier experience of more critical and judgmental men and thereby lessened the grip of his harsher, more exacting superego introjects. My hypothesis is that in the context of his emotionally engaged work with this patient, who could be looser and more playful than the analyst and his mentors, a shift silently took place for the analyst that gave him a new freedom from the strictures of past identifications. Stimulated by his patient's comment, he consciously engages in personal work. I suggest that in the course of their working together, the analyst has also unconsciously responded to the manifestations of the stance the patient put in words. The combination of these multiple modes of personal work results in his being "looser and more responsive" with patients. This shift in his behavior is something he has long desired but previously had not been able to effect personally. It may be that the patient's confrontation was the impetus for him finally to come to grips with his "tightness." He is able to see how he changed with his patients, but he is not sure if there were reverberations in his personal life.

Analyst 21: Confrontation with Avoidance of Staying with Pain

In the context of a regressive experience caused by a massive illness in the analyst, he comes to grasp the accuracy of a patient's complaint. He recovers early affects and comes upon new understanding of his previously and currently puzzling behaviors. An increased freedom in his capacity to stay with both his patient's pain and his own affective yearnings develops following his self-reflection.

> I had a woman patient whom I had treated for many years who frequently and increasingly belabored me for my failure to stay with her pain. Particularly painful to her was the attention her parents had given to her siblings. I'd point out to her how much hard work she had done that would justify her expecting to have gotten attention from her parents for all her accomplishments.

And she would berate me for staying focused on her accomplishments and turning away from her experience of pain. She felt that I defaulted on her and deserted her by focusing on what her parents had done or not done. She wanted me to stay with her experience of rage, anger, pain, and hurt instead of turning to her history. Now I could sort of see what she was saying, but I did not really understand it. I couldn't really see how what I was doing could account for her feeling so distressed with me.

Then a series of life events—a massive illness and regression lasting some five months—pressed me toward fresh knowledge about myself in deep and enigmatic ways. One outcome was that I came to a better grasp of what my patient and others like her had been trying to have me see.

For a year prior to my acute illness, I had struggled with an obscure bacterial enteritis. I was debilitated and had much weight loss. I had begun to think about retiring. Then came a mild coronary occlusion. I was hospitalized for ten days and then well enough to be eager to get back to work and start coronary rehab. I returned to my patients. I noticed that when I spoke to patients about fears and wishes that they might feel uneasy or ashamed to discuss, I would first speak about some pleasure I detected in them regarding their assets and accomplishments. This counterpoint to speaking about negative matters had come to feel like a useful technical gambit. It struck me that while it was therapeutic, I was doing more of this than I had done in the past. I figured I was struggling to regain a sense of my own competence. But I could also see I didn't get the results with my patients that I'd hoped to get—something fell flat. One patient referred to my trying to fluff him off when I spoke of him as so excellent in his accomplishments that he might well have expected to receive this affirmation. Besides, it was puzzling that he seemed to draw so little self-affirmation from all that he achieved.

During this time of my early convalescence, I had to deal with a big break in our hot water plumbing and trying to mop up the damage. I pushed myself into atrial fibrillation. This turned out to be a pretty serious complication for which I was subjected to a series of unsuccessful medical efforts to put me back in rhythm, treatments that seemed only to worsen a partial heart failure. I began to alert my patients that I was going to retire some seven months hence. I noticed it was much harder to tell my women patients than my men patients. I felt quite a bit of concern and a sense of abandoning them, most of whom had been in treatment for a long time. I noticed I was more casual with the men patients, as if this was something they ought to be able to take in stride.

A month later, there occurred a serious housebreaking by a young and agile man. We were able to fend him off, and it gave me, although still in fibrillation, a strengthened conviction of being a survivor with a stout heart. I felt pretty tough and that I was really making it. . . . Ten days later I was hospitalized for the purpose of being started on a new antifibrillation medication . . . it gave me my rhythm back and then a severe bilateral allergic pneumonitis. I was on full oxygen, at bed rest and struggling to survive. I lost a huge amount of weight. I had to be treated like a baby, bowels and bladder and all the things that don't work for a child didn't work for me. . . . I finally got out of it in an emaciated state. I have since recovered quite well.

What struck me was that from the start I had received a wonderfully warm reception by the nursing staff. The in-hospital experiences I came upon in this period of illness, which I need to dwell upon, began on my admission to a cardiac care floor. They treated me with respect and dignity and caring. I had a huge and immediate sense of surprise, pleasure, and questioning. Do they do this for everyone? Why me? As the medication took its toll, I became profoundly dependent on them for very basic survival care and was expected not to make it. I had to go through a slow period of recovery. I had to learn to regain sphincter control and to feed myself again. It struck me I was like a little kid coming back up through the stages of development. My mood was pretty good, partly because of the huge amounts of cortisone I was on. I was giddy and talkative or pulled way back into myself, vigilant, remote, and watching. This was exactly the way I experienced myself during the break-in. I've known I can do this at times of great stress. I could take some comfort to be in that quiet place of watchful coping.

I began to yearn for my wife's visits. She was coming frequently and very caring. At the same time she was badly buffeted about by what was happening to me and was sort of dutifully doing what she could, and I could sense a kind of detachment, a preoccupation. It made sense because I was aware of her desperation. On the other hand, I became very invested in getting visits from the nurses . . . who I felt were fully there with me. They were generally young, pretty, lively, very friendly, and solicitous, and they seemed to like to linger and talk. In retrospect I could see that I was very courting and engaging of them. I was determined never to complain or wince, just to cheer them on. I had a sense of delight in what was happening. They gave me the finest possible responses . . . I began to wonder why I so much wanted to be liked and appreciated by them. . . . In near delusional moments, I thought I could hear them make allusions to me in the background: "He's a fine man, bet he's a good doctor. He's so caring." I had a sense of joy, relief, gratitude. Then I had a dawning that the words I heard them say were ones that had been spoken about my father. My father died when I was an infant—died with his boots on, taking care of patients in a flu epidemic. The few people I came upon who knew him would use those words about him: "What a fine person." . . . "He cared only about his patients." It struck me with a real whack, *that* was my goal in life, and it had always been, not to be famous or make a lot of money but just to be a dedicated doctor who cared a lot about his patients. What came with that with a real smack in the head was that these fragments were all I had ever heard about my father. My mother would quote this praise . . . but that was all she said about him. My uncle, his brother, who came so much to our home, never spoke of him. My sisters didn't either. I somehow knew not to ask. I never knew a personal thing about him. Later when I was in my 20s another uncle told me about going hunting and playing football with him. These were the first pieces of information of what my father was like. There was this big gap about my father. Yet I'd worn my hair like him and wore a tie with a tiepin even when I played tennis, just like he wore in the picture of him on my mother's dresser. I'd just idealized him unbelievably. There were loss and hurting to feel I was never able to talk with anyone about him. I got to the immense pain of having a mother who didn't talk much, who was too preoccupied with all the jobs of parenting . . . reawakened by my wife's understandable preoccupation with practical financial matters she had not had to deal with when I was well, while I was dependent on others to take care of me. The thing that was going on within me about my wife and the nurses [then] fell into a focus. I recalled many instances in which I'd been sitting with [my wife] in a restaurant, and she's a very pretty woman, and I love her deeply, but invariably I'd get a fix on some unknown, attractive woman at another table, and I'd glance at her with intensity while we were eating, and I'd wonder what is this about. Then I recalled something I'd been told: a young woman [name] had come and stayed with mother and us primarily to take care of me while mother was taking care of the other kids and grieving [my father's death]. She stayed between one and two years. I have no recollection of her except that she was said to be pretty and very young. I have a feeling of warmth when I think about that name. So this led me to see that I had made a connection between this young woman of my early years and my pull toward these pretty women in the restaurants and now the caring I was getting from the nurses. I asked one particularly capable, pretty, and caring young nurse, "How do you do this? You are so wonderful with us strangers. You manage to convey how caring you are." She was nonplussed. A day later she came back and said, "We are trained to be like that. Some of us are better at it than others. But you make it easy. You don't complain. You treat us with respect and kindness. You are easy to like." That felt good to me to the point of tears, and something then fell into place.

I did a lot of crying. I became keenly aware of my self-deprecation as a lifelong trait. People would often comment, "How come you don't seem to show personal pride in what you do?" I saw now what a strong sense of uncertainty I had carried about my worth, my lovableness, my right to claim anything. It was more than that family edict of "don't blow your own horn." No boasting. It took me back to my thinking about my mother's not talking about my father and how that put him out of my reach. He was forever enshrined in her and not available through her to me in any way; I could not take his measure or feel his humanity. He was so idealized. I remembered when my mother was dying, I got there in time for her to die in my arms, which was wonderful for me. She died murmuring, "Oh, [diminutive of name]," which was not ever *my* name; it was my father's. So I went into this intense crying over having lived with a mother who I knew had loved me but had no way of saying it to me without getting too caught up in her own pain. She kept things pretty matter-of-fact and down-to-earth. I was crying with a mixture of pain and anger and some relief at what I was beginning more fully to grasp. I was so grateful to these women who had given me this care and were allowing me to tap into how I was always unobtrusively seeking to be assured . . . that what I hoped was so but couldn't quite grasp . . . that I had made it in some fashion that was OK . . . that I guessed I had felt, but didn't remember, with the young girl who gave me much of my early care. . . . I was greatly comforted by that. It made sense that I'd always handled my intensity of affect by a good deal of solitary reflection and special pleasure in solitary crafting of beautiful and practical things. I did it with some sense of an audience in mind, as with home things done for my wife or son or for our home. It was my way of doing something like my uncle but more than he could do, something I would imagine my father might have done . . . my way of trying to be as I imagined my father would have been. . . . It's been this way with my writing. I take great pain and then pleasure in writing papers and watching how they turn out. I know I'm accomplishing something quite good at times, but then I'll shrug it off. I make no appeal to be held superior or knowing. . . . It's more an appeal for fellowship, a shared experience. "Are you finding it like this?" I take pleasure in hearing others know what I'm talking about or differ here or there in ways that show me they have read with respect.

Now the clinical spin-off that followed from this has been subtle but sustained. I came out of this much more open to my own affective state than I've ever been before and much more comfortable with them [patients]. I did some crying . . . I hadn't cried in years. With my patients I [now] had a real keen sense that for a long time I'd been reluctant to stay with the pain of narcissistic yearning for affirmation. I could stay with it for a while, but I'd recede into quiet waiting or counter the pain with allusion to the pleasure in that patient's hard work and accomplishments and how they'd sustained them. I saw now that, of course, I was talking about myself. It was what that woman patient of mine had been trying to tell me and I couldn't quite hear. . . . I've been able to resonate much better with a patient's pain. This has, of course, been coming up more in the closing months of my work—this craving for affirmation, afraid of not finding it, being discovered to be trying and caring so hard for it. I'm much better able to stay with, and help, patients articulate that pain. Resignation has come not to connote failure; it has to connote a different and calming solution. I saw that my technical rationalization had been that for a patient to hear something wounding, I had to offset it with something positive and affirmative. I hadn't seen how in a personal way I had been taking care of my own stuff, my own pain and yearning, that I had been quieting down and dampening my own urgencies in those areas. It was a pretty profound experience for me. I don't any longer shy away from the pain, especially with the male patients, where previously I would have tried to get them through that by shifting their focus to what they have been able to do for themselves, which was my way of having handled it for myself. Once I could see more clearly how I had used my excellent adaptations for defense purposes, I didn't need to use this way very much. After this the sequences of what I did with patients became different. I'd stick with the immediacy of the pain and only after we'd been through that, would I remind this woman what a really fine person she has proven herself to be. It grows out of the relief I can see the patient feeling, out of having seen into the greater depth of some of the misery she was having. With men patients, too. Once he's been through that, he's able to feel it, and I'm able to say it. Before, when patients weren't eager to stay with their pain, I wasn't that eager to stay with it myself. When I'd focus on pain of narcissistic loss and the parents failing to give affirmation, I'd be focusing on accomplishments, I'd be moving away from the pain.

With this woman, I'd kept telling her how important I thought it was that she tried to get her parents' attention through her hard work but that her parents had failed to notice this. She would berate me for this shift in focus from her pain to what her parents were doing. I had done this. She wanted me to stay with her in the pain because that's what her parents didn't do. Going into intellectual reconstruction of the past, I was shifting away from her immense rage and anger and hurt. My doing that actualized her experience with her parents. The linkage to me was the focus of my accomplishments. My family didn't boast, didn't give much praise. Words, storytelling, repartee were allowed in my family but not the words that acknowledged from the heart. It's a very big difference. We never spoke personally about anything. The whole question of who really values you and for what was a big thing in my life. My uncle who came around all the summers of my boyhood, who taught me all sorts of things, went away when I was 12, and I didn't see him again until I was all grown. He went to the West to marry. He even took the rifle that he had given me for my 12th birthday. I loved that man deeply, but when he came back in his 80s, he took a look at me and said, "You must be [mother's name's] son, I guess." The fact that I could remember him down to the last detail, and he could only remember me in only a generic sense . . . I had a rueful, hurting . . . I handled it just as you'd expect, saying, "Now isn't that something, how differently people remember each other." I obviously meant much less to him than he to me. But then he had a whole passel of nieces and nephews to remember. But it did hurt. It was another instance of feeling I didn't quite make it.

I talk with an analyst friend in another city regularly, at least once a week. He had a group of us together to talk about the more personal aspects of clinical work. I also do this with my study group. I talk about how patients get to me, like with this woman patient. She really made me look and try to see where I was defaulting on her. I have usually reflected more on my own musings to myself in solitude, reflections while I'm doing manual work and less talking with others as a central source for my self-inquiry. I'm in contact with my transference figures—my analysts, mother, uncles—as I do my woodwork or gardening. I've said more to you about this than I've said to anyone else, no doubt because of your caring interest. But I came out of this experience determined that I was going to talk to a small group because it seemed so powerful. I have never talked to my wife about my cases. I do that only in a study group or with analyst friends. In this particular instance I haven't even talked to my wife about these more personal discoveries because she's been so stressed out by this that I know it would burden her. So I wouldn't do that for now.

It's a delight to me to have someone write to me and say, "Oh, you put it so well." I love the feedback. But there was this diffidence of not knowing, because of the awful silence of all those years. I feel I have the right to speak of these things when I put them in the context of your book or my writings. This gives me a legitimate reason to speak about myself. It's not OK to do so for my own ventilative purposes. I have it better now since this hospital experience. I feel so much freer to have my own feelings. The affirmation opened things up when I was in this regressive position, this being cared for by strangers opened me to those early days . . . when I felt in a sense I'd been a stranger in my own home, unable to talk about things that were terribly important to me. Maybe it's illusory, and maybe it's real, but writing notes about my experience and talking to you about it give me a broader comprehension. It gives me a sense of perspective. It's not just talking to somebody; it's talking to somebody who really wants to hear about things we knew but didn't know and now we know in a different way.

This analyst had been confronted by his patient about the way he moved away from her pain. His reflections on her complaint did not enable him to deepen his appreciation of why she was so distressed or the accuracy of her observation about him. Rather, a life-threatening, regressive experience reawakened childhood affects and helped him to reconstruct early memories and uncover deeply repressed yearnings.

In this instance the life event, more than the work with patients, facilitated the change in the analyst's perspective and stance and increased his freedom of affect. The analyst nonetheless frames his shifts in terms of his work with his patients. He remains diffident in speaking of himself. Based on his own report, none of his self-discovery or internal shift would be related to others were it not for the context of work and others' potentiality to learn from his experience. His patient's confrontation of his previously limited ability to stick with her pain becomes the point of reference for discovery and change.

Confrontations by patients about some characteristic or behavior of the analyst focus these analysts on a particular aspect of themselves. The first analyst had denied and avoided facing a personal conflict; the second analyst was well aware of the conflicted area, but it had not been the particular focus of his self-scrutiny or self-analytic attention at the time the patient made his observation. The third analyst had intellectually registered the patient's perception. He did not affectively integrate its personal significance until his illness created a regression in the context of which the patient's reaction could be understood. When these analysts recount the impact of their patients' observations, they emphasize the sharpness of focus it gave them to pursue their self-explorations.

While countertransference reactions and recognitions of similarities also bring a problem area of the analyst into the center of attention, with these triggers for increased self-awareness, analysts are more likely to describe the recognition of the conflict area as a first step. They then continue to elaborate the means by which they begin to work on this newly focused problem area. In contrast, when the stimulus for recognition is the patient's confrontation of the analyst with a personal difficulty, the analyst's description places more emphasis on the assimilation of this information. In these examples, the analysts place their first efforts of self-scrutiny on establishing for themselves that what the patient had observed about them could be substantiated by other information they had about themselves. The first analyst knows about her tendency to "muscle" her way through difficulties and quickly detects the emergence of rivalrous feelings with their historical roots. The second analyst is familiar with his tendency to be hesitant to speak and actively recalls its developmental models to impress on himself more clearly its maladaptive aspect. The third analyst discovers his need for distancing himself and avoiding painful yearnings only after he actually experiences these previously evaded feelings.

When patients interpret to their analysts, there is a reversal of role. The analyst, while usually able to tolerate the changed role and attendant ambiguity about whose conflict, defense, or shame is central at this moment, is not usually "cool" in his or her emotional reaction to these confrontations. In fact, such confrontations usually occur when transference–countertransference engagements are relatively heated, and the analyst's initial response, albeit unspoken, may be relatively tumultuous.

These analysts describe their process in a rational, orderly fashion. The unsettling sense of confusion, of temporarily, at least, being unclear about whether this is more about them or about their patient, and of feeling threatened, while not totally absent, is not central to their narratives. I think it is unlikely, however, that they failed to experience this sense of tumult at the time of the actual incidents.

The analysts have recounted these incidents at a time that is distant from their actual occurrence. They indicate that they spent considerable time rethinking and reworking what took place with their patients. It seems likely, then, that their relatively contained descriptions reflect an order and control that have been achieved over time rather than the actual portrayal of an experience that was at the moment responded to so smoothly. The third analyst does convey the intense pain of recovered affect. Part of his work focused on reweaving his discoveries in connection with his patient's observation of him.

The first and second analysts elaborate more fully on how their self-exploratory work changed their behavior with their patients than on the personal ramifications stemming from their self-inquiry. Having behaved in a manner with their patients that they regret and that the patients made apparent that they had observed before the analyst did, they are eager to make clear that they have behaved responsibly toward their patients. They take their patients' observations seriously, work on absorbing their accuracy, and offer their patients the benefit of their more acutely self-aware abilities. The third analyst also makes clear that he had seriously considered his patient's perceptions. Once they had an emotional resonance for him, his stance toward his patient changed.

Shifts in work with patients are undoubtedly easier to effect than shifts in one's personal world. Even though work with patients can be extremely emotionally demanding and requires both great self-control and capacity for intimacy, the requirements are restricted in time. For stretches of 50 minutes, it is more possible to offer our best, most modulated, and available selves.

While analysts are aware that they reveal both their "foibles and strengths" in their work with patients, they are also aware that when they learn about themselves and are motivated to change, this may more easily be accomplished in an arena where there are fewer personal stresses and demands. All three analysts state that their manner of relating changed not only with a particular patient but with other patients as well.

While these changes for the first two analysts were conscious and planful, really being "looser and more responsive," as the second analyst describes, cannot be effected only by cognitive means. If analysts do change in their style in work, if this analyst has actually become "looser and more responsive" with his patients, is it possible that there is *no* carryover to his personal life? When our patients change in relation to us during the course of analysis, we assume that these changes will also make their appearance in their relationships outside the analytic relationship. Why would we not assume that this would also be true for the analyst? Conversely, if changes are not also reflected in at least some small way in the analyst's personal life, are the changes that the analyst reports occurring in treating patients actually taking place, or are they mostly wishful? It is, of course, possible for the analyst to be "looser and more responsive" with some people than with others, but it requires more reflection to understand why this would be restricted exclusively to the work setting. It is also possible that the analyst has actually attained more freedom in his outside life that he is not yet aware of. I return to this question of self-report and psychological change at the conclusion of the book.

The third analyst describes a much more intensive and extensive personal process taking place from which he achieved more freedom of affect. For this analyst, of course, the stimulus for reflection was not primarily the patient's confrontation but a major, life-threatening event. In this respect, analyst 21's account is different from the others reported in this book. For the other analysts, their work with patients is the stimulus for self-discovery; for this analyst, his self-reflections stimulated by work with the patient serve to confirm and reinforce his recognition of his defensive stance, but the affective discovery comes from a life, not work, experience.

CHAPTER 8

Countertransference Responses as Stimuli for Self-Reflection

Of the 194 examples offered by the analysts in the questionnaire, 118 were instances of countertransference reactions serving as triggers for stimulating self-exploration. Since analysts are trained to be alert for deviations in their usual analytic stance, these disquieting countertransference reactions, occasions when they recognize that they are not "with" their patients but instead are reacting to them with unexpected affects, often and quickly catch our attention.

When analysts recognize a similarity between patients and themselves, it may, or may not, be troubling; when patients have a quality their analysts lack but can freely admire, without the intrusion of too much unconscious envy, it is reported as primarily inspiring. When analysts are confronted with an aspect of themselves by their patients, it causes them to reflect, but they may defend temporarily, decide eventually that the relevance comes more from the patient's issues than from their own, or do both. When analysts, however, experience their own countertransference, either through recognition of an enactment or through a conscious affective experience in which they see that they have brought an aspect of themselves into their work that has interfered with their intended interaction with their patients, then they know further self-reflection is required.

These moments are an inevitable part of treatment. Most often they occur subtly and nondisruptively, sometimes remaining unrecognized.

In fact, if they do not occur at some point in the course of an analysis, the analyst is unlikely to be sufficiently engaged in the process. Countertransference reactions are most often about heated affect—love, hate, anxiety, fear, envy, shame, guilt. The analyst is gripped by something he or she does not yet understand. These are moments of great opportunity for patients. If the analyst and the patient do not back away from explorations of these occasions, they can enable the analysts to regain perspective and recoup their professional selves, as well as provide opportunities to learn more about themselves.

In the examples that follow, analysts recount their experiences of self-discovery, the impact that their patients had on them, and the reverberations from their insights. They recount their perceptions of the psychological changes in themselves that occurred—changes in both their personal and professional functioning. The analysts' descriptions of the processes that they report led to change vary in the amount of detail about both the particular conflicts or characteristics that changed and the process in which they engaged that they believe facilitated these psychological changes.

Analyst 22: Recognition of a Current Grievance with the Analyst's Wife through a Recurrent, Erotic Countertransference Fantasy

The work this analyst describes primarily loosens the grip of an old conflict and ultimately enables him to reengage actively and affectively with both his patient and his wife.

> [The analyst first offered a brief description of his manner of approach before describing the details of the process of his self-discovery.] When a response of mine commands my attention, I try to think about the patient who stimulated this reaction, to think about the response and the situation that engender it. . . . I notice something about the patient that I persistently failed to understand . . . became overly interested in or something about myself that I became alerted to that was a little bit out of the ordinary . . . usually something I noted in my reaction to the patient . . . fantasies about that or my associations that accompany listening to that. . . . I find myself returning to some response either about the patient or about myself that captured my interest or curiosity and that then leads to some kind of exploration of why I've become interested in this particular facet of the patient's character or narrative or my own response or fantasies or affects.

[He would try to understand both the origin in the past of his response and its current use.] When countertransference reactions arose, there was usually something going on actively in my current life that I was not addressing ... an unresolved issue in my current life. ... What I see leads me to reexamine the conflicts in the patient's current life that he or she may have been avoiding because of similar conflicts that reverberated with my conflicts.

[He then went on to describe how a persistent erotic countertransference fantasy was employed by him to mask a current grievance with his wife. The analyst found that he was having fantasies about a married female patient.] I imagined running off with her, making love to her, maybe marrying her. My first intellectualized, theoretical explanation was that I felt a certain interest in her as I had in my mother, that there was a triangle with her husband and that this was some expression of some oedipal conflict on my part that had been reawakened. ... I felt rivalrous with the patient's husband ... doubts whether I was good enough for the patient, and felt I could surpass him as a husband, and lover.

[In the next stage of his process, the analyst notes that his fantasies persisted despite this explanation.] I asked myself, Why this patient? Why did it persist? I thought it persisted for a couple of reasons. One was that there were some difficulties in my relationship with my wife at the time that I either wasn't fully aware of or quite facing up to. ... Maybe at another time, when I didn't feel that kind of problem arising, the same kind of content or similar content from another patient or the same patient might not have evoked such a reaction. ... That then led me to wonder what this fantasy in my own life was a substitute for or an avoidance of in terms of facing my own relationship. ... That led me to think about the ways I might feel somewhat dissatisfied and the ways in which I was fearful of giving voice to that dissatisfaction, and that led to a whole reconsideration on some level in self-analysis of my relationship with important women in my life and the kind of fears of speaking up or making my wishes known directly. [Self-reflection brought to the analyst's awareness that he had a grievance with his wife at this time.] I felt she was not being attentive enough to my needs ... I then recognized that these fantasies about my patient had direct correlation to my unexpressed frustration with her. I then wondered why I was so reluctant to be direct and clear about my dissatisfaction with my wife. Was I afraid of my anger or her response to it? [These thoughts led to further self-analysis in relation to his past. He recognized that old

fears around separation and ultimately deeper fears around abandonment were aroused in relation to expressing anger to a loved
one.]

[Along with his self-exploration, the analyst continued to reflect
on how these fantasies and conflicts of his own related to what was
going on in his patient's life.] As I began to think about my marital
relationship . . . I then began to think about hers . . . and realized
that I was also experiencing something that was not only pertinent
to my own history and my own current situation but might be pertinent to her situation. So as I began to look more closely at this. I
felt that there was a way in which my patient and I were at that
moment in the analysis somewhat alike. Whereas currently I had
some difficulties in stating my own needs, I felt that she had all
along been hinting at her own dissatisfactions [in her marriage],
which, when I had tried to address them, she had dismissed or cov-
ered over or denied in some ways . . . I realized I had accepted her
defenses against realizing some aspects of her marital situation. . . .
I had accepted her defenses rather than challenging them more. I
could only do that once I challenged myself and my own relationship. . . . That led me back then to think about what she had been
saying about her marital relationship. . . . Also, clearly, I had to
wonder, Did she have fantasies about me? It was true, she did, but
the main point for me was to help me focus on something that I'd
been aware of but not taken fully into account. . . . Going along
with the patient's making light of it and dismissal of the depth of
her difficulty. So that once I worked through the issue more for
myself, then I could more truly be helpful to her in asking her and
helping her confront the issues of her own difficulties in asserting
herself and her wishes in relation to her husband.

[Self-reflection had enabled him more easily to see and interpret
his patient's fears of confronting her own wishes and making them
known to her husband and in the transference to her analyst. The
analyst's insight increased.] I began to see how my fantasies were
not only a substitution for my discussion with my wife but also a
substitution for the interpretation of my patient's defenses, which
were at that moment too close to my own. . . . I was then also able
to speak with my wife about my concerns. . . . In both instances,
my direct expression of concerns was met with satisfactory
responses. . . . my fantasies about my patient ended.

The fantasies of intimacy with the patient served several different functions. They were a substitute for what was missing with his wife and a

defense against dealing with it. They also enabled him to recognize that he and his patient were both afraid to express directly dissatisfaction to someone they loved. Once the analyst was able to pinpoint his inhibition, he felt freer to say what he felt. What had emerged for him was not something new; he had worked on these issues before. He knew that the deeper origin of his fears of self-assertion was linked to his fear of separation and still deeper and earlier fears of abandonment. His self-exploration sensitized him to how this conflict reemerged. What he learned about himself he then discussed with a colleague/friend with whom he shares experiences of countertransference.

In another part of the interview the analyst states that he often discusses his self-discoveries and process with a peer group, a colleague/friend, or his wife. He thinks the expression of conflict and its resolution need affirmation and confirmation. Communication not only serves as catharsis but also keeps one on the right track and helps one avoid being self-deceptive.

The example offered by analyst 22 is more subtle than most of the other reported instances of countertransference in this study. While the analyst's deepest underlying anxieties reflect the same intense, early issues as those conveyed by others, this analyst did not describe coming to grips with his fears of abandonment based on what he discovered in relation to his patient. The analyst was already aware of this issue and had done much previous work around it. Instead, the example illustrates the tenacity of previously established defensive strategies and how easily they can be reevoked by current difficulties. The reemergence of old defenses is especially likely to occur when the difficulties of the present resemble past conflicts. The analyst describes a process by which he disentangled the present from the past. Through self-reflective work, he clarified the reasons he was having difficulty in stating his own needs. The analyst then is able to be more risk-taking interpersonally. His enhanced capacity to state his own needs suggests that there has been a shift in his tolerance of wanting, of needing, and possibly of shame. An expansion of self seems to have occurred.

Analyst 23: Reawakening of Incompletely Explored Feelings Toward the Analyst's Deceased Parent Stimulated by a Countertransference of Anger and Frustration

Self-inquiry enabled the analyst to gain perspective on a residual conflict and to disentangle it from feelings stirred in relation to both her patient and her personal life.

A male patient in analysis wanted help but experienced that everything I did for him was wrong and got very angry with me. For the first six months of the analysis, his berating me did not get to me, but his barrage of complaints went on and on, and I found that I couldn't get through to him. After one session, I found myself crying and realized how upset I had become. I wanted to say to him, "Don't you know I'm trying to help, to be a good person." It was then I recognized this as a familiar experience that sometimes occurred with my husband; it had often occurred with my father where I felt misunderstood. . . . He failed to recognize that I was trying to be good and helpful.

[These connections gave the analyst a new understanding of what the patient's transference had stimulated for her in the countertransference.] I had been frustrated with the patient . . . and this was about my needs. . . . Then I was able to focus on the patient and what were his needs . . . encourage fuller expression of his feelings and reactions toward me.

[The new awareness also led her to further self-reflection.] I tried to give myself time to think and not be involved in anything else, to free-associate and follow any feeling attached to a thought and sometimes did dream analysis. . . . My father had died two years earlier, while I was still in analysis; it had opened a lot about my feelings of anger and frustration in relation to my father. . . . But I was no longer in analysis, and working with this patient, I came to recognize a deeper sense of anger and frustration and not feeling loved by my father. It was a point of turmoil. It helped me to appreciate again how frustrated I had felt not to be acknowledged or accepted. . . . These recognitions did not all come at once but evolved through the work. Their ever-sharper recognition helped me to work through my feelings and see how I got pulled into similar feelings with my husband. . . . Telling my husband what I recognized made a big difference. It made the historical basis for my reactions to him explicit between us . . . and made me feel my new perspective was more realistic and solid. . . . I felt a change in myself, . . . a greater sense of being able to let the feelings go.

This is an example of an analyst's being caught unaware by an intense countertransference reaction. It may be that the pained and frustrated response existed long before she recognized it consciously. The analyst offered support for this speculation in that as soon as she recognized her reaction, she was immediately able to relate to the patient differently and also talk with her husband about what she had understood about their relationship. A "deeper" level of her feelings became accessible through an appreciation of the power of her transference to her patient. She was then able to recognize "real" ways in which both her husband and her patient were critical of her. Having been able to separate out the extra dose of criticism that she projected from the past, she developed an increased tolerance for their criticism in the present.

Analyst 24: Recognition of Primitive Anxiety Through a Countertransference Dislike in an Initial Consultation

Working with this patient and other similar patients, the analyst learned about unconscious, anxiety-laden facets of himself. Through his self-exploration over time he found more comfort with these more primitive features in himself.

> [When the analyst was seeking his third supervised case, a therapist referred one of his therapy patients for low-fee analysis.] I did not like him and felt he did not like me. I thought the patient had been dumped by his therapist, who I assumed also must not have liked him. . . . The patient was much sicker than someone I thought would be a good analytic case. The patient was very, very anxious and very narcissistic in his way of presenting himself. He wanted me to be available at his beck and call, even during the consultation period. . . . I needed a control case, but I worried about taking on a patient I felt I did not like. [Further self-reflection, however, led the analyst to consider the countertransference meaning of his reaction.] I began to wonder whether I was feeling that I didn't like the patient because I was feeling threatened by the whole situation. If this didn't work out, I'd have to find another case. It wouldn't reflect well on me. . . . I realized my dislike really reflected my anxiety. [He also began to consider whether the anxiety he was feeling, in addition to reflecting his own concerns, was] informing me about my patient's state. I began to wonder whether my prospective patient might be feeling terribly anxious because he was, to a certain extent, being dumped . . . and very skeptical about starting with a new person, especially someone who, in his mind, was inexperienced and second-rate compared to the more experienced per-

son who was referring him. So he was frightened. [The analyst then used his countertransference response to help him with the treatment.] I thought about what I would need to feel all right about proceeding if I were in his place. . . . I would need to feel secure and not threatened, . . . and I came to realize this patient would need to feel the same in order to proceed to work with me. . . . I realized that I had to analyze all this in order to feel comfortable and recognized that nothing but an analysis was ever going really to touch this kind of material in this kind of man in any really meaningful way. [He took the man into analysis. The analysis lasted ten years.] He became one of my most successful and enjoyable analytic cases.

[The experience with this patient stimulated the analyst to reconsider assumptions he had made about his expectations of analytic patients and the qualities he had thought were necessary for someone to be suitable for analysis.] I saw that I was frightened of primitive wishes and began to realize that this was because if I examined them, I'd have to recognize certain primitive aspects in myself, which in this instance had to do with my own wish to be taken care of, by my patient or people who referred patients to me, and my own fears of people making primitive demands on me. . . . I knew it didn't mean that I had to gratify those wishes, but I had to be aware of the way in which they created certain kinds of primitive anxieties within me. [After these reflections, he found himself becoming much less frightened of, and more comfortable with, primitive wishes and anxieties.]

The experience with this patient opened up a lot for me. I began to treat a number of patients whom one might think of as more sick than one usually sees in analysis, with uniformly good results. . . . Each of these cases enabled me to confront what I would think of as more primitive aspects of my own psyche, which ultimately led to my feeling more comfortable with myself. . . . I had no organized way of working on the material that was stimulated by these patients. . . . A lot of it goes on while I listen to patients. . . . I allow myself a lot more freedom to reflect about myself and my own experiences while listening and attending to the patient's experience. . . . I think that seeing my patients struggle with primitive aspects of themselves leads me to think about those parallel aspects in myself, which I then begin to explore.

This analyst, now quite senior and experienced, reflected back on an incident at the end of his training that had a continuing influence on his subsequent feelings about analytic work and his sense of himself. For

the analyst, two different levels of anxiety had been stirred. His conscious concern was that he might not be able to treat such a primitive
patient successfully and would be thought less of if he did not succeed,
manifestly a performance anxiety; his initial dislike of the patient concealed his anxiety that the patient's primitive wishes might stir primitive wishes in himself, an intrapsychic anxiety.

This analyst was trained in an era when oedipal conflicts were viewed
as the central organizing feature of all analyses. The absence of an organized oedipal neurosis and the presence of a more "primitive" psychological organization in this patient alarmed the analyst and made him fear
that the patient might not be a "good" analytic patient. At the time of his
training, most training analysts focused their attention on oedipal, rather
than preoedipal, material. While, of course, there were exceptions, many
analysts failed to appreciate the complex relationship and interweaving of
the earlier and later developmental issues. Performance anxiety was more
likely to be familiar territory from an analyst's own analysis. For this analyst, like many others, after his own formal training had ended, he learned
about the more primitive aspects of himself through first exploring these
primitive wishes as they were expressed and explored by his patients. In
another part of this interview, the analyst reported that over the subsequent years he had increasingly talked about his awareness of anxieties in
himself with a group of his colleagues and, as time went by, found that he
became more comfortable with himself.

Analyst 25: Recognition of an Unconscious Identification with a
Negatively Viewed Aspect of a Parent through a Countertransference
Enactment

The analyst reports reintegrating a previously unconscious aggression
and transforming it into constructive assertion that she used for her
patient's benefit. A changed perspective and increased tolerance for her
own behavior led to a new, more benevolent view of her mother.

> The patient was a significantly ill woman who felt that I was shov-
> ing ideas, feelings, interpretations into her. She vociferously com-
> plained that my interpretations were suffocating her. And I began
> to feel as if I was suffocating and had an anxiety attack in the ses-
> sion. . . . I hadn't had an anxiety attack in years; I had anxiety
> attacks before analysis, but they didn't happen anymore after
> analysis. . . . I could not understand my experience but assumed
> that something that was going on for the patient was also going

on for me. . . . I talked to a close friend who is an analyst, someone I am comfortable with who knows a lot about me. This analyst/friend knew I had an early trauma, but at that moment I had no memory of it. My friend reminded me of it. . . . I was surprised I'd put this memory out of my thoughts and had needed my friend to bring it back to me. . . . I wondered why it had not been more easily accessible. I had learned about my own early experience only as a result of a difficulty I had with my infant son. So I knew it had previously been repressed.

When I had given my four-month-old son cereal, he had had an autonomic reaction—pushing it out of his mouth. So I didn't do it again for a while. But when I did, the same thing happened. After the third time this occurred, I mentioned it to my mother. . . . My mother responded by telling me that the same thing had happened with me except my mother was breast-feeding me. I had developed teeth early, bit my mother, and so my mother had weaned me abruptly. I had resisted taking a bottle and began to look like a failure-to-thrive baby. When my mother fed me cereal, I did the same thing my son had done—push it out. [Unlike the analyst, who backed off, her mother had force-fed her.] My mother put the cereal back in my mouth and held my mouth shut until I swallowed it. My mother reported this incident as if she were relating how she had saved my life. I was shaken by my mother's failure to sense how I might have experienced this as an infant. I felt very angry with her and put even more emotional distance between us than I had before—though it was already there.

[This information, once again in her awareness, led her to reconsider her interactions with her patient and her unconscious identification with her mother.] I thought my interpretations to my patient were helpful and competently and sensitively given, but my patient felt I was shoving things into her. [Based on her early experience, she now had to question her unconscious motivation.] I must have been feeling so anxious because I wanted to shove something down my patient's throat; . . . this was a highly conflicted thought since this was not something I would consciously want to do; I know I employ reaction formation against my aggression. . . .

A year later, the patient again experienced herself as drowning and saying I was shoving things at her. [This time the analyst was clearer about her own motivation.] I was consciously aware of wanting to give the patient something—a lifeline. My manner of

offering this may have been shoving aggressively, but I knew that
the motive behind it was to give my patient something I believed
was essential for her. . . . Realizing that my intent was different
from my manner I knew was a major internal shift for me. My
patient, too, came to understand what I intended, and a shift of
feeling occurred for her too. . . . The patient had never conceptualized a nonaggressive reason to be preemptive. She now understood my behavior as being helpful in taking over. Throwing the
lifeline was something I had done aggressively, but the intent had
not been aggressive. . . . I then reopened looking at my early experience with my mother and understood both my own behavior
[with my patient] and my mother's [with me] as a helpful taking
over. . . . I still see my mother as insensitive, highly aggressive,
and out of touch with her anger and intolerant of any aggression
from anyone. What I could see was, my mother could not contain
her own anxiety . . . a terror must have underlain what felt [to me]
like cold indifference. But my mother probably didn't consciously
want to frighten me.

[The work with this patient is ongoing, and the analyst is
unsure what other changes in her may emerge.] I believe that
work with this patient pushes something in myself that leads to
my opening up and reworking aspects of myself.

When her friend/colleague connected the incidents, the analyst was
stunned to see the similarity between herself and her mother. She was
aware that while this piece of history was not repressed, neither did it
readily come to mind. She knew the memory of her mother's telling her
of this occurrence had been upsetting to her and was not surprised she
had put it out of her thoughts, but she realized she needed to explore
why it had remained inaccessible prior to being reminded.

She had seen herself as being very different from her mother, and
this incident made her reassess this perception. Both of them had
viewed what they were doing as "helpful"; both had been unaware
how the person they were consciously trying to help had experienced
what they were doing as assaultive, and neither of them had been conscious of having any aggressive intent. Previously, she viewed herself
as unlike her mother; she was "trustworthy, sensitive, self-aware, and
had benevolent intent" toward those in her care. In contrast, she had
seen her mother as "very aggressive, insensitive, lacking in insight
about herself, and not to be trusted as a caretaker." Her conscious negative identification with her mother had masked an unconscious identification with her. The analyst was greatly distressed by this

recognition, since she consciously wished to be someone who helped and did not hurt. The patient's confrontation of her with her aggression had forced her to face a disavowed aspect of herself.

The extent of the analyst's own self-criticism needs to be considered. She had been oblivious to the forcefulness of her style of intervention because of her unconscious partial identification with her mother. She may not, however, have been "force-feeding" her patient. Her identification with her patient may have made it difficult for her to distinguish what she as the analyst had actually done from what her mother had done to her and how she had felt about it. The analyst has recognized a previously split-off aggression in herself, but she may be overinterpreting the extent to which she outwardly displayed it. Her description indicates that her tendency is to turn this aggression back on herself.

While the analyst had a brief insight, she did not continue to work consciously with it. The analyst has a repressive style; what she learned seems to have been assimilated unconsciously and gradually over time. Only when a similar situation arose did she become aware of the change in herself. At this point, her perspective changed. She modified her perception of her mother and herself as fright-engendering people. In the first instance when this patient accused her of assault, she identified with her patient and gained an increased empathy for her patient's experience. On the second occasion when the patient experienced being assaulted, the analyst identified with her mother and gained increased empathy with her.

Because of her affect-laden, shorthand style of presentation, the quotes from the analyst might make it seem that her views of her mother and herself were oversimplified. A previously uncomplex view of her mother fueled by anger had led the analyst to view her mother as lacking in "benevolent intent." Her changed picture of her mother does not exclude her mother's insensitivity or her mother's or her own unconscious aggression. Rather, the change in the analyst is that she is now able to have a greater sense of complexity and see that her mother's *conscious* intentions were benevolent and that anxiety contributed to her behavior.

Analyst 26: Discovery of Previously Unexplored Feelings Toward a Parent Awakened by Countertransference Reaction of Terror and Rage

The analyst's self-scrutiny enabled him to decrease defensive distancing behaviors. Self-exploration and work with the patient led him to increased tolerance for primitive affects in himself and more intense affective displays from others.

The patient was an intimidating, . . . explosive man of powerful intellect and temper . . . much smarter than me. He treated me with a narcissistic indifference to my state . . . and expressed an explosive rage toward me. . . . After a long period of distancing myself from the patient's anger by an icy withdrawal because I initially felt unable to withstand its intensity, I found myself able to allow the patient's fury to build more without interrupting or defusing it. I knew I had a tendency to become cold inside and not let myself feel in response to fear, and I worked consciously not to deaden my own response to the patient. . . . When I would start to feel this coldness, I would ask myself, Why was I having to do this? The questioning itself helped me not to withdraw. . . . Once I was able to overcome my icy response, I came to feel a rage and terror in response to my patient's behavior that I had never knowingly experienced anywhere else. I found myself going to the mirror after my sessions with the patient and realized later that I was struggling to feel if I existed in the face of my patient's total refusal to see and accept me in any way as a separate person . . . literally checking to see if I were still whole and still existed; . . . I was experiencing the power of the patient's rage as shattering and fragmenting.

I had not had this kind of patient while I was in analysis; the level of intensity was greater than anything I had previously known. . . . Most of the initial working through was done running and obsessing and thinking, Why was I wasting my time with this patient? And working it out over and over again until it became more powerful and less fragmenting personally.

[As he became better able to tolerate this experience, the analyst could also begin to consider how his countertransference reaction informed him about his patient's experiences.] I'd think more about what went on in the patient. I came to understand that this terror was what the patient had experienced growing up. The patient had used his explosive rage to keep others away. As the patient became aware that I was less blown away by the rage, . . . the patient also became less afraid of destroying everyone and everything else and became better able to stay with his feelings. [The analyst increasingly understood the value of having withstood and faced his own terror.] Only by facing my urge to disconnect could I stop myself from going cold with the patient. When I went cold, I had no idea what was going on for my patient. . . . Once I was able to let myself feel the terror, I gradually found myself able to bring in pieces of my own history. . . .

Whatever the nature of the experience, it would be filled in with either a memory, more genetic material, a kind of fuller understanding of something that I'd done all my life . . . got filled in mosaic-wise over time. . . . I saw that disconnecting and becoming cold were habitual ways I'd dealt with conflicts that were similar to my experience with this patient.

[After reaching these understandings about himself, the work with the patient proceeded without these intense reactions on the analyst's part. Toward the end of this patient's analysis, the analyst's father died.]

During the first phase of the patient's termination process, the work had seemed to be unremarkable to me, and I felt complacent. The patient began to talk about being very angry with me in a way he hadn't been. He talked about my not being with him. . . . At first I listened relatively complacently. I thought I knew that what was going on was a repetition of an aspect of the patient's early experience with his mother; it was an expected part of the mourning process. But as the patient continued to complain rather stridently and was filled with rage, saying, I "just wasn't with him!" there was something about the nature of his complaint that suddenly took on a different quality. . . . It wasn't just a repetition; there was something happening between us that made me more curious about what was going on. . . . I became aware that my complacency was kind of peculiar because I wasn't feeling empathic at all—feeling it was no big deal. That was not how I usually felt when someone was terminating. Once I had this recognition, I literally felt something lift inside me, and I became overwhelmed with sadness. . . . Until that moment I hadn't recognized the degree to which I had been fending off a lot of my own grief about my Dad's death and my own sadness about this guy's terminating. We had been through an enormous amount together, and . . . I had learned an enormous amount from him, so there was this kind of dual hit. . . . Feelings of love and grief about loss . . . so intense. . . . It struck me that in many ways I had a countertransference to the patient because his way of relating was not all that different from my father's . . . so who had the transference and who had the countertransference at times was a good question.

[After the analyst had this realization, there was a change in the patient's experience in the transference.] Without my saying a word, the patient relaxed and said, "You're with me now." There followed from that a whole series of sessions about a person very important to the patient who emotionally withdrew whenever he disapproved of the patient.

[In the course of describing his reactions and discoveries about himself through work with this patient, the analyst came to a new realization. He saw that he had had a father transference to this patient. I'm wondering if I have to retract my statement about never having had this kind of rage before consciously, because what I was just thinking is that maybe this was some of the rage I had with my Dad, who in my eyes was very powerful and was built like this guy. He also carried a monumental intellect, and there was no way I could hold a candle to him.

[These factors made the analyst feel like a little boy in the patient's presence. The analyst had not been consciously aware of this aspect of his experience before recounting it in the interview. The link to the experience with his father when he was a child emerged as a new discovery.] This is something that has just come to me now. What I've become aware of is just how much of a transference I had to this person.

I knew that something very important had shifted for me; after my work with this patient, a kind of primal terror of the other is no longer so easily evoked in me. I feel a sense of my own separateness is much firmer now. I can now sit with patients who want to obliterate me and not feel obliterated. . . . I no longer need to disconnect from this kind of patient to feel intact. . . . I also have a keener sense of when feelings of discomfort are coming from myself and am less likely to view these feeling incorrectly as projected from patients.

[Changes also occurred in his intimate relationships.] I find I have much more tolerance for my own affects and more ability to reflect on them. . . . Growing up, my family had been inexpressive of affect except for my explosive father, and strong affective displays had been disquieting to me. Now I am also much less reactive to the emotionality of members of my adult family. I feel I can be more intimate. . . . My wife notes the difference and appreciates that I am less reactive.

The analyst was aware that analyzing this patient had "made a very strong impact" on him. This awareness of the changes in himself had led him to volunteer to be interviewed for the study. Only in the process of reporting on these changes, however, did he connect the experience with this patient with his childhood feelings in relation to his father.

This man's powerful intellect—"he was much smarter than me," the analyst said—and physical attributes that resembled the analyst's father had contributed to the analyst's feeling like a little boy in his presence. At this point we can see that the analyst's response to the patient is based on countertransference.

Projective identification, at least in its more narrow definition, is an incomplete description of what the analyst had experienced (Gabbard, 1995). Even before the analyst made a conscious link between the patient and his father, he reported a change: he had "a keener sense of when feelings of discomfort were coming from myself, and I was less likely to incorrectly view these feelings as projected from patients." The recognition of this change suggests a preconscious awareness of the transference phenomena that became articulated in the interview.

While the analyst did not know me well, we had discussed some mutual interests previously, and he viewed me as someone who would understand, respect, and respond positively to the ideas and experiences he conveyed. Before the interview, he had had the powerful experience of shifts within himself, but in this interview they became newly understood in the context of his personal history.

This analyst shares his thoughts and feelings and is generally open with his intimate experiences. In another part of his interview, he described that he talks freely with his wife and with a close friend, who is not an analyst but is analytically informed. The insight he attained in the course of the interview may have emerged because he discussed the patient in more analytic detail than he might have with his wife and friend, since they were not analysts. Had he talked about the patient with an analytic colleague at an earlier time, he might have arrived at this insight then. He does not share as frequently with any analytic colleague; this may be due to geographic circumstances or possibly some more personal issues of particular incompatibilities with the perspectives of his colleagues at his institute. He believes he would be open about himself, provided the person to whom he confided was someone who he thought would be understanding, respectful, and responsive. His not sharing personal reflections with analytic colleagues at his own institute may then represent a fear of exposure of vulnerability in an interpersonal context that does not feel safe enough.

Previously, his focus had been on the nature of his defense and how it diminished. In the context of sharing his strong affective experience with me, another aspect came more into focus. He became aware of a transference to his patient as his father. While the acquisition of this new awareness in the course of our interview could be seen as a transference response to me, I think it belongs among those aspects of transference described as "nonobjectionable," which can, and do, develop in a situation felt as safe.

What occurred for this analyst in the interview does not represent a psychological change. Based on his description, a shift in him had previously taken place, but a deepened understanding of why it had occurred and why it had been so emotionally gripping now ensued. Our theory would maintain that this insight will further consolidate the changes that have occurred and help him further reintegrate past experiences with present ones.

Analyst 27: Recognition of Early Unmet Needs and Fears of Passivity through a "Sadistic" Countertransference Response

The analyst, through a combination of self-reflection, ongoing processing of his own experiences with a colleague, and the actual work with the patient, becomes more tolerant of his own intense affects and passive longings. He develops a comfort and pleasure in passive experiences. He shifts his theory of analytic technique, which is then reflected in his changed manner of working with patients.

> The patient was a hysterical woman who, after much struggle and hard work in her analysis, had been able to feel and express her love and erotic longing for me. . . . I was my stuffy self. My patient said, "All you have to do is say thank you." In retrospect, I thought it was courageous passivity on her part to let things flow and that someone different in my place could also let the positive things flow. To my distress, instead I felt a sense of sadistic satisfaction when my patient cried in experiencing the intensity of her frustrated wishes. . . . I was deeply disturbed by my recognition of this reaction in myself. . . . When I get sleepy, bored, tired, anxious, stimulated, . . . I realize that something is going on in the interaction, and I pay acute attention. . . . I have one friend, also an analyst, whom I talk with about things troubling me. We confess and confide in each other. I make my discovery with the patient. Then after the hour, I reflect by myself and also with my analyst friend. We have done this for many years. Then the synthesis takes place during the session with the patient.
>
> [His response to this patient led him to undertake the process he described. His reflections resulted in his remembering and reexperiencing genetic material related to his reaction. At the time of the initial interview he was not specific about this content. In a

subsequent contact, he told me more, but the specifics were too personal for public disclosure.] My memories got me in touch with being an intensely wanting and frustrated child whose desires were not being satisfied. . . . My revived experience was not about erotic desire; it was about separation. . . . I then began to consider that the patient's positive transference in its erotic longings was not just around genital wishes but reflected earlier yearnings as well. I saw that my sadism was a defense against feelings of reawakened pain and longing related to separation, that I was feeling it was better to be needed and have someone need something I couldn't do, better to have someone else crying than to face the experience of an unmet need that was in me. . . . My sadism was defending against the experience of passivity, of being the one who needed from someone else something that might not be forthcoming.

[As he and the patient worked on the transference–countertransference experiences, the treatment deepened.] Both of us became increasingly comfortable with staying with the intensity of our affective experiences without having actively to do anything about it. . . . I came to trust the unconscious process that is stimulated in analysis. . . . allowing previously inaccessible longings to rise to consciousness. . . . The synthesis that developed as these wishes were reexperienced and reworked then seemed to me more the agent of change than the impact of my active interpretations. . . . I began to question whether my earlier adherence to being an active interpreter was based on the same reversal, namely, the fear of feelings that were stirred when I was in a position of passivity. . . . Increasingly I focus the interpretations I do make on what was going on between the patient and myself. . . . The countertransference I had experienced with the patient had led to an internal restructuring for me in which I became much better able to give up the control of trying to direct the process and was able to let it flow. [Other changes have followed for him.] I feel myself to be much more comfortable and actually to enjoy experiences where I am passive.

[Describing the changes he had observed years after analysis, he said,] Something changes in the self. We put it together on the inside first and then do it on the outside . . . reshape it . . . an enactment of internal restructuring . . . an ego synthesis. . . . We make the world like we make the mind. . . . Increasingly I respect the transference–countertransference and interpret what is going on between us . . . "the between us" is where the work happens.

The analyst's response was disrupting to his sense of himself as a caring, benevolent person, consciously intent on helping to ease pain, certainly not wishing to create it. Central to his experience and his patient's pain was a state of helplessness, a state in which each was unable to feel any sense of efficacy, in which the satisfaction of his wishes was totally out of his control and depended completely on the response of someone else. For both the analyst and the patient, the someone who could release them from this painful, powerless position was a person who was loved. Precisely because this person was loved, the state of dependent longing had come about. Once the analyst recognized that he wished to escape from these painful feelings of helplessness, of being unable to get the other to respond as he wished, he saw that his countertransference reaction was based on a wish not to recognize and reexperience a state that was similar to his patient's. He was defending against his identification with her—as he said, "better that anyone rather than I should experience this painful passive state."

Being actively interpretive in his analytic work, he then saw many arenas in which he took charge in order to prevent, reverse, and evade being in the passive position. He had not been so conscious that his stance as the active interpreter of the analytic process had been employed for this personal reason previous to this experience. Yet, what he had seen in this stark and dramatic experience with this patient he could see had been true previously in much more subtle form in his work.

This analyst had believed in an ego psychological theory that supported his active interpretive stance, a theory that many analysts would subscribe to, but he came to see the personal purpose it had served. Being actively interpretive was not "wrong," but in his case, it was an active avoidance of being passive, of letting experiences wash over him and become integrated in a slower, more gradual way. He saw that he had been frightened not into actively grabbing hold of what he understood but into mastering his affects through understanding them instantly. His need had been to take charge of the process both for his patient and for himself.

The analyst has labeled his response "sadism." Certainly, there is a continuum in regard to what we view as sadistic, and this analyst's response seems to be only a flash of it. Sadism implies a wish to inflict pain and a pleasure in seeing that one can do this. While I understand that the analyst was upset to see his experience of pleasure in the patient's painful frustration, I do not think he was primarily describing a wish to cause pain. Rather, he was experiencing pleasure in not being the one who had come to experience an excruciating, helpless place.

Perhaps when we really understand the origins of someone's sadism, this construction is often found to underlie sadistic reactions.

What he has identified seems primarily the defense of turning passive into active. That he had done this more broadly and reflexively than he previously had known was made clear by his uncharacteristic reaction to this patient's distress. This recognition freed him to be responsive to the patient in a new way.

His mutual "confessing and confiding" over a professional lifetime with a colleague friend suggest an openness and receptivity that foreshadow his epiphany in recognizing the freedom and pleasure from allowing himself a passive experience. In one way, he had been doing it all along with his colleague friend, but because it was a mutual process, he had not recognized this aspect consciously.

In the next chapter I discuss these transference–countertransference interactions in the context of the therapeutic action of psychoanalysis. I show how these analysts' examples illuminate the therapeutic effect of the analytic process on the analyst.

CHAPTER 9

The Therapeutic Process
for the Analyst

In transference–countertransference interaction more than in other situations that analysts describe, the analyst's experience parallels the patient's experience. A therapeutic process is set in motion that potentially can occur for the analyst as well as the patient. Here analysts, like their patients, are caught by unconscious aspects of themselves.

Transference–countertransference interactions were by far the most frequently cited examples as triggers for self-discovery. As stated previously, they constituted 66% of all the examples provided. Because they are the most complex and most frequent stimulus for self-discovery and self-reflection, it is in relation to countertransference recognitions that I will describe more fully the ways in which the parallel impact from the analytic process can take place for the analyst.

The analyst enters the treatment situation with a sense of safety that the patient needs to establish before allowing more involvement. This difference at the outset is to be expected, since the patient, not the analyst, has sought help and feels vulnerable. The analyst's awareness of personal engagement is most often ushered in by the recognition that a personal conflict has been stirred. Once the analyst is aware of an internal struggle or a disturbing affect that requires deeper exploration, the analyst is engaged in a process that parallels the patient's process: a disquieting inner experience needs to be understood. For some analysts, familiar defensive operations first alert them to a need for self-scrutiny.

The process of analyzing defenses is usually the first step undertaken in analytic work after the establishment of an atmosphere of relative safety. The analyst with the erotic countertransference and the analyst with the countertransference fear of his patient's powerful rage both first perceived their disequilibrium by the appearance of familiar defenses.

For the analyst with the erotic countertransference, a familiar defensive expression of the analyst's attempt to avoid dealing with a conflict—for him, a turn to fantasy—alerted him to search for an area of disturbance. His self-inquiry allowed him to understand the reason for his defensive avoidance and to interrupt its elaboration. In this instance, he described the process of the continuing work that occurs in order to elaborate and rediscover a conflict that is already familiar and previously explored, that is, the fear that confronting dissatisfaction could result in the withdrawal of affection and, on a deeper level, a feared separation or abandonment. For the analyst with the countertransference fear of his patient's rage, his feeling withdrawn and "cold" warns him that some old issue is diverting him from his work with the patient. This recognition is sufficient to interrupt his defensive withdrawal.

Recognition of the activation of a defensive reaction stimulates self-exploration for both these analysts, but their reflections lead them to different depths of affect and insight. For the analyst with the erotic countertransference, the affect and intensity of his reactions were relatively mild, and what he recognized about himself was not as personally, emotionally shaking as it was for most of the other analysts in this study. Presumably, he had experienced much greater intensity around these issues at an earlier point. At this time, what the analyst was primarily illustrating were his interruption of a defensive process and reengagement in the process of both analyzing the patient and keeping in touch with his own ongoing issues and their vicissitudes. When analysts are familiar with the difficulties that surface within themselves, the model described by this analyst may represent a frequent kind of experience.

While this analyst does not report a working-through process, the reexperiencing of early issues may actually be a miniloosening of the affective ties to past beliefs. This loosening occurs because the analyst has the experience of not having his past fears confirmed. In this instance, he receives a double disconfirmation. Neither his wife nor his patient reacts as he had expected based on his past, originally unconscious and currently preconscious, remobilized fantasies of separation, abandonment, or both in response to his anger. The lack of confirmation of his fears may make the analyst ever so slightly less reluctant to address irritated feelings the next time they arise in him.

In contrast, the analyst who recognized his "icy" withdrawal initially is confronted by a newly discovered terror. Once his defensive reactions were interrupted, he experienced powerful and frightening affects as he worked with his patient. The analyst not only allowed himself to experience intensely frightening affects but also was able to tolerate and not be "blown away" by them. This change in the analyst's capacity was then paralleled by the patient's increased capacity to stay with his own affects, and his rage and terror then also abated. Although the analyst does not detail the process between them, it sounded as if what occurred was a mutual exploration of what each could tolerate from the other. This exploration was affectively enacted, not just put into words. The analyst's experience in the treatment, if not as powerful as the patient's, was close to it.

Sometimes what comes to the fore more powerfully than a recognition of defense is an intense affective reaction to the analyst. The transference, rather than the resistance to the transference, claims center stage. Instead of a gradual unfolding, the patient and analyst are plunged into an affective engagement that catches both of them by surprise. Backtracking is necessary at a later point to analyze defensive retreats. The patient has experienced or enacted the very thing that was frightening in this early phase but has done so before the patient and the analyst have enough information to understand what is occurring.

Personal analysis should have sufficiently informed the analyst about his or her own conflicts that most intense reactions reevoke an awareness of some historical referents. Memories of related past events or interactions can relatively quickly be brought to the analyst's mind. These reflections, along with all the insight previously achieved, provide a perspective that prevents the analyst from being as flooded and confused as the patient is when caught unaware by a transference reaction.

The analyst whose countertransference was to feel angry and frustrated in reaction to feeling unloved and unappreciated, the analyst whose countertransference was to "shove something down her [patient's] throat," and the analyst whose countertransference was a "sadistic" response to his patient's erotic transference were all caught by surprise about the intensity of their affective reactions to their patients. The analysts experienced responses to their patients that were totally discrepant with their expectable analytic selves. They temporarily lost their position of empathy with their patients' struggles and responded instead as if their patients were a threat. The analyst whose counter-transference was to withdraw faced a similar situation and experienced his rage and terror once he had relinquished his defensive stance. The analyst with "primitive" patients also suggested that similar "primitive" states were stirred for him once he let himself more fully participate in the process with his patients. Most of these analysts were then able to reflect on their own histories and use their previously acquired understanding about themselves to regain perspective and an internal professional stance toward their patients' material.

All analysts are, of course, familiar with the process by which they reclaimed their psychological equilibrium, but I elaborate it to emphasize the parallels for the analyst. Each analyst had to step back affectively and reflect on what had occurred in the interaction that stirred this response. Stepping back and reflecting are skills that patients employ to help them gain perspective on what transpires. Similarly, analysts use what they see and what they know about the patient and themselves to deepen their insight. While the experience is intense with affect, the process usually remains more active and cognitively controlled for the analyst. The analyst progressively gathers data: first from his or her response to the patient, next from the exploration of the patient's memories from the past, and then from the placement of what is learned from the past against what the patient knows about herself or himself and her or his mode of relating and working in the present. In countertransference reactions or enactments, the analyst's cognitive control is lessened. The analyst then has a greater need both to evoke these skills and to gather comparable information about himself or herself for his or her own benefit.

Insights can both stimulate and consolidate psychic shifts. Such new integrations can take place when a person feels safe and understood. Our concept of therapeutic alliance is based on this assumption (Zetzel, 1958; Greenson, 1965b; Meissner, 1989). Analysts have both learned about themselves through their own analyses and developed the skills to continue to do analytic work, the most notable being the ability to associate freely. It is, therefore, not so surprising that they would be able to continue their emotional growth and deepen understanding of themselves as new and different situations arise, such as those affect-laden issues with which their patients confront them.

Analysts are aware of the necessity to establish conditions of safety for their patients. If their patients are going to be able to hate, love, and fear them, they must be able to trust them enough to do so. The situation for the analyst again is different. The analyst may well come to trust his or her patient, but the analyst expects, and in the context of wishing increased freedom of expression for his or her patients welcomes, the intensity of both negative and positive affects being openly and forcefully directed toward him or her. The analyst expects the patient to contain actions but not the expression of feelings. In contrast, the analyst expects to be able to contain both actions and the shape and intensity with which his or her own feelings are expressed to the patient.

Although, once less defended, the analyst with the "icy" withdrawal is initially "blown away" by his reaction to his patient and believes that his patient is preconsciously attuned to this fact, he did not enact this response to his patient in any blatant form. Nonetheless, his "coldness," his experience of "feeling overwhelmed," and his unawareness that his experience of his patient is connected to childhood events with his father all indicate a relative loss of control on the analyst's part. Ultimately, through self-reflective work, he regains his balance and keeps treatment "safe enough" for his patient. Initially, however, he does not feel safe himself, and the patient, sensing this, does not feel safe either.

While countertransference enactments are no longer viewed as impeding treatments, when they occur, their initial effect may not necessarily be therapeutically beneficial to the patient (McLaughlin, 1991; Chused, 1991; Kantrowitz, 1992). The patient is likely at least temporarily to experience a loss of safety. Until perspective is recovered, the patient may experience a frightening reliving of previously painful events. Only when the analyst is able to regain self-control and learn about himself or herself, the patient, and their relationship from the interaction can countertransferences enactments be of benefit. If increased understanding does not ultimately result from enactments, then they are likely to be detrimental to the treatment.

It is not surprising, therefore, that when analysts get caught by intense affective reactions to their patients, they wish to talk with some trusted other person about their analytic experiences. Patients may often talk with other trusted people about what they are experiencing in analysis. Often they do so to dilute the intensity of the analytic work. For the patient, this may be a resistance to something developing in the transference; alternatively, it may be a way to enable them to remain in analysis without becoming overwhelmed by its intensity, or it may be some variant of each of these factors. For the analyst, talking with others also may be a way to dilute the intensity and gain some perspective on transference–countertransference interactions, but, at times, this may also detract from what might be experienced and learned in the undiluted analytic involvement with the patient.

Most communications of personal struggle stimulated by analytic work or self-discoveries attained from it are initiated to help the analyst contain his or her affective reaction, gain perspective on the experience, or provide a reality check on the analyst's self-perception. When countertransference reactions are very intense, confiding in a trusted person may be an ongoing accompaniment to the analytic work. All the analysts interviewed who offered countertransference examples as the source of recognition of personal issues described discussing their self-exploration, discoveries, or both with at least one other person. The analyst with the angry, frustrated countertransference reported the need to communicate her self-understanding to another person in order to derive a fuller emotional benefit from what she had learned about herself. In this instance, her feelings about the person whom she told were also tied up with her own painful self-representation. Telling her husband what she had understood about herself, she began to free their relationship from some of its transferential burden. Her acknowledgment of the part she had played in projecting negative feelings about herself onto him and then responding with anger may have created new space in their relationship for his positive feelings for her and her ability to perceive and respond to them.

The impact of her communication on her own experience of herself is clearer in this case because her relationship with the person she told was linked to her self-perception and her sense of well-being. In most instances, the analysts' descriptions of sharing their self-explorations have been less transferentially related than in this example.

The analyst with the countertransference of rage and terror reported the containing and sustaining function of describing his frightening experiences to the two people he believed knew and understood him best. Later, these same confidants provided confirmation of his own sense of personal change. Relating his experience to me provided the stimulus for this analyst to attain a new insight that enabled him to place his reaction in a historical context.

The analyst who had the countertransference of "shoving things down [her] patient's throat" when she talked with a friend/colleague was provided with a crucial piece of her own history that she had not consciously linked to her reaction to the patient. As a result of their discussion, she not only felt her affect better contained but had the equivalent of a genetic interpretation that facilitated her deeper understanding of the patient, herself, and their interaction. The analyst described this aspect of her relationship with her colleague/friend as close to mutual analysis. While the analyst was not suggesting that they had told "everything," she indicated that they had had a relationship of mutual trust that had lasted over many decades in which they freely talked about their vulnerabilities and discoveries of unconscious issues when they emerged. She viewed this relationship as contributing to her continuing to work through her personal issues.

Working through issues involves a lessening of affective charge and a gradual reintegration of previously unacceptable or disavowed aspects of the self. This process occurs in different ways and with different degrees of intensity and depth for different analysts. Two steps described so far are the analyst's private self-reflections and the sharing of conflict, affect distress, insight, and work in progress with a colleague or psychologically informed friend or mate. Some analysts engage only in the first step and are systematic in these explorations, and others are not. A third step occurs in the actual work with the patient. Work occurring in this arena is likely to occur simultaneously with one or both of the other routes to achieve self-knowledge and affect management.

Many of the analysts interviewed described a process that involves a reverberation with the patient's and the analyst's issues that takes place during the actual analytic work with the patient. Since each analyst has his or her own specific constellation of characterological and conflictual issues, of which only a particular array will be stimulated, depending on the nature of the "match" with the patient, the content that is reworked varies for each analyst and potentially in each analysis.

The safety of the analytic setting permits a regressive process enabling usually suppressed or repressed affects and fantasies to become available for both patient and analyst. The "play" that becomes possible in the context of such safety creates the opportunity to rediscover identifications and to become more conscious of their formation. Then, in relation to a new and different object, shifts in self- and object representation become possible. Concomitantly, shifts in defense, availability or tolerance of affect, and the more conscious shifts in attitudes, values, or beliefs also may occur.

The analyst with the "primitive patient" stated that he had no organized way of working with what was stirred in him in the process of analyzing his patients. He thought that what occurred was that as he listened to the patient, he simultaneously allowed himself the freedom to reflect on his own experience. He seemed to be suggesting that as the patient's more "primitive" aspects were expressed, explored, and reworked, he allowed these "primitive" experiences of the patient to stimulate an awareness of the parallel experiences within himself. To the extent he was able to be aware of similar affects, experiences, defenses, and fantasies in himself, he permitted his newly conscious "primitive" wishes to reverberate with the patients' exploration of his or her related states. In the context of an intense affective relationship between patient and analyst, old wishes were revived, reworked, and reintegrated in a new, less split-off, manner. The result was greater comfort with himself.

The process of working through conflicts stemming from previous painful relationships is illustrated by the analyst whose male patient described her as failing to help and revived her experience of what she believed was her father's view of her. Although she did not elaborate the details, she indicated that these reactions were played out in the transference-countertransference interactions between her and her patient. In this interplay between herself and her patient an increasing clarity evolved about her feelings of being unloved, unappreciated, angry, and frustrated. She seemed to be suggesting that she came to recognize that unconsciously she had been experiencing her patient's rejecting and unappreciative stance as if it were literally about her and had been failing to keep its transferential meanings in focus. Her discovery of its unconscious meaning to her came only when she found herself in tears and heard herself using the same words in relation to her patient as she had in thoughts about her father. Once she had seen her loss of perspective, she was better able to facilitate her patient's expression and exploration of his feelings. She was then able to understand his perception of her in the context of his history and, at the same time, to use his reactions to consider and reflect upon the similarities and differences between her sense of his perception of her and her father's perception of her.

Once she was able to see how she fused and confused these experiences with her patient and her father, she could also begin to see how she had done something similar in respect to her experience with her husband. Communicating her self-discoveries to her husband served to solidify her changed feelings about herself and to enable her still further to let go of her anger and frustration.

The analyst with "sadistic" countertransference to the patient's erotic transference, once he recognized the defensive aspect of his need to be in charge, subtly shifted his stance from active interpreter of the process to being a mutual participant in the process. This shift did not mean that he relinquished his role as an observer or that he ceased to value his understanding and conceptualizing of what transpired. He came to believe, however, that the centrality of the work resided in the transference–countertransference experience and came to trust in the unconscious process that was stimulated in analysis.

By focusing on what emerged in the interaction with his patient and by allowing the relationship to evolve, instead of trying actively to direct it through interpretive activity, the analyst found that "previously inaccessible longings" rose to his consciousness. The analyst described allowing himself to become fully affectively involved with his patient. Once having done so, he was open to having the analytic process work for him in much the way it worked for his patient. The patient was not the interpreter of his process, though some patients may be so; the analyst believes that interpretation was a much less central agent than "the synthesis" that developed as his and the patient's wishes were reexperienced and reworked in the context of their work.

As his patient explored her experiences of helplessness and frustration in her unmet longings, he could allow himself to resonate with them rather than fight against this experience in himself. Permitting himself to remain connected to the painful state of his patient facilitated the recall of parallel states of helplessness and painful frustration for himself. Staying affectively close to his patient in her pain, reexperiencing his own parallel pain, and simultaneously appreciating the inevitability of his role as the agent of frustration for his patient's pain, he found that an internal restructuring took place for him.

"Letting it [the process] flow," he believes, enabled a resynthesis to take place. In other words, where formerly he had taken active control, he now let himself become fully emotionally engaged with his patient and permitted his empathic feeling for her to emerge; he allowed himself to be passive in relation to what occurred. The more he was able to allow this to occur, the easier it was to let it occur again. Earlier painful experiences gradually became less toxic as they were reexperienced in this relationship. Each time they rose to consciousness, they were not only newly understood but newly reexperienced in the context of a relationship. This relationship, while not actively and directly gratifying the longings that arose, allowed both participants to remain connected and trusting of each other. The patient verbally expressed this experience of longing, while the analyst privately explored a similar state. The analyst said that he came not only to feel much more comfortable but actually to enjoy experiences in which he was passive.

Some analysts are quite conscious that a process of transformation is taking place, but others are unaware that an aspect of themselves has shifted until they see themselves responding differently. The analyst whose patient felt she was "shoving things down her throat" did not recount the process of her work; she was aware of the outcome but not conscious of how it occurred. Although it was not directly in her awareness, in the course of describing this patient and the treatment, the analyst conveyed how she had come to appreciate the intensity of this patient's struggles and to respect her for her capacity to face "unpleasant" aspects in herself and withstand psychic pain. We know from the example that she identified with her patient's sense of being assaulted, that she resonated with the experience of being forced to "swallow" something unwelcomed. While it must remain speculative, it does not seem too much of a stretch of the data to suggest that the analyst's shift in her sense of herself came about through a reworking of her own issues that paralleled and mirrored the patient's issues as the patient explored and expressed her experiences. This example seems to support the idea that changes may occur without being recognized.

Some analysts are acutely aware of what is transpiring in the process. They place what occurs in an intellectual framework and try to explain why it occurs. Other analysts, like the one I have just described, are far less focused on trying to conceptualize the nature of therapeutic action for themselves. They are likely to analyze the countertransference interferences but may have less interest in grappling with the more theoretical ideas about process and change. Instead, their affective participation in transference-countertransference encounters may result in changes for themselves without any conscious registration. They become aware that such changes have occurred only when they find, as this analyst did, that she was responding quite differently to a situation that previously had been a source of distress.

The psychological changes that occur when analysis is successful occur in areas that are embedded in the process. Broadly defined, these areas are intrapsychic, interpersonal, and related to work. In each of these areas, attitudes, values, beliefs, affect availability and tolerance, self- and object representation, and sense of self play a role. To understand the curative aspect of analytic work, it seems necessary to tease apart two aspects of this work. One aspect has to do with affect availability and tolerance and the other has to do with object relations—the interface between intrapsychic and interpersonal relationships. The noninterpretive aspects of the analytic work occurring around both these variables are experiences that occur for the patient and have many direct parallels for the analyst.

Several factors contribute to making the analyst's tolerance of frustration and affect modulation less an issue in the analytic setting than is the patient's. In the analyst's own analysis, even if self-control has not been a direct focus of the work, the experience of frustrated wishes must have occurred and been endured. So even if, in the unlikely but most idyllic scenario, life circumstances or choices have limited the amount of frustration the analyst has had to withstand, the analyst has had some practice with tolerating disappointment and frustrated wishes as an adult. In addition, in the current analytic situation where he or she is the analyst and not the patient, the degree of frustration experienced is likely much greater for the patient than for himself or herself. Also the material that is the focus of attention is the patient's and not hers or his. Nonetheless, each analytic treatment potentially reopens the experience of managing frustration and disappointment for the analyst as well as the patient.

In the example of the analyst with the "sadistic" countertransference, the dreaded state of passivity, of being dependent on another to relieve one's pain and frustration, was a similar problem for patient and analyst. The patient's directly experienced and expressed acknowledgment of this state stimulated the analyst to explore and find his own previously disavowed similar pain in a passive state. Both patient and analyst then knew that there was an affect state that they dreaded experiencing and had difficulty tolerating. In fact, the patient initially may have been able to tolerate this state somewhat better than the analyst since the patient could allow herself to experience and express it before the analyst "knew" about this state in himself. In his "sadistic" response, he was trying to distance himself from "feeling" it. The patient and analyst were sharing a difficulty in bearing the painful experience of frustration.

As the patient described and explored her state of frustrated pain, the analyst, by then alerted and open to vicariously experiencing the similarity of their difficulty, had a "taste" of that experience. He listened empathically, no longer distancing himself, and addressed himself to his patient's pain in some manner that allowed her to know that he had understood her distress. His staying with her in her experience of pain enabled her to bear her frustration better. Her analyst was not gratifying her wishes, but neither was he leaving her to tolerate them alone. His understanding presence allowed her to contain her painful frustration better. Her better containment was also vicariously experienced by the analyst. As his patient was increasingly able to experience, express, explore, and tolerate her painful feelings, the analyst in his identification with his patient around this area also became increasingly tolerant of his own affective states.

He has a "taste" of her mastery, her increased capacity to contain and bear her experience, as well as her pain. These "tastes" of his patient state and mastery can be thought of as trial identifications (Fliess, 1942), generative of empathy (Schafer, 1959). The analyst's "aim is to understand, to enhance the reality of the other person through his own experience and awareness of that person; that he thereby enhances his own inner world does not detract from the object-related nature of empathy" (Schafer, 1959, p. 353). This analyst viewed the process that evolved as one in which previously inaccessible longings rose to consciousness in the context of the patient's discovery and tolerance of her own unmet longings and then became resynthesized. Not only did what was disavowed become reintegrated as part of the self, but tolerance of the affect experience itself changed as a product of the work for both patient and analyst.

A related but slightly different situation existed for the analyst with the countertransference of rage and terror in response to the patient's powerful anger. In this analysis, the analyst is more deeply immersed in the intensity of his affective distress than is commonly the case. The analyst permitted himself to regress in this manner in order to help his patient. He knew that if he maintained his defensive distancing, he would not become flooded, but he would also not be able to understand or help his patient. He, therefore, faced and overcame his affect inhibition and allowed himself a fully affective engagement with his patient. He trusted himself enough to take this risk. The patient began analysis with a transference in which he perceived his analyst as an enemy to be destroyed. He was the kind of patient Winnicott (1954) described as ruthlessly aiming to annihilate his analyst and Bird (1972) described as having wishes *actually*, not symbolically, to inflict harm on the analyst.

Until the analyst could allow himself to experience the "fragmenting" terror and rage, it seemed the treatment, if not the analyst himself, might be destroyed because the analyst in his defensive withdrawal had backed out. The analyst's ability to acknowledge his defenses and face himself reversed this outcome. The analyst believes that his patient had been able to perceive that his analyst had backed away from him in response to his powerful rage. He also believes that his patient preconsciously registered both the analyst's terror and his ability to withstand it. Once the analyst no longer retreated, the patient was no longer "blown away" either, since he could then be less afraid of the effect of his rage on his analyst.

Seeing that his analyst was not destroyed, the patient had to modify his belief in his destructive powers; such a modification can be relieving only when the conditions under which this ruthless, aggressive stance toward the world feels no longer necessary for safety. The patient found, it seems, that his analyst not only was not destroyed but was also not about to try to destroy him. He was then able to experience and express feelings other than rage and successfully explored and came to understand these affects and experiences.

The analyst, for his part, had powerfully revived, but not cognitively registered, early childhood experiences of terror and rage. He reacted and recognized his reactions but did not know the origin of his terror. Now a grown man with physical, intellectual, and emotional strength that he did not have, and could not have had, as a child, he was determined to face and not flee his terror. Why was he willing to do this? Both professional and personal factors contribute to the answer and may not be totally separable in this instance.

As the patient explored the feelings that lay behind his rage, the analyst was able not only to feel less afraid but also consciously to empathize more with his patient, and perhaps unconsciously more with his father, whom he only much later realized was the person affectively evoked. The analyst came to understand that the terrifying, bullying patient was himself terrified; this understanding also served to decrease the analyst's fear. Much later, in the context of the interview, the analyst realized his own father must have been similarly afraid. Having forced himself not to flee, the analyst found he was better able to withstand the terror. The more he withstood it and found he was not destroyed, the stronger he felt. His increased strength was perceived by his patient, who was calmed by it. The gradual calming of the patient further increased the analyst's sense of strength, effectiveness, and mastery.

A comparison can be drawn between these two patient–analyst pairs. For both, the power of the treatment is in their interaction. In their work, the analysts were overcome by an intense affective reaction that paralleled the patient's, and both patient and analyst learned to withstand and ultimately regulate their affective experiences. Unlike the analyst with the "sadistic" reaction, who quickly recalled the relevant history for his reaction, the analyst who experienced rage and terror "felt" the familiarity of his affective distress and reactive pattern of coping but did not recover a historical context until our interview. He withstood the affective intensity by focusing on his understanding of personality organization, by recognizing his defenses and their repetitive nature, and by committing himself to master his fear and help his patient master his. Most important, it seems, his sense of increased strength and ability to cope came from seeing that he was progressively more and more able to do so. He illustrates the view that changed behavior precedes insight (Ferenczi, 1955; Gedo, 1991). For the analyst with the "sadistic" reaction, the process is the reverse. He first understands and then is able to change his behavior, though only gradually was he able to rework his affective experience. This analyst more quickly recognized his identification with his patient in her affective distress and understood that he needed to struggle with the same problem his patient faced. It took a longer time for the analyst who experienced rage and terror to grasp that his present experience was what his patient had felt growing up. Until he realized that both he and the patient were struggling with the same issue, he experienced the patient as a threat to him. Only later could this analyst learn from the patient in the reverberating manner that occurred for the first analyst.

Increased tolerance of painful affect does not occur outside the context of a relationship. Shifts in affect availability and tolerance may precede or follow shifts in self- and other-representations. A change in the analyst's capacity to tolerate and modulate intense affect and a change in self-representation are related. A greater sense of an ability to be self-regulating increases a sense of competence and self-esteem. For some analysts this means achieving a greater sense of self-control, while for others it means being looser. A new integration that includes changes in self- and other-representations occurs after the analyst with the countertransference rage and terror confronts and struggles with the modulation of his aggression.

Not only is there a mastery of early terror, but there is also an unconscious reintegration of his sense of self in relation to his identification with his father. Change in affect availability and tolerance facilitates a change in self- and object representations. The analyst in choosing to become an analyst had selected a field of work where he actively sought to help others ease their pain and fear—again suggesting he had selected a life work that would support a mastery of early pain. Unconsciously, it seems this choice may have also been based on a negative identification with his representation of his father: he, the analyst, would ease fears by analyzing and mastering them, not create them as he believed (unconsciously) his father had in him. Once the analyst perceived his patient differently—no longer just a terrifying bully—unconsciously, he must have also perceived his father differently. The analyst with the "sadistic" countertransference was horrified at his response to his patient's pain. Self-reflecting, confiding in his trusted colleague, and reworking his own fear in the course of the analytic work with his patient led him to new views of his mother and himself. He recognized that what he is struggling against are his own fears of passivity. An interpersonal terror then became understood as an intrapsychic terror and paralyzing fear, or a "sadistic" reaction became replaced by anxiety that could be grappled with and understood.

For both these analysts, the transference–countertransference was viewed as the dynamic pivot facilitating psychological change. In the words of the analyst with the "sadistic" countertransference, "what is going on between us . . . the between us is where the work happens."

While analysts are usually deeply involved with their patients, we do not assume that a patient is likely to have the centrality in an analyst's life that the analyst does for the patient. Indeed, if this should occur in any sustained way, there are likely to be untoward consequences for the treatment; however, the degree of personal involvement that an analyst feels with his or her patients varies depending on the nature of each particular patient–analyst pair. The more areas of personal overlap, perhaps especially when these overlaps are in areas of shared difficulties, the more intense the analyst's personal involvement is likely to become.

Under the conditions of this increased emotional involvement, transference–countertransference engagements are likely to be more heated and to have a more powerful impact on both participants. While the patient's difficulties are the focus, the analyst becomes a participant in the struggle as the patient's transference intensifies. The analyst increasingly feels, not only understands, what the patient has been describing. Sometimes this affective understanding is in empathic resonance, but sometimes it is not. Both the position of being "inside" the patient's experience and the position of being "outside" in the role of "the other" provide data about the patient and oneself. Allowing oneself to participate actively in the affective life of a patient means being open to one's own affects, fantasies, hopes, and fears.

Although the asymmetry of the relationship means that the analyst by definition is in a "safer" position than the patient, once the analyst permits this emotional openness, the analyst is engaging in an emotional risk. Without this emotional risk, no psychological change can take place. To be truly engaged is to allow oneself to be vulnerable to another person. Once engaged, the interaction that occurs between the patient and analyst provides an opportunity for the analyst, as well as the patient, to change.

Such engagement is not lightly undertaken. It requires trust—trust in the analyst's own capacity to withstand the intensity of the patient's affects and the intensity of what these fantasies, wishes, and fears evoke for, and from, him or her. The freedom that the analyst can permit is dependent not only on the extent to which he or she trusts himself or herself but also on the extent to which the analyst believes he or she can trust the patient. The analyst's spontaneity and emotional openness are likely to increase, the more the analyst believes that he or she can rely on the patient's capacity to express freely the thoughts, feelings, and fantasies stimulated by the analyst, the analyst's interventions, and the analytic situation. The character of the particular patient and the extent to which the analyst feels a personal resonance with the patient are also apt to influence the analyst's sense of trust. While it is not the patient's obligation to maintain confidentiality in relation to anything that he or she learns directly or indirectly about the analyst or what transpires between them, the manner in which the patient deals with all such material undoubtedly affects the analyst's sense of safety and freedom in the analytic setting. The greater the sense of safety, the greater the trust and the greater the possibility for change to occur.

If psychological change comes about, at least in part, because what transpires between the analyst and the patient is different from what the patient previously experienced—namely, that frightening or disappointing expectations about the other, oneself, or both are not repeated or, if repeated, are reworked, reunderstood, and then relived with a different outcome—then something parallel is likely to occur for the analyst. The analyst cannot reasonably expect that the patient will contain and control his or her reactions to the analyst in the same way the analyst tries to do so in relation to his or her patient. In fact, the analyst hopes that the patient will come to feel free enough not to contain the expression of these feelings, albeit the expectation is that they will be put in verbal form. Given this dramatic difference in expectation, how can this relationship benefit the analyst beyond a further recognition and clarification of some of his or her own issues?

The answer is that if the analyst is really emotionally engaged, and if this engagement is around an area of mutual difficulty, the interaction between patient and analyst entails a mutual reworking of past expectations.[1] The analyst not only sees and experiences his or her patient's reliving these expectations in relation to him or her but has the opportunity to be in both roles and affectively appreciate the complexity and ambiguity of experiences. At one moment the analyst is identified with the patient, as the analyst with the "sadistic" countertransference becomes with his patient in her painful frustration; at another moment this analyst is experiencing himself as the perpetrator of this pain. In identifying with her, he reexperiences the pain of being hurt and disappointed and maybe also feels betrayed. He feels anew unsatisfied longings, unrequited love, frustrated rage, fury at being frustrated, panic at fearing being abandoned, punished, castrated, rejected, and so on. But when he experiences himself on the "outside," he sees himself

---

[1] Weiss and Sampson's (1986) view of psychoanalysis as the testing of the patient's "pathogenic beliefs" is similar to the point I make here.

as being represented as causing all this distress.[2] Indeed, at times, he may reciprocate any of these feelings toward his patient, but he also maintains an awareness of how he simultaneously does not. The analytic situation allows him to see and experience both points of view, the patient's perspective and the perspective that he ascribes to the other. For the analyst whose countertransference was rage and terror, his fluctuation between the experience of rage and terror ultimately facilitated his developing empathy for his patient, which deepened as he was more fully able to move back and forth between these states.

The analyst's trial identification with the patient, which enables the analyst empathically to explore the patient's difficulties, also provides a vicarious experience of these issues for the analyst. In a sense, when an analyst enters a patient's world in this way and tries to understand and grapple with the patient's experience, if the issues the patient is struggling with parallel issues for the analyst, the process that evolves offers the analyst a chance to work on these difficulties in a once-removed fashion.

The analyst holds the patient's construction of herself or himself, of the analyst, and of the analytic relationship and juxtaposes this against his or her own perspective of himself or herself, the patient, and their relationship. The analyst does not do this to determine which is "true" but rather to explore and expand his or her understanding of each of them and their engagement. The discrepancies are likely to be the areas where central work occurs for both of them.

When the analyst with the "sadistic" countertransference experienced pleasure when he saw the intensity of his patient's frustration, he almost instantly had this experience of pleasure replaced by an experience of acute pain and distress. In the first moment of this interaction as it is described, he is identified with his mother, and the patient is identified with his childhood self. He initially refuses to reenter that painful childhood place. But almost as soon as he feels the distance from that childhood place, he is horrified to think he could be doing what he felt was done to him, even if only in his thoughts and fantasies. Through his self-reflective work, his position shifts. When he rejoins his patient

---

[2] There are, of course, other transference–countertransference possibilities, such as complementary ones (Racker, 1956). The analyst could also experience himself as some other qualitatively different, benign rather than sadistic, person from the patient's life. The point I emphasize here, however, is that this particular transference–countertransference grips the analyst because of his own particular issues. As Bird (1972) states, there are as many (counter)transferences as there are analysts. The specific affective reaction that is stimulated in the analyst depends not only on the patient's conflicts but on the analyst's. Sandler (1976) makes a similar point when describing role-responsiveness.

in identification with his childhood self, he has an awareness and knowledge of what it felt like on the other side. It is not quite how he had imagined it as a child. He, in the role of the perpetrator, was not as unfeeling, as unresponsive as a child feels the adult is when the child is hurt, frustrated, or disappointed. If he continues to frustrate his patient, it is not because he wishes to make her suffer; it may even be that he would wish to gratify her, but his greater sense of caring about her means that he would also have to frustrate himself rather than do this. What he is coming to see is that not only are things not necessarily the way his patient thought they were between them, but they are not necessarily the way he had constructed them and may have continued to construe them based on his past relationships. At the same time, he must, of course, also be very clear with both her and himself about why it is understandable that she and he came to view things as they did— both determined by their history and by the nature of what transpired between them. In other words, he has developed an empathy for both perspectives.

What is being played out interpersonally is also intrapsychically represented, that these two perspectives of patient and analyst are externalizations of intrapsychic representations. What we see as an interpersonal struggle is also an intrapsychic conflict. Therefore, as the patient and analyst become more empathic, understanding, and open to these multiple and at times conflicting points of view, complexity and ambiguity increase, and the sense of conflict diminishes. The disowned aspects of the self are able to be reintegrated because they are no longer experienced as so toxic; they are experienced as less lethal because they are no longer seen as so "black and white." The reintegration creates a new synthesis with slightly expanded capacities for self-acceptance and acceptance of others and their differences.

For the analyst whose countertransference terror and rage were stimulated by his patient's powerful rage, only in the termination, which coincided with his father's death, did the analyst affectively experience how deeply attached and how sad he felt at the prospect of his patient's leaving. In parallel, he experienced how attached he felt to his father and how sad he was at his loss. Still later in the context of feeling trust and safety in relation to recounting the example, he made the cognitive link between his experience with his patient and his father and recovered the memory of early terror.

The analyst reported that his experience with his patient changed his tolerance for affect both professionally and personally. He no longer found himself withdrawing or so frightened by patient's rage. He had a much keener sense of when discomfort was his own and was less likely to assume it was a projective identification. In addition, in his personal life he was no longer so reactive to emotional expression of his family members. He had grown up in a household where affect was very muted and had previously felt disquieted by the much more intense affect and volatility of his adult family. Following the analytic work with this patient, he found himself much more comfortable with the emotional expressiveness of his family and much more tolerant of his own affects and had a much greater subjective sense of intimacy. His wife has spontaneously observed how much less reactive he is to the expression of intense affect.

Another analyst described the effect on the analyst of analytic work, especially when the affective intensity is great:

> I think every successful analysis induced changes in me. The most striking ones have come about in relation to some more disturbed but analyzable patients. There comes a time when one has to 'go to the wall' with them. I mean a time when one experiences—particularly in terms of primary aggressive encounters—a confrontation in which the analyst overtly or covertly refuses to either back away from an interpersonal conflict or overtly or covertly attack in a nonanalytic way. . . . I believe that such encounters occur with more or less regularity with ordinary patients in often small and not-noticeable increments.

The analyst who discovered his "primitive" feelings became aware that his expectations about himself and about what constituted analyzability needed to be modified based on his experience of successfully analyzing a "primitive" patient. The initial countertransference anxiety was understood and enabled the analyst to proceed to take on the case for analysis. He could do this despite his fears, in part, because the analyst's self-exploration led him to believe his fears were irrational. The first effect that this patient had on this analyst was to make him question and reconsider his assumptions and beliefs in relation to analytic work. Ultimately, his work with this patient led to his changing his beliefs not only about the criteria for analyzability but also about the danger stemming from "primitive" wishes. This change in the analyst represents a cognitive shift; the analyst changed some of his beliefs about both his work and himself.

The second shift began with the analyst's reconsidering the inadvisability of analyzing someone with a "primitive" psychological organization, but the discovery of the analyst's own "primitive" wishes occurred in a more gradual way. When the analyst realized that he felt that this patient had been "dumped" on him, he also realized soon after that he had wished to be taken care of, that is, given a high-functioning patient, not a "primitive" patient. Self-inquiry resulted in his seeing that he feared the patient's "primitive" demands, but once he recognized that he feared the "primitive" wishes that became stimulated in himself in response, he also saw that the experience and expression of "primitive" wishes were not synonymous with having them enacted. Over the years, then, this analyst used this change in his own beliefs to allow himself to take more "primitive" patients into analysis with "very good results." In the analyst's words: "Each case has enabled me to confront more primitive aspects of my own psyche." The result of this work, he believed, was more comfort with himself.

As indicated earlier, the analyst with the "sadistic" countertransference reevaluated some attitudes about how he conducted analytic work once he understood his need to defend against being in a passive-dependent position. Having understood the dynamic reasons he had valued being the "active interpreter" of the process, he became open to the patient's having an impact on him as well as his having an impact on the patient and saw the curative power of the work residing in their transference–countertransference interactions.

Although it is not possible to know how deep or far-reaching the transformations are when analysts report shifts in their attitudes, values, or beliefs, these phenomena have a conscious representation; at a conscious level we can accept that the analyst has changed. Whether or not earlier attitudes, values, or beliefs continue to persist unconsciously and influence the analyst's reactions and behaviors in ways he or she is unaware of is not something we can assess in this material.

I am not suggesting that when the patient and analyst share an area of difficulty, the analytic work will result in the same psychological changes or even the same areas of psychological change for each of them. For all their similarities and overlaps, the differences between them mean that each participant will make use of the work in his or her own particular way. What a particular interaction means for the patient and what he or she learns from it may be very different from what the analyst learns from it, even if there was a similarity in their initial construction of its meaning. In this instance, both patient and analyst experienced being in a helpless state of longing as intolerably painful. We know that the analyst was initially self-critical, seeing himself as taking pleasure in her state; we do not know if this is what the patient believed he was doing. The analyst learned both how this was and wasn't true of him in the course of their analytic work. The patient may have learned the same, but she may also have learned something very different, something more relevant to her particular history and dynamic organization.

In every analytic situation that succeeds, some form of intense emotional engagement occurs at some time in the analysis. How much of it the analyst allows to occur for himself or herself probably depends not only on similarity of conflict areas but likely also on similarity of values. This does not necessarily mean that the patient needs actually to be like the analyst, only that the analyst can find a place of respect and regard for the patient. Most analysts describe that the longer they work with patients, the more these feelings of regard increase as they come to understand better what their patients have struggled with and why they have come to the solutions they have chosen. The more the analyst comes to know and respect the patient, the more the analyst trusts[3] the patient and is able unconsciously to move closer and be more open and vulnerable. I am not suggesting that this occurs in the content of what the analyst says, though at times it may, but I am alluding to something nonverbal that is communicated in subtle ways. This is an area of our work that deserves further consideration.

In trying to elucidate the nature of therapeutic action, it is clear that many factors play a role, though their relative importance remains to be determined. The recent emphasis on the experience of analysts during analysis has begun to document how the analytic process impacts on both participants to the extent to which they are open to this process.

---

[3] As indicated earlier in this chapter, many specific factors about any patient–analyst pair influence the extent of the analyst's trust.

Therapeutic Action of Psychoanalysis
Exploration of Its Impact
on the Analyst

As stated at the beginning of this book, attitudes toward the analyst and the analyst's role have undergone a change in America during the past 15 years. Many analysts have come to regard analytic work as an interactional enterprise (Gill, 1982; Greenberg, 1986; Modell, 1986; Stolorow, Brandchaft, and Atwood, 1987; Stolorow and Lachmann, 1988; Dorpat and Miller, 1992; Mitchell, 1993; Stolorow and Atwood, 1992; Skolnikoff, 1993; Goldberg, 1994; Hoffman, 1994) influenced by, and impacting on, both participants. While this view has become a mainstream belief in America only in the last decade, the idea that the practice of analysis has a therapeutic effect on the analyst is not new. In response to Glover's 1940 survey investigating analysts' views on psychoanalytic practice, a majority of analysts considered the dominant effect of analysis on the analyst to be therapeutic. It was recognized that in the analytic situation was continuous stimulation of conflict for the analyst; therefore, most analysts assumed that there would be temporary exacerbation of conflict that would require self-analytic work. Glover termed this effect "countertransference therapy," which occurred for different reasons for different individuals (p. 79).

While the analyst continued to be perceived as centrally influencing, and being influenced by, the analytic process in the British object relations schools (Bion, 1962; Baranger and Baranger, 1966; Balint, 1968;

Winnicott, 1969; Guntrip, 1975; Little, 1981) and in the interpersonal schools of psychoanalysis (Sullivan, 1940; Fromm-Reichmann, 1950; Levenson, 1983), during the next 30 years in America, the perspective of the analyst as participant in, much less potential beneficiary of, the analytic process faded from prominence and was replaced by a model that viewed analysts as "blank screens" and relatively interchangeable (Arlow and Brenner, 1964). Cultural forces, referred to earlier in the section on self-revelation, such as the increasing distrust of authority, and a move toward egalitarian ideals developed in the 1960s. The influence of philosophic ideas (Habermas, 1964; Ricoeur, 1974) about the permeability of boundaries between subject and object and scientific views about the effect of the observer on the observed (Heisenberg, 1934) have likely contributed to the shift in scientific attitudes. An early 20th-century belief about the possibility of studying and understanding an individual independent from the impact of his or her environment has been replaced by an appreciation of codetermination. Psychoanalysis in this country did not remain immune to these changing ideas. The analyst and his character and conflicts—no longer only his skill and training—were soon regarded as central to the process, a codeterminer of the outcome of the psychoanalytic work.

By the 1980s, analysts and their role in the analytic work became a focus of study (McLaughlin, 1981, 1988; Gardner, 1983; Kantrowitz, 1986, 1992, 1993; Kantrowitz et al., 1989, 1990c; Baudry, 1991; Jacobs, 1991). The contemporary perspective on the analyst was quite different from the views of Fliess (1942) and Isakower (1974). Countertransference (Spruiell, 1984; McLaughlin, 1988, 1991; Jacobs, 1991; Schwaber, 1992; Agger, 1993; Skolnikoff, 1993; Weinshel, 1993) and enactments (Boesky, 1982; Chused, 1991; Renik, 1993) increasingly engaged analysts' attention and interest. Hoffman's (1992, 1994a) social constructivist model went still further in emphasizing how analyst and analysand jointly constructed meaning and understanding in the analytic endeavor.

In this section of the book I have used the analysts' interviews to discuss the effect of the analytic experience on analysts in light of their role and maintenance of their function as analysts. To preserve this function, the analyst must apply a consistent self-scrutiny. Conflicts, affect-laden memories, and fantasies and affect provoked by patients require that analysts continue to find some effective means to rework their own history of conflict. I propose that a by-product of this self-scrutiny and reworking of personal material, although not the reason for undertaking the analytic work, is personal change in the analyst. In the previous chapters, I illustrated how the analysts in their descriptions of the impact of their patients on themselves illuminate aspects of the effect of the patient–analyst match that further illuminate the therapeutic impact of analysis on analyst. Now, I briefly review current perspectives on analytic work in relationship to the role of the analyst. In addition, I discuss the relative possibilities and limitations in our considerations of psychological changes occurring for the analysts as an outcome of their work with patients.

Because of the momentum of increased interest in the analyst and the analytic process as an interactional engagement, some analysts worry that patients will get lost as the focus of analytic attention. Most analysts, however, are aware of their own role, retain their primary focus on their patients' inner world, and use their countertransference awareness to monitor themselves in their work. The shift in emphasis, however, has led to increased attentiveness to the analyst's process. Particular life events, such as illness (Abend, 1982, 1986; Dewald, 1982; van Dam, 1987; Clark, 1994) or pregnancy (Fenster, Phillips, and Rapoport, 1986; Beiser, 1984; Friedman, 1993) sometimes stir transference–countertransference reactions in treatment that, in addition to illuminating aspects of the patient's conflicts, stimulate analysts to scrutinize themselves more closely. Through careful self-observation, analysts become aware of previously unrecognized aspects of themselves. As noted, however, relatively few analysts have described the reverberating effects of their patients' influence on them and thence on their work with the patients, McLaughlin (1981, 1988, 1990, 1993, 1995) being a notable exception.

Many analysts report an increased self-awareness growing from their analytic work (Gardner, 1983; Spruiell, 1984; Poland, 1988). Other analysts (Goldberg, 1994) echo the ideas expressed in the Glover (1940) survey that analysts are changed through their work with patients: "We do not leave an analysis the same person as we were when we entered" (p. 28). Some analysts (Smith, 1993) believe that the analyst not only becomes more self-aware but actually is shaped by the nature of the engagement with patients, whether or not this shaping is consciously recognized. These statements, however, remain abstract and insufficiently documented. Analysts, like patients, may idealize their own sense of change. There is a need for data to support such convictions.

Psychological change is difficult to assess. The validity and reliability of the perceptions of these shifts are often open to question. While analysts believe from their clinical practice that psychoanalysis substantially changes the quality of their patients' inner experiences and frequently changes the nature of their engagement with others and with their work, very few formal outcome studies substantiate their clinical convictions. Only two studies (Wallerstein, 1986; Kantrowitz, 1987; Kantrowitz et al., 1990a) have had formal preanalytic assessments that were used as a basis of comparison with multiple postanalytic evaluations. Both studies indicate that the stability of psychological changes is dependent on the vicissitudes of life circumstances, for better and for worse, over time.

Apart from formal studies, anecdotal reports of psychological shifts remain the source of knowledge about the impact of psychoanalysis. Patients and analysts can each describe what they believe has changed for the patient. They do not always agree on what they perceive (Kantrowitz et al., 1987a), and even when they do agree, independent external assessment of their perception may find it inaccurate and collusive (Kantrowitz, 1986; Kantrowitz et al., 1987b).

However flawed analysts are in their assessments of the patient's psychological change, it is an assessment based on a comparison of the knowledge of the patient at two distinct times—pre- and postanalysis. When considering psychological changes in the analyst, there is no comparability in this respect; there is no clear starting or ending point. The analyst is likely to be engaged in several, if not many, analytic treatments of patients at the same time. The analyst may believe that one analysis more than another has had a profound impact, but it may also be that other analyses have offered the analyst an opportunity for reworking the issues stirred from the other treatment. Some analysts report that psychological shifts are often not clearly detectable at any one particular time but accrue gradually in slow, nonquantifiable increments in the manner of working through conflicts.

In addition to there being no one definitive time to use as a marker for "pre" and "post" comparisons, no one individual has a baseline knowledge of the analyst that is comparable to the analyst's knowledge of the patient. With regard to the patient, there are two views about psychological change—the patient's and the analyst's; with regard to the analyst, there is only one view—his or her own. Family members, colleagues, or friends may, in fact, note a change in the analyst, but they are unlikely to know what to attribute it to or when to date its emergence. Factors outside analytic treatment may contribute to psychological changes, but the effect of nonanalytic factors, of course, applies to psychological changes in the patient as much as in the analyst.

A subjective sense of change is meaningful even when it lacks clear external validation. It is unlikely that most analysts would engage in analytic work if they did not believe this to be true. If psychological changes could be demonstrated, and the analysand felt unchanged and unmoved by the analytic experience, most analysts would question the meaningfulness of the objectively assessed change. Similarly, since in the previous chapters the only source of data is the analyst's self-report, readers may question the reliability or validity of these analysts' self-evaluations of change. What cannot be doubted, however, is that these analysts *believe* they have been affected by their work with the patient whom they describe for this study. Their self-reports provide descriptions of transformations that, even if only subjectively verifiable, constitute genuine change in their sense of themselves. For this reason, I have discussed their accounts of their work with patients in terms of the effect of the treatment process on them, and I accepted their reports of psychological changes as valid, if not validatable.

Changes in the analyst due to his or her participation in the analytic process would seem expectable once analysis is viewed as an interactional process. Investigation of the nature and extent of the influence of the process on analysts may serve to illuminate further the contribution of various factors as therapeutic agents. It may also extend our understanding of how psychological development builds on analytic work and continues after formal analysis ends. The examples in the previous chapters provide data to explore the role of various components of therapeutic action and to support the belief that analytic work influences the analyst's personal development.

In order to consider how this influence occurs, it is necessary to review current beliefs about what constitutes the therapeutic effect of psychoanalysis. Examination of elements assumed to be the agents of therapeutic action, as I have tried to demonstrate, also involves delineating which of these factors may affect the analyst as well as the patient and the difference in their impact on the two participants. Consideration of these factors and how they affect the analyst is now reviewed in light of the clinical examples.

Psychoanalysts have continually debated the relative importance of factors contributing to the therapeutic effect of psychoanalysis. They have tended to polarize in a controversy between an emphasis on the cognitive-affective value of making the unconscious conscious—a focus on content (Freud, 1915; Strachey, 1934; Glover, 1937; Bibring, 1937, 1960; Eissler, 1953; Loewenstein, 1956; Blum, 1979; Goldberg, 1979; Blatt and Behrends, 1987; Meissner, 1989; Gray, 1990; Kris, 1990a, b; Kernberg, 1992)—and an emphasis on the primary importance of affective-attachment's creating support and promoting growth through a benevolent presence—a focus on the relationship (Freud, 1916–17, 1937; Sterba, 1936; Spitz, 1956; Reich, 1960; Loewald, 1960, 1979; Stone, 1961; Gitelson, 1962; Kohut, 1965, 1977; Modell, 1976, 1993;

McLaughlin, 1981, 1990; Basch, 1983; Blatt and Behrends, 1987; Schwaber, 1990; Pine, 1993). Outcome studies of psychoanalysis (Wallerstein, 1986; Kantrowitz et al., 1990a) have documented that supportive factors play a greater role in therapeutic benefit than previously had been thought. Pine (1993) specifies the aspects of the analyst's participation in the psychoanalytic process that universally have the effect of support. These mutative factors in the analytic relationship stem from the analyst's reliable presence, neutrality, abstinence, relative anonymity, and focus on the patient. Kris (1993) defines the analyst's activity as support when it counters the patient's self-criticism.

The particular conflicts or areas of distress for which patients seek help have great variety and have stimulated psychoanalysts to develop many specific theories of cure, including the power of making the unconscious conscious (Freud, 1915), the influence of the affective bond with the analyst (Freud, 1916–17, 1937), the gradual working through of conflict (Freud, 1916–17; Fenichel, 1937, 1941; Greenson, 1965b), the provision of a new object as a model for identification and a facilitator of organization (Loewald, 1960), the provision of a selfobject to enable self-soothing and a sense of continuity of the self over time (Kohut, 1984), the acquiring of missing psychological skills, such as tension regulations, setting personal priorities, and accepting realistic limitations (Gedo, 1979, 1988), the ability to arrive at one's own interpretations (Gardner, 1983), the integration of affect and validation of perception provided by the analyst's subjective responses as a source of information (Stolorow and Lachman, 1978; Stolorow, Brandchaft, and Atwood, 1984; Stolorow and Atwood, 1992), the beneficial effect of regression to reopen hope (Winnicott, 1954, 1965), the power of assimilation of experience through play (Waelder, 1932), the integration of hate and love through the unraveling of interlocking systems exposed in the transference (Joseph, 1989), the corrective emotional experience from a focus on the "here and now" experience in the transference (Gill, 1982), and the self-understanding that emerges from an appreciation of the cocreation of meaning (Hoffman, 1991, 1992, 1994).

Regardless of the particular theoretical orientation or content chosen as the focus for the analytic work, all analysts agree that experiences of painful disappointments and frustrations need to be revived and repeated over and over again in the context of the analytic relationship. Most analysts believe that reopening painful past experiences requires a regression. Under optimal circumstances, each time there is an increased understanding of the historical antecedents, the present-day behavioral and experiential ramifications of these earlier determinants can be more deeply appreciated. The differences between the past and present situation can then be more readily grasped.

The steps in achieving the therapeutic impact are most often described as first requiring an analysis of resistance and a making of the unconscious conscious through interpretation, along with the establishment of the affective bond between patient and analyst. Next there is the repeated experience of powerful past relationships in the transference. Gradually, through understanding, explanation, and ever-increasing tolerance for the affect stimulated, a new sense of self and possibilities evolves.

The analytic work has emotional power for both participants, but they enter this situation with different experiences, expectations, and intensity of involvement. For the patient, ideally this entire process of discovery, affective engagement, and working through occurs during the course of analysis. For the analyst, the situation is different. The analyst has been analyzed previously and should already be familiar with his or her character, conflicts, and defensive and coping strategies. While it is, of course, possible that new conflicts, defensive maneuvers, or characterological tendencies will be discovered, it is more likely that previously known aspects of the self, partially resolved, will be revived. The analyst's involvement, while at times intense, is rarely of the same magnitude as the patient's. If a regression occurs for the analyst, it is rarely as deep, extensive, or difficult to rebound from.

Explanation, clarification, understanding, and interpretation are not comparable experiences for patient and analyst. Apart from the patient's observations about the analyst and interpretations of the analyst's countertransference, the analyst will not receive interpretations. Although some analysts find patients' observations very informative, most do not believe this is the source of deeper learning about themselves. As the patient's transference emerges, and focus is placed on the analyst, the analyst has the opportunity to consider what aspects of himself or herself have contributed to the patient's current experience in more subtle ways. Many analysts believe that in these subtler and more nuanced interchanges, they come to recognize more about themselves. Analysts, of course, maintain a focus on the patient's experience. Even when the analyst's contribution becomes the center of attention, most analysts still analyze this in respect to the meaning it has for the patient. This remains true even when the analyst privately considers the accuracy of the patient's observation or transference representation.

Nonetheless, if conflicts or other painful affective experiences are revived for the analyst in the transference–countertransference experience, I maintain that the situation does allow for the possibility of the same kind of reexperiencing and reworking of issues for the analyst as it does for the patient. The frequency, depth, and degree of intensity in these occurrences vary among analysts; for those analysts for whom revival of conflicts or other distress occurs, its quality and intensity depend on the nature and extent of overlapping issues with the particular patient.

The sense of safety is, of course, much higher for the analyst, since the patient's material, not the analyst's, is the focus. The analyst is also less vulnerable because he or she is not expected to reveal thoughts, affects, fantasies, and reactions to the patient. While these added factors of safety make the regression less likely, the greater sense of safety may also permit the analyst more freely to explore all these responses privately.

Potentially, however, the process of working through is available to the analyst. Since the experience is less powerful, both because the meaning and affective intensity of the analytic relationship are less for the analyst than for the patient and because the analyst's issues are less a central focus of the dyad's attention, the sense of greater safety and previously acquired self-knowledge create the conditions for the analyst to work through issues as part of the analytic engagement. Just as Winnicott (1965) describes the patient as selecting, according to his or her particular need, only certain among the many interpretations offered by the analyst, so the analyst selects, consciously or unconsciously, those aspects of the patient's experience that have an emotional resonance with his or her own as a stimulus for further personal work.

The recognition of similarity may often be the first step for deeper self-exploration. Sometimes the work that follows is conscious and systematic. On other occasions, something spontaneous occurs to lead the analyst to new discoveries without the analyst's actively working on, or thinking about, what has been awakened. Often analysts help their patients with issues that they themselves have not mastered. Working with their patients on these shared struggles, they come to see and understand things about themselves of which they previously had only a glimmer. This glimmer comes into clearer focus and gains dimension and texture as the patient is able increasingly to articulate, explore, and expand his or her self-knowledge.

Sometimes similarities of situation may dramatically evoke previously repressed memories or affects. More often a vicarious reliving of similar experiences, an empathic attunement with various affective states, or appreciation of a shared mode of defense permits the analyst to rework aspects of himself or herself in displacement. As a participant in the patient's struggle with these known or partially known similar issues, the analyst is able to revive them affectively for himself or herself.

Once the analytic process is under way, the reverberating nature of what transpires between patient and analyst often makes it difficult to tell where the process began. Working at this edge of the analyst's own self-knowing, the analyst sometimes consciously, sometimes not consciously, may exert an extra energy to encourage the patient to explore more deeply and fully in this overlapping area of mutual investment. The patient's ideas, thoughts, affects, and reactions stimulate the analyst's. The patient's increased self-knowing and courage to explore may facilitate something similar in the analyst. Comparing and contrasting the patient's experiences and responses with his or her own, the analyst learns more about himself or herself. Sometimes patients have found more creative and adaptive solutions and sometimes they have found more restrictive and less successful solutions than the analysts have found. In either case, the analyst gains a greater appreciation of relative strengths and limitations, and the range of possibility increases a complexity of understanding about the dilemmas faced.

The patient's feelings as he or she grapples with similar concerns also enable the analyst vicariously to contain and tolerate affect stirred around an area of distress. Since the current situation is usually more central to the patient's immediate concerns than to the analyst's, the affect mobilized for the patient will be a great deal more intense. The analyst has less affect to contain and modulate. He or she can achieve greater mastery because he or she has less to deal with than when more powerful affect related to his or her own struggles is mobilized. Along with having less intense affect to manage, the analyst has the benefit of a vicarious experience of the patient's increasing capacity for managing affective distress. Both these factors aid the analyst in achieving a greater tolerance for, and mastery around, the similar, previously painful experiences.

As the patient and analyst explore the patient's development and the evolving nature of coping mechanisms through identifications and counteridentifications, they come to be much better understood as they play themselves out in the transference. While this work with the patient is going on, the analyst has the opportunity to clarify and reassess how he or she has evolved and adapted in comparison with the patient. Something similar takes place for all parents as they watch their children develop. It is another powerful opportunity to reunderstand one's own development, to rethink how one has understood one's parents and their role in relation to oneself (Benedeck, 1959). While the analyst, however, is a participant observer with the patient, the parent is much more deeply and less objectively involved with his or her child. The emotional intensity of the parent–child relationship provides one of the greatest opportunities for personal insight and growth for the parent. Yet, paradoxically, because of that intensity, it may be difficult for many parents to extricate themselves affectively so as to have the perspective necessary to learn.

The analytic situation, if it is going as one hopes, is hardly affectively cold for the analyst, yet compared with the intensity of the parental role, it is much more objective. This increase in objectivity may allow the analyst to clarify and better understand not only the nature of his or her own past struggles as seen through the patient's struggles but the relative effectiveness or ineffectiveness of some solutions the patient arrived at compared with the analyst's own solutions.

The process of working through is gradual for the analyst just as it is for the patient. A slow, steady repetition of previous pain in the context of an emotionally intense relationship, over time, leads to the diminution of the pain and increased tolerance for it when it occurs for both participants. In addition, when the patient perceives the analyst as the inflictor of this pain, and the analyst's conscious identification is with the patient, the analyst has an opportunity to revisit this experience from a different perspective. Sometimes this creates a new empathy for those persons in the analyst's life whom he or she had experienced as disappointing or frustrating. On other occasions, it may help the analyst more fully to understand or empathize with his or her earlier situation when he or she had previously tended to be more self-critical.

Studying the effect of patient–analyst match (Kantrowitz, 1986; Kantrowitz et al., 1989, 1990c) provides a means to further our understanding of the therapeutic impact of analysis and the factors that impede or facilitate and enhance psychological growth. This framework also serves to illuminate the impact of the patient on the analyst. Overlapping characteristics or conflicts and similarity of values, attitudes, or beliefs can, and often do, result in "blind spots" preventing certain areas from receiving analytic inquiry. Differences between patient and analyst along these same dimensions may pose another kind of interference. Too little resonance can result in an experience of affect distance and potential failure of understanding and communication. Conversely, when these similarities and differences become the center of analytic attention, both participants may learn a great deal. For the analyst, the recognition of areas of overlap or tension offers the opportunity to reconsider and potentially rework previously neglected or partially resolved aspects of the self (Kantrowitz, 1992, 1993, 1995).

What evolves in any analysis, then, although it is, to some extent, determined by the character and conflicts of the two participants, is not predetermined but context-dependent. The interaction of the specific character and conflicts of the two participants brings out different aspects in each other. Since the patient brings the material that is the focus of the work, it is likely that analytic work with most skilled analysts who do not have a "blind spot" in the patient's central area of conflict will address the most troublesome areas. The depth, range, and development in other areas, however, would vary depending on the particular patient–analyst pair. For the analyst, however, the areas of personal conflict or distress that are revived and explored are more dependent on the overlap with the particular patient; therefore, some analyses more than others contribute to the development of further self-understanding and growth.

With situations of similarity when the analyst feels generally in harmony with the patient, the patient's work on the issues seems to synergize with the analyst's. The patient's explorations consciously or unconsciously stimulate and facilitate the analyst's parallel reworking of similar issues. Active self-analysis or other methods of exploration may or may not accompany these reworkings for the analyst. On these occasions, the analyst may be thought to have the patient as a tacit partner in this work.

With enactments or countertransference reactions, the initial experience of the situation is usually quite different. While sometimes enactments may come as a result of a conscious identification, more often the patient at this point is experienced as "the other," providing the stimulus for the recognition of some unwanted aspect of the analyst. Under these circumstances, the first jolt of recognition of being caught in an emotional reaction causes distress. The analyst sees that he or she is not in conscious control of his or her affective reaction to the patient and that the reaction has had behavioral or distressing experiential consequences.

Since analysts enter this work to help their patients, their work ego ideal, at the very least, is temporarily disrupted. Active efforts to understand why this situation has occurred are usually sought. The analyst needs to find out what has been stirred in order to resume his or her position as analyst; in addition, as discussed in earlier chapters, the analyst has an opportunity to learn more about some either unrecognized, previously known and presumably repressed, or temporarily inaccessible aspect of the self. The analyst cannot usually resolve this just within the analytic hours. As elaborated previously, self-reflective efforts, along with talking to colleagues and sometimes friends or spouse about the personal, emotional distress stemming from the situation with the patient, are employed by the analyst to regain perspective in the analytic work. They are also undertaken to relieve personal discomfort.

Although the initial experience for the analyst is very different depending on whether or not enactments or countertransferences arise, or if there is an empathic resonance, the actual process of work is not so different once the analyst becomes aware of what has been rekindled. When the patient represents some emotionally important figure for the analyst in his or her countertransference, the reworking of earlier experiences is most parallel to the patient's reworking. The patient, however, unlike the analyst, has no reason to be empathically attuned or responsive to the personal meanings stirred in the analyst in reaction to him or her. The determinants for the patient's character and conflicts or motivations for current behavior are undoubtedly at least somewhat, if not very, different from those of the figure whom the analyst once experienced as he or she now experiences this patient. Nonetheless, the situation offers the analyst an opportunity to reconsider assumptions about previously or currently emotionally important people and the nature of their relationship. Finding the differences between the patient and this affectively important person whom the patient now represents and working on understanding and engaging with the patient in the present enable the analyst to gain a new perspective on the past.

Reintegrations and new self- and other-representations may occur unconsciously or preconsciously or be explicit and detailed in self-reflective work. Reconstructions may emerge accompanied by reflections shared with the person(s) in whom the analyst confides. In other words, the facts, details, constructions, and reconstructions about the analyst's actual life are actively explored outside the analytic setting. For the patient, of course, these "facts," details, constructions, and reconstructions are all actively explored in the analytic work. As stated previously, working through affects and experiences once they are revived is a slow process that requires considerable time and is similar for both patient and analyst.

The conquering of fear of disappointment and frustration requires the development of trust, which also takes time, and repeated exposure over time. The patient enters the analytic situation with the hope and expectation that the analyst could be a needed, reliable figure; the analyst has no such conscious expectation for the patient to be this, apart from coming to the sessions and paying the bills. Yet if the analysis goes well, a rapport develops between patient and analyst in which the analyst can, and does, increasingly count on the patient with his or her ever-increasing capacities to be reliable and trustworthy. Usually, the analyst does not *need* the patient to be that way, but the fact that the patient is, or becomes, this kind of person as a consequence of the work they have done in analysis has an impact on the analyst. The analytic situation potentially is one of great intimacy, though the affective bond varies in its intensity for each patient–analyst pair. The impact of the patient on the analyst derives its power from the affective involvement; the degree of the patient's impact on the analyst varies depending on the intensity of engagement, which is determined by the nature of the overlapping of their character, conflicts, values, and beliefs.

Particular aspects of character, coping strategies, attitudes, or values may be admired by either participant in the other. Part of the lasting power of analytic achievements has been assumed to derive from the patient's identification with the analyst's analytic function. As the more personal nature of the patient–analyst engagement is recognized and acknowledged, it becomes reasonable to consider that the analyst may identify with more personal qualities of the patient as well. Patients enter analysis because of some area(s) of personal dysfunction, but this by no means suggests that they do not have many areas of personal strength. Their analysts do not necessarily have the same strengths or the same degree of development in these other areas. The power of the affective tie between patient and analyst makes the patient, as well, a potential model for identification for the analyst.

The focus of this chapter has been on the therapeutic effect of the analytic process on the analyst. I have described various ways the analyst may benefit from participating in the work. But along with the possible benefit are potential risks. Just as patients are sometimes harmed, rather than helped, by their treatment, so may analysts be damaged, rather than enhanced, from their analytic work. In the next chapter, I discuss the negative changes that may occur for the analyst as a consequence of his or her work with patients.

CHAPTER 11

The Darker Side
The Potential Negative Impact
of Patients on Their Analysts

Change is bidirectional, and there is no reason that this should not be true of the psychoanalytic situation. The analysts in this survey have almost exclusively reported positive psychological changes in themselves that they believe resulted from their work with patients. The fact that analysts choose to report positive and not negative outcomes is not surprising. A contributing factor may be that the way the questions were posed did not invite responses about negative changes. To obtain descriptions of unfavorable outcomes would have required that I inquired in fairly specific ways about patients' potential negative impact on their analysts. Future projects might do this; however, I suspect the return will be low. Analysts, like all people, are likely to be eager to relate occurrences that they are proud of, since they enhance self-esteem; they are less likely to volunteer to relate experiences that they regret, that they wished had had a different, more favorable outcome.

Analysts overcome this sense of personal discomfort when they report negative outcomes of treatments; they presumably do so for the benefit that potentially exists for the scientific community of psychoanalysts. Others can learn from mistakes that they have made. But when the analyst believes that he or she has been changed for the worse by the patient as a consequence of their work, the pain, the disappointment, and, probably most intensely, the shame are likely to make him or her reluctant, if not out-and-out resistant, to communicate this experience.

Several analysts who responded to the survey wondered if any responses indicated that therapeutic work with patients led to disturbing experiences or damaging enactments. The answer is that they did not. Probably, for the reasons just cited, if analysts had such experiences, they would not have responded to this survey at all. The closest thing to a negative outcome was provided by one analyst who described analytic work in terms of the painful feelings that it kept alive for him:

> I am not convinced this work is "therapeutic" for me. I often feel it activates conflicts that otherwise might cause me a lot less trouble. I believe a good deal of analytic work entails efforts to restore a lost object and is ultimately doomed to disappointment, although a great deal can be learned along the way.

This analyst's response directs our attention to two different, but equally painful, consequences that can occur as a result of undertaking analytic work. One consequence is the "trouble" it may cause for the analyst; the other consequence is the pain, sometimes leading to despair, in repeated disappointments when facing inevitable limitations. By "trouble" this analyst meant pain, but for some analysts the trouble may be greater due to "damaging enactments." I address this more external life consequence first and then return to the more subjective sense of pain raised by this analyst.

NEGATIVE CHANGES

Although no analysts responding to this survey offered illustrations of a negative impact of therapeutic work with a patient, many analysts, if asked, could think of examples that they personally knew where this occurred. While reports of such accounts suffer from incomplete data, some general categories providing an overview of these experiences seem important when considering the effect patients may have on their analysts. In the broadest form the negative changes described by analysts about colleagues can be classified as accounts of weakening of superego constraints. One type of loss of personal and professional restraint occurs when sexualized transference–countertransference reactions cannot be contained, integrated, mastered, or used for analytic purposes, and the analyst and patient become sexually involved with each other. An unfortunate vulnerability on the part of the analyst has been stirred. The analysis crumbles. Most often the results are devastating.

The present-day view of enactments, of which Sandler's (1976) view of the analyst's role-responsiveness was a forerunner, takes into account the participation of both patient and analyst in their transference and countertransference responses to each other (McLaughlin, 1991; Chused, 1991; Roughton, 1993). The assumption is that conflict within both patient and analyst has been stirred when enactments have occurred. It is clear from what I have written throughout this book that I do not share the view that enactments inevitably lead to untoward consequences; however, sometimes they do. My thesis is that the outcome, except in cases of extreme psychopathology in either the patient or analyst, is influenced by the match between them, in this instance, their intersecting vulnerabilities.

I do not mean to suggest that patient and analyst bear equal responsibility for boundary violations. It is always the analyst's responsibility to maintain an ethical standard when treating patients. Analysts are expected to have internalized ethics of care that help them keep their footing even when subjected to great personal stress. Analysts are expected to see and heed danger signals and seek help in doing so when unable to do so by themselves. The analysts responding to this survey have illustrated many of the methods that they employ to regain perspective when heated affects or impulses are aroused. Unfortunately, as Gabbard and Lester (1996) describe, not all therapists are able to make use of these or other methods for protecting their patients from boundary transgressions.

Gabbard (1994a) shares my perspective that the "goodness of fit" between the residual conflicts and self- and object representations within the analyst and what the patient projects onto the analyst is likely to determine whether or not an analyst responds to a patient's "coercion" (p. 206). Having evaluated and treated more than seventy cases of therapists who have had sex with their patients, Gabbard cautions analysts not to assume that they are, or will remain, immune to the temptation to exploit patients. He states that it is common for therapists to view their colleagues whose behavior has involved unethical transgressions of boundaries as "impaired, sick, and most of all different" from themselves (Twemlow and Gabbard, 1989, p. 73). Such reductionistic divisions are employed to relieve analysts of anxiety about their own potential for engaging in similar behavior. Careful study of sexual exploitation of patients has led Gabbard to believe all therapists and analysts are potentially vulnerable to these transgressions, as well as other kinds of boundary violations with their patients (Gabbard and Lester, 1996).

According to Gabbard and Lester, analysts' susceptibility to boundary transgression[1] may stem from responding to their patients as an externalized, idealized part of themselves (Ogden, 1986) with which they fall in love; enacting an unconscious attempt to rescue a depressed parent of the opposite sex in their effort to cure their patients (Apfel and Simon, 1985); erecting a manic defense against the experience of mourning and grief evoked in the process of termination that revive earlier conscious or unconscious experiences of painful loss for the analyst (Gabbard, 1994b); attempting to validate the gender identity or sexual orientation of analysts who are insecure about their masculinity or femininity (Gabbard and Lester, 1996); wishing to be transformed by the patient (Bollas, 1987); defending against their own aggression, leading to a masochistic surrender in which the analyst becomes intimidated and controlled by a demanding patient into boundary violations as a means to prevent a suicide (Eyman and Gabbard, 1991); or a narcissism in which the analyst's grandiose belief is that only he or she can heal or save this patient.

Analysts who tend toward action more than reflection are also seen as particularly vulnerable to ethical transgressions. The capacity to engage in fantasy formation seems crucially related to sustaining the "as if" nature of analytic engagement. Failure to make use of fantasy is seen as an ego impairment, whereas many of the other vulnerabilities to enactment are viewed as disturbances in the formation of the superego in which values have not been fully internalized.

While being clear that they are not blaming patients for their analysts' unethical behavior, Gabbard and Lester (1996) note that patients who have a history of incest "often consciously or unconsciously convey to the analyst that nothing short of a repetition of the original incestuous relationship will be helpful" (p. 117), a situation that makes them a particularly high-risk group of patients for exploitation by their analysts. The authors make clear, however, that most patients with whom analysts enact these unethical behaviors were not incest victims. Pope and Vetter (1991) found that only 32% of patients who had sex with their therapists also had a history of sexual abuse in their childhoods.

Other examples of loss of superego restraint relate to money. Wealthy patients are reported to have tempted analysts to make use of their money in ways that do not accord with professional ethics. Sometimes, according to these analysts' anecdotal statements, the

---

[1] Analysts who cross boundaries may also suffer from psychotic, psychopathic, and paraphilic disorders. The formulations the authors propose that I review have excluded analysts suffering from these more severe psychopathological disturbances.

patients have actually taught the analysts ways to conceal their taking these funds. Other less dramatic accounts, but still devastating to the lives of the affected analysts, describe analysts whose envy of their patients' wealth, power, or sexual exploits stimulated them to try to seek similar experiences for themselves, often in ways that seriously disrupted their lives. In still other instances anecdotal stories included descriptions of analysts whose envy of people who "don't have to play by the rules" was heightened by patients who shared these feelings and acted upon them, resulting in these analysts' emulating their patients in these slightly or not so slightly "corrupt" ways. All of these accounts need to be viewed with a critical eye in terms of their actual veracity. In addition, I am uneasy thinking of patients as being in any way responsible for their analysts; influence, however, is not the same as responsibility. Once we accept that there is a bidirectionality of influence, it is necessary to acknowledge that the patient's impact on the analyst can potentially lead to a change in the analyst as well as the other way around, for better or worse outcomes.

FACING THE INEVITABILITY OF LIMITS

Another change that may occur as a result of the analytic work is the analysts' increased awareness of the inevitability of human limitations. The present survey investigates analysts' belief in change, but the change I am now describing is reflected in some analysts' increased pessimism about what can change, about how short-lived any changes are likely to be, and about their despair in the face of acknowledging their limited ability meaningfully to help another person feel or behave in a different way. Some analysts find that confrontations with the limits of their power is chastening. To experience pain, if it leads a person to become clearer about reality and to gain perspective on the past, if it enables a freer sense of choice for the future, is expected and desired from analytic work. For analysts responding to this survey, the pain they felt was offset by the self-esteem they gained from facing their previously unrecognized and unacknowledged omnipotent or omniscient fantasies. The benefits of coming to terms with hubris were described by one analyst:

> During what seemed to be an impasse in termination with a patient who continued to have a painful area of difficulty in life—that had not changed despite our analytic effort and understanding of the root causes—I became intensely preoccupied with needing to help her with this. The patient pointed out

to me that there were some things about her I would never understand or should never understand. This helped me to become aware of a consciously held belief that I could understand anything, but concealed an unconscious belief that I could fix anything and therefore avoid feeling helpless or vulnerable to certain kinds of loss.

The analyst was confronted by her patient with the limits of her ability to understand, a limit that seemingly troubled the analyst more than the patient. Confronted with her difficulty in accepting a limit in her capacity to "know" another, the analyst reflects that she consciously has held a belief that she "could understand anything." She then uses the patient's acceptance that she cannot be fully known by her and cannot be fully "fixed" by her to see that the analyst herself had unconsciously believed her own powers were much greater than she had consciously acknowledged. The analyst quickly grasped that this omnipotent belief served to keep her from feeling helpless and enabled her to deny the possibility of "certain kinds of loss" occurring. She does not state whether or how this recognition changed her, but a new recognition of such limits is likely to have an impact, at least temporarily. Such insights are painful and may quickly be rerepressed or put to one side of conscious thought. The tone of the analyst's account suggests that she views this new awareness as an achievement, but she does not address the pain that likely accompanied it. As the analyst who was quoted earlier stated, facing the inevitability of loss cannot really be evaded in doing analytic work if the analyst is committed to working in depth. As such, analysts cannot sustain a denial that many others can indulge in because denial does not directly impinge on their effectiveness in their work. Since analysts value "knowing," not being self-deceptive is a strongly held value that offers some balancing comfort for what otherwise might seem a searing acceptance and need continually to face "reality." In addition, I speculate that the patient may have served a parental role for the analyst around this issue. It was as if the patient were saying, "You don't need to save me from this difficulty. I can stand it, and you can stand not fixing it." The patient's stance may be relieving to the analyst since it both provides a model of tolerating human limitations and also gives the analyst permission to be relieved of an impossible task.

Facing personal limits and the limits of the human condition, that one in certain respects remains inevitably separate and alone and eventually will die, can free people to live more fully; it may also lead to despair. For some analysts defensive overoptimism or "grandiose" ambition may be replaced by depression and despair. A swing too wide in the opposite direction may have occurred. Again analysts who feel despairing are not likely to have responded to this survey. They may also have abandoned doing analytic work. It is not likely that any one experience of working with a patient would produce such great despair, but there are anecdotal reports of analysts who have had a patient suicide that colleagues believe led them to leave the field. I do not mean to offer an overly simplistic view of why analysts may give up their work, cease to believe in the value of their training, or succumb to a sense of existential despair. A multiplicity of factors is likely at work. I am merely suggesting that one contributing element may arise from the feeling of being ineffective in one's work, which may reach a crisis in relation to some particular patient.

Shortly after completing this project, I had the opportunity to interview an analyst in training who felt her first supervised case had had a profoundly negative effect on her. The patient was a divorced woman who was angry, frightened, and depressed. She was caught in a "messy" custody battle for her child. The patient had taken on the responsibility of caring for her family while she was growing up. The analyst thought that she had not felt appreciated but had never acknowledged any resentment or anger about her childhood experience. In the analysis, the patient expressed her rage in relation to her current troubles. The analyst felt an inability to work effectively with her patient.

> I really felt at a loss. . . . I felt like I never knew what to say that would further the analysis. . . . When her complaining would escalate, I would feel that I had done it wrong. I was always feeling, if only she could feel that I understood, that I wanted to understand, she would let go of some of her sort of ranting. The part of wanting to be helpful and being unable to was the issue that was so difficult for me.
>
> I would feel . . . as if I reenacted some of that in supervision. . . . I tried to talk about that, but that never was helpful. . . . I felt my supervisor to be much more critical than he was; in fact, I know that. Part of it was him. . . . Although I think he liked me, it wasn't in his personality to be supportive. . . .
>
> I was finished with classes when I started the case, so I never presented it. Part of what was so hard was that I was so isolated with this case. . . . I went back to see analyst's name, and I said, "I think something's wrong, but maybe this is . . . just what life is like," and he said, "You're really depressed." I really know that. . . . Most of what made me get depressed was things that I

hadn't really talked about in analysis that I finally looked at in a much more naked way, but I think that my experience with this patient was really part of it.

I had an idea, that I wanted to be an analyst. . . . I thought analysis was very helpful. . . . I thought I knew more or less what I was doing, but it didn't resonate. It was very disturbing, and it was hard to . . . get any help.

I have less faith in analysis than I did. I think I had an idealized notion of analysis before, but I don't think that this was an optimal disillusionment. . . . I still find myself thinking, How could I have done something different?

It brought my self-criticism into my work in a more intense way. It really exacerbated it. I don't think my self-criticism was so intense in my work before working with this patient, and certainly not in my ability to think of myself as an analyst before.

If there had been a case that went wrong in a different way, maybe it wouldn't have affected me quite as much. She had terrible self-criticism but hid it. . . . I suppose maybe that's part of what made it so hard . . . the fact that she dealt with it by externalizing. Her self-criticism was—so different from me. Maybe that was part of what was so uncomfortable about it, that I could easily be attuned to her self-criticism, but her attunement was blocked by something in her way of dealing with self-criticism that was so foreign to me . . . not so foreign to me, but intolerable to me, the kind of blaming she did. . . . We dealt with our masochism in such different ways. That was part of what was so painful about the experience of being with her. If I would feel annoyed with her, then I would turn even more on myself. It was much harder, maybe, because she was simultaneously like me and very different.

The fact that the questions about analysis and the limits of it are associated with such painful affect . . . makes it hard. I loved my analyst and being in analysis. It was terribly disappointing not to be able to provide some of that to someone else. I don't think I mean that I wanted to be like my analyst—though in ways I did, just as I had the fantasy he would know what to do. I felt something more profoundly disturbing. I don't think I mean I wanted her to love me as I loved him. I think I wanted to be able to offer her an environment in which there was room for love. She felt she'd not been allowed to mother her child the way she thought she should. I think I felt in a similar position—I wanted to be able to take care of her in some ways. Somehow the experience of not being able to contact her felt as if it invalidated the love I had for my analyst. I knew I had loved him, but I could no longer find it in myself. . . . I think it's a terrible thing to be frustrated in the wish to love, and I think that was my experience with my patient. I wanted to be the bearer of hope, but it seemed the only way she felt understood was for me to agree that the situation was hopeless . . . that she would never find satisfaction.

This young analyst and her first analytic patient seem to have shared a problem of self-criticism, but as the analyst notes, they employed it differently. The analyst was determined to master and overcome her difficulties, while the patient clung to a sense of hopelessness and despair. Ultimately, the analyst feels she was more affected by the patient's stance than the patient was by hers. Many factors seem to have contributed to this unfortunate outcome, some possibly preventable, others not. Nonetheless, the analyst places a primary emphasis on her interaction with this patient for dampening a sense of optimism, hope for the future, and belief in her capacities. This analyst's experience offers a window into the kind of negative outcome that can result when treating patients.

Paradoxically, a positive outcome of treatment might also have a negative effect on some analysts. The analysts who responded to this survey primarily experienced their admiration for their patients as supportive of their own personal development; however, analysts could also experience these discrepancies between themselves and their patients as deflating. They may have been able to help their patients around some issues, but they could still feel pained and despairing about achieving or becoming like the patients along other dimensions. Analysts' envy of characteristics or accomplishments that they believe are unattainable has the potential to corrode their self-esteem and sense of well-being if a corrective perspective cannot be attained. Conversely, a negative treatment outcome might then be used to elevate analysts' self-esteem. Rather than focusing on their failure to help the patient, analysts might view the patient's difficulty in making effective use of treatment as reflecting poorly on the patient, not on themselves. Such analysts might employ the discrepancies they perceive between the patients and themselves in a self-congratulatory manner and take taking pride in having even tried to work with such difficult patients.

Just as changes in a positive direction are strongly influenced by the particular match of patient and analyst, so are the negative outcomes influenced by the interactive impact of the characteristics of participants. While the character of the analyst is likely to remain relatively stable despite being buffeted by the intensity of patient difficulties, as Gabbard and Lester (1996) warn, no analysts should assume they are immune. Again, the parallel of negative changes with positive ones needs to be retained: the extent and nature of the negative impact depends on many factors, such as the particular stage of the analyst's life, the nature and extent of supports and satisfactions outside work with patients, other past and current experiences with patients, and the particular match between the analyst and the patient.

Many of my comments in relation to negative change are speculative. The topic of negative change was not investigated in this project. To make any serious assessment of the negative impact of patients on their analysts, a systematic exploration would need to be undertaken. While it would likely meet great resistance, a future project could be designed to try to evaluate the kind of negative changes analysts have experienced as a consequence of their work with patients.

PART IV

Epilogue

Concluding Thoughts

In concluding this presentation of analysts' perceptions of the ways in which their patients have affected them, I want to review and reconsider (1) the nature of self-report data, (2) the meaning of psychological change and the extent to which it can be assessed, (3) the relationship among life circumstances, discussion of personal, affect-laden issues with significant people in the analysts' life, and analytic work as agents of change, and (4) the role of the match between the patient and analyst as a central determinant of the extent of the patients' impact on the analyst.

As I have already acknowledged, self-report data cannot be validated. The material collected reveals only what a group of analysts have chosen to report about what they think about their patients' effect on them. Since an observer bias is always present, they are more likely to claim they have been affected by their work with patients if they view this as a desirable outcome of their work and less likely to claim an impact if they view it as undesirable. Abstract statements are notably unreliable. In part, the unreliability is related to the lack of specificity in the definition. In this study, the lack of precise definition in the term "change" was intentional. As I stated in the first chapter, I wanted to encourage reflections on the widest range of constructions of what constituted change. There was no requirement that analysts agree on a definition of change. It was my hope, however, that they be able to illustrate what they meant by change in relation to themselves. My assumption was that illustrations would be more illuminating than any definitions they might offer about the nature of their changes.

Often analysts reported experiences that they felt as powerful, sometimes transformative, but for many it was hard to find words that described how they felt they had changed. A relatively large number of analysts answered the first item on the questionnaire affirmatively and claimed they had been changed by their work with patients but then offered no material to support this statement. Some of these analysts also checked the specific areas in which they believed changes had occurred. Were these analysts merely stating what they thought would be the desirable thing to say? Perhaps. Social scientists (Schuman and Kalton, 1985) report that even with anonymous data, people's responses are influenced by what they believe are the desired or "right" answers.[1] If many analysts answered affirmatively for this reason and could not later support their statements, it could be assumed that they lacked the actual data. It is also possible that these analysts did not want to elaborate this material, possibly because they felt it too personal even if anonymously reported. Still other analysts may not have provided illustration because they did not want to devote any further time to this project.

A large number of analysts who did offer examples failed to provide data that addressed the idea of discovery or change. Their examples indicated only that the analysts recognized that they were caught in a countertransference reaction. Were these analysts defining change in a wishful way, viewing being stirred by an interaction as an indication of some internal shift? Perhaps. If an analyst did not provide substantiating data, it does not mean that the analyst failed to change, but it does mean that as readers we have no evidential reason to believe that he or she has changed. When analysts profess to have changed and do not document the change, they may be trying to impress others; they may be self-deceptive; or they may lack a sharpness of focus, the evocative language adequate to describe their experiences of internal shifts, or both.

---

[1] The authors do note, however, that the effects of social desirability bias in self-reports may be overestimated. Studies indicate that the majority of respondents assume that their own attitudes are shared by many others. The respondents' tendency to project their own attitude onto a wide population means they assume their own views to be the socially desirable ones. Such assumptions serve to preserve the candor of their responses.

The analysts who provided the illustrative material certainly believed they were offering examples of personal changes. Certain readers may accuse some of these analysts of being self-deceptive. Yet the analysts who volunteered to be interviewed all believed that learning about themselves and changing as a result of work with patients were desirable and so were biased to believe they were the beneficiaries of this process. The reader is likely to believe each analyst to the extent the analyst is able to describe convincingly a process in relation to an outcome.

While I am not asking readers to suspend critical judgment, I do want them to be open to the possibility that there are different learning styles and different modes of "knowing" and of "expressing" what is known. Clear, logical, linear presentations that are detailed and precise and take the reader step by step through an analyst's process are most likely to be experienced as convincing. In contrast, discoveries and changes emerging from enactments, when no specific process of reconstruction from the past material or construction based on later work is proposed, are less likely to be persuasive. People with repressive styles, however, have a harder time holding on to and expressing what they know, but they often know aspects of themselves in feeling without precise words. People with obsessional styles often know facets of themselves that they can describe with precise words, but they are much less clear about their feelings. Both these statements are, of course, oversimplifications of a very complex topic, but I want the reader to be aware of an understandable tendency to overvalue the command of language and possibly confuse it with self-knowledge. The point is that clear, elegant constructions about psychological change no more guarantee that the purported changes have actually occurred than do affect-laden, impressionistic descriptions of such changes. In the absence of any independent, reliable, external source of confirmation, validation remains absent. The questionnaire itself could have contained items that would have allowed a check for internal inconsistencies, but I think this would have revealed only that these analysts' self-perceptions were complex and at times contradictory. Extended interviews potentially might have provided material that made each analyst's view seem more or less credible.

This material offered by these analysts needs to be read on the terms it offered: it represents *analysts' perceptions* of what happened as a result of work with patients. Even if it is self-deceptive, it remains the analyst's *belief*. Narratives are created to make sense of experiences. When analysts present a picture of themselves, they offer a construction that intermingles disparate parts to make a cohesive whole. People may not be telling themselves the "truth" about themselves because "there is often no single truth . . . perceptions depend heavily on subjective definitions and . . . attitudes may be deeply ambivalent. Answers to survey questions are not answers to research questions, but only one starting point in a serious attempt to understand human action" (Schuman, 1995).

The psychological effect of a belief, even a self-deceptive belief, is a topic too large to address here. Follow-up studies have indicated, however that "transference cures"—cures based on an attachment to the analyst without a concomitant accrual of insight and "structural change," cures that might be viewed as "self-deceptive"—have had more stable and enduring therapeutic benefit than had been assumed could occur (Wallerstein, 1986; Kantrowitz et al., 1990c). The limited nature of what self-reports provide needs to be acknowledged, but the benefits that may be learned from these personal accounts also need to be appreciated.

While all the analysts interviewed seem to have full and satisfying lives in both work and personal relationships, none of them view themselves as without residual conflict or believe they have learned all they can about themselves or changed in all the ways that may still be possible for them. A presentation of themselves as open to continued psychological change may also be viewed as offering a picture that corresponds to what they view as a group ideal. It may also represent what they actually believe.

Most of the analysts who offered examples and all of the analysts who were interviewed believed some internal shift had occurred within them as a result of their work. Often they themselves did not know whether or not anyone else would notice these changes, but patients completing analyses, it should be noted, often state something similar.

The psychological changes described by most of these analysts are subtle. A few analysts described symptom relief, such as analyst 9, whose recovery and exploration of a repressed memory resulted in a decrease in her night waking. Most analysts, however, even when they recovered previously repressed memories, affects, or impulses, report lessening of inhibitions and greater comfort with their affects, conflicts, fantasies, and themselves in general rather than specific, concrete changes. They report diminutions of self-criticism and enhancements of self-acceptance and self-esteem. Changes in attitude, sometimes belief, are also recounted. These shifts in cognitive stance were frequently viewed as the vehicles leading to, or possibly creating, psychological changes.

I have indicated many reasons that the reader should be suspicious of these self-reported changes. In the chapter on changes in the analyst and their assessment, I have discussed the ways in which the assessment of changes for patients and changes for analysts differs and is more limited in relation to the analyst. I remind readers of the limitations of our ability to assess change, even with patients.

Outcome studies of psychoanalysis indicate that most patients obtain therapeutic benefit, but only approximately 40% show a change reflecting an integration of analytic understanding derived from work in the transference (Erle, 1979; Erle and Goldberg, 1984; Wallerstein, 1986; Kantrowitz, 1987). The Menninger and Boston outcome studies, both prospective and longitudinal projects, provided the most rigorous measures to ascertain change to date. Pre- and postanalysis evaluations allowed for objective comparisons to be made about the patient's psychological state, conflicts, and defenses at two different points in time, with psychoanalysis as an intervening event. We have learned that "transference cures" are more stable than we had been led to believe and, in addition, that the psychological gains accrued by the end of a psychoanalysis may be less stable than we had previously thought (Wallerstein, 1986; Kantrowitz et al., 1990a).

While it is, of course, desirable that analysts establish reliable, verifiable methods to assess the impact of analysis, most of us would not be willing to say that we do not believe in the changes our patients and we have experienced just because we have not yet established this level of rigor for evaluation. Perhaps we need to reconsider how we think about our criteria for change as we reflect on these analysts' reports.

When an internal shift takes place, the person experiencing it is not usually so focused on whether others will recognize it. Of prime importance is how it is experienced by the person who believes it has occurred. The fact that such criteria lack scientific rigor does not invalidate their importance. What are reliable and measurable may not always be the most meaningful changes.

Based on our current ability to assess psychological change, we cannot assume that even those changes that can be documented are necessarily attributable to analytic work for either the analyst or the patient. To make such a claim, we would need a control group. This is a difficult, probably impossible requirement, since baseline states, psychological complexity, the effect of the "fit" with the particular analyst, and the presence of other life supports all would need to be matched. Factors other than treatment can, and do, facilitate psychological change for patients. Likewise, analysts have many other opportunities for discovering and reworking issues apart from their work with patients. As stated in the introduction, it is likely that most analysts believe they have learned and changed the most from their relationships with their spouse and children and from critical life events, such as births, deaths, and major life transitions, achievements, and disappointments.

Most of the analysts in this survey reported discoveries about themselves in the context of work with patients; however, many of these analysts described working on what was discovered outside the treatment situation. While analysts sometimes felt the need to return for formal treatment, it seems, based on the reports in this survey, that they more often continued their self-inquiry through a combination of private self-reflection, confiding and exploring with trusted friend/colleague(s) or spouse, and working through and reintegrating issues as part of their work with their patients.

To the best of my knowledge, analysts' published descriptions of their self-inquiries have not included information about their sharing their personal discoveries with others. The role other people play in stimulating, supporting, and consolidating self-exploratory work has not been discussed in the psychoanalytic literature. It is understandable that the content of such communications is kept private, but the fact that many analysts engage in these intensely personal exchanges also seems to have been treated as relatively confidential. It is as if analysts assumed they were expected to complete their self-analytic work on their own. Yet Freud (1937) advised analysts to return at least every five years for more analysis, since working with patients would likely stir conflicts. While Freud encouraged analysts to continue their self-analysis, he also cautioned them about its limits. One problem was always the transference. Although few analysts claim to follow Freud's recommendation for such regular reanalysis, anecdotal reports suggest that more analysts return for treatment than the present data might lead the reader to believe. The analysts responding to this survey may feel less inclined to seek further treatment because many of them found their continued psychological growth facilitated by personal communications with colleague/friends.

While few of the analysts referred to the specific emotional importance of the person or persons with whom they shared their self-discoveries, almost all of them made it clear that the recipients were people trusted to be respectful, accepting and nonjudgmental and to view the analyst with positive feelings. These qualities are essential for intimacy; they are necessary in close friendships and in therapeutic engagements alike.

A great deal that these analysts learned about themselves in their self-explorations was painful; they saw aspects of themselves that previously had been disavowed. Telling another person(s) about some aspect of themselves that they had only newly come to recognize and take ownership of puts them at risk for again experiencing shame. These shameful affects had only recently been overcome enough to allow these perceptions to become conscious. This may be why one of the analysts described the telling as "confessing." Communicating intimate, painful, often unflattering qualities about oneself to another person creates a situation of closeness, often of great intimacy, but also of great vulnerability. It may stimulate intense transferential experiences in relation to the person(s) to whom it is told.

All present-day relationships are, to some extent, influenced by previously emotionally important relationships. Psychoanalysis capitalizes on this fact and creates conditions that accentuate this tendency. In nontreatment relationships, people try to see the person with whom they are engaged as clearly and accurately and as uncontaminated by the effects of transference as possible. Yet the personal history of past relationships always has some bearing on how people perceive and react in present relationships.

The tension between the pull from old perceptions and patterns and the push to respond clear-sightedly in more adaptive ways to the present is ever active. Loewald (1960) has described the dual nature of the analyst's role as both a transference figure and a new object. The progressive push is evident in how our memory can be remodeled "in accordance with current and immediate experience" (Treurniet, 1993, p. 210). "The curative power of the transference can be seen as an extension of the curative power of love. From this point of view, the psychotherapeutic setting may be thought of as a means of concentrating those curative forces that are present in ordinary life" (Modell, 1990, p 26).

The analysts in this survey who "confess and confide" in their peers have chosen to use life, though a very particular form of life engagement, rather than a therapeutic setting to pursue self-reflections. They have found the experience of this depth of sharing with peers helpful, both for their patients and for themselves. If they are no longer engaged in their own analytic work—and most of them, at least in this survey, were not—then how can they reach the optimal level of self-awareness and sense of support for their self-scrutiny and not risk being swamped by regressive transference and countertransference intrusions into those relationships?

Most of the analysts in this survey who described sharing their personal material stated that there was a mutuality in their communications: those in whom they confided also confided in them. Mutuality increases intimacy and decreases the likelihood of regression that is not in the service of the ego. In the majority of analysts who described sharing their self-discoveries, the people in whom they confided had been analyzed and were mainly analysts themselves. Understanding the nature of transference and keeping its impact in mind also serve to decrease its potential nonadaptive, regressive effect on the relationships of people who "confess and confide" in each other. All intimate relationships leave the participants more open in their vulnerabilities but also enriched by their engagement. The balance between vulnerability and enrichment for people actively engaged in intrapsychic exploration of others and themselves probably shifts and varies over the course of time and is likely renegotiated in each new, or at times old, relationship.

The particular time of life may also influence the manner in which analysts decide to pursue their self-explorations. Anecdotal reports suggest that in the years immediately following graduation from an institute, analysts are more likely to return for more analysis than when they are more senior. In part, the reluctance of older analysts to seek more treatment may be that there are fewer analysts in the community who remain distant enough from their lives. Older analysts may also have already had more than one or two analyses and feel that they have gained as much as they expect to from this form of relationship, though not necessarily as much as they can from employing an analytic process.

Sociological changes may have helped make younger analysts more ready to be self-revealing, but it is unlikely these changes have eradicated narcissistic vulnerabilities. The content of what is experienced as shameful may shift, but the experience of feeling shame is not apt to disappear. In this survey, although the younger analysts seemed more relaxed and open about their sharing personal material with peers and saw value in this openness, in general the older analysts provided the most detailed, personal material about themselves. These older analysts had come to view such self-disclosures as beneficial for psychoanalysts. It was not uncommon for them to share their skepticism that most of their colleagues would share these views.

As described earlier, a number of the analysts used the interview process in this study similarly to the way they engage with their colleague/friends. They used the observations I offered to deepen their own reflections and form new ideas. Most of these new constructions were about themselves, but sometimes they were about the patients. New learning for most of these analysts seemed to occur in an interpersonal context.

None of the analysts commented on any awareness of a transferential aspect in their self-exploration or in their exploration with their colleagues and friends or with me. It may be that because these relationships are experienced as primarily nonregressive, supportive, and facilitative and as one of the most satisfying forms of collegial friendship, the analysts do not conceptualize them as transference.

Although the analysts themselves do not refer to the transferential aspect of their relationship with the colleagues with whom they engage in self-explorations, transferences are part of all relationships and thus are bound to be part of what transpires between them. The benefit analysts attain from their mutual quest for self-understanding is likely enhanced because both participants have previously become in touch with, and explored, their own unconscious processes. Analysts are impressed at how easily and rapidly former analytic patients can reopen formerly explored areas of unconscious conflict and reenter transference experiences (Pfeffer, 1959, 1961, 1963; Schlessinger and Robbins, 1974, 1975, 1983; Oremland, Blacker, and Norman, 1975). Anecdotal reports by analysts of reanalyses of former analysands support these findings.

In the context of mutual respect, regard, and trust, friend/colleagues who have both familiarity with, and access to, their own unconscious experiences have the potential to explore their psychological processes in depth. The mutuality increases the intimacy between them, which facilitates the deepening of the experiences. Their training, self-awareness, parity, and mutual esteem for each other enable them to maintain the boundaries that make it safe for them to experience and explore their regressive experiences together.

Stein (1981) observed that in treatment, such cooperative, collaborative aspects of the patient–analyst encounter often remain unaddressed and unanalyzed, to the patient's detriment; however, the conditions and aims are different in the mutual explorations of colleagues. It may reduce the likelihood of nonadaptive regressive phenomena to maintain a focus on the content they share rather than the complexities of their reactions to each other. Nonetheless, in times of tensions between them, the extent to which they are able to explore these responses may determine the limits of their sharing.

Most of the analysts described their experience of regressive phenomena primarily in relation to affects, fantasies, impulses, and defenses stirred in relation to their patients. As their material demonstrated, these countertransference responses were the stimulus to this process and often the place where the analysts actively reworked their own issues. They experienced the reawakening of conflicts with their patients and explored, examined, discussed, and interpreted it in their self-reflections and with their colleagues and friends.

Although some of the analysts illustrated a very complex process that evolved over time, many of the examples are organized around a single incident, often an affectively intense moment for the analyst. Some analysts have described these incidents as either the beginning or the culmination of a process of a slow, less dramatic lowering of defenses and gaining of insights. It may be that the analysts whose accounts are dominated by these focal moments have also engaged in these more ordinary and gradual modes of discovery and reworking but understood their task as a survey respondent to be the relating of those pivotal occurrences from which an insight was suddenly grasped.

Illustrations that focus on the single incident convey an oversimplified picture of how the therapeutic effect can occur. Since these examples convey so little of the process of working through newly discovered contents, they may be artifacts of the presentations rather than actually reflecting the analysts' process. It is not uncommon for spontaneous verbal communications of affect-laden material to be more superficial and impressionistic than written communications, in which more time can be taken for more reflection. Should the analysts' processing actually be restricted to moments of epiphanies, considerable skepticism would be in order about the enduring nature of the psychological changes. Even the hard-won shifts that come from working and reworking old painful conflicts or undesired characterological tendencies may be lost at moments of stress. The most recently acquired skill is often the one that disappears most quickly. Newly discovered facets of conflict or character may hold the analyst's attention because of their affective power but are unlikely to lead to any sustained psychological change unless they are slowly integrated over time.

Most apparent in the clinical illustrations is the fact that the analysts have been attuned to some aspect of their patients that resonates with some aspect of themselves. The overlapping characteristics and conflicts repeatedly catch the analysts' attention and focus their self-reflective efforts. These qualities of match between patient and analyst determine which patients the analysts have chosen to present. These patients often pose the greatest challenge for analysts, since the work requires that the analysts be free enough from these personal issues to "see" them in their patients and not confuse what they see with what they know about themselves. I have tried to demonstrate that patient–analyst overlaps potentially are a source of mutual benefit, provided the analyst remains conscious of, and committed to, exploring the area of overlapping difficulties. The situation is Janus-faced with pitfalls and opportunities.

Just as an individual's psychological organization is unique, so is the working unit of each analyst and patient pair unique. Each analysis then provides a different set of possibilities of what analysts may learn about others and themselves. Each analyst will highlight and bring out slightly different aspects of the patients. The material brought to the fore will then stimulate different aspects of different analysts, whether silently in the hour, saved for later exploration, or expressively conveyed to the patient. These verbal and nonverbal responses to the patient, in turn, stimulate further reactions from the patient that are particular to the patient–analyst pair. In other words, the codetermination of what occurs is not replicable. Just as patients can have beneficial analytic experiences with many analysts, though each in a slightly different way with a slightly different outcome, so analysts may learn things about themselves and change with many different kinds of patients. Because the process evolves, with each interaction influencing the interactions that follow, it is not predictable in advance when and to what extent it will be enhancing or impeding. Skill and experience on the part of the analyst are always assets that make it more likely that both the patient and the analyst will benefit from the process. But the effect of the overlap between their respective psychologies does remain an issue; it fuels their relationship, for better or worse, depending on their capacity to make use of it. Analysis is a powerful tool and, when responsibly and effectively employed, offers the potential for lifelong development in analysand and analyst alike.

References

Abend, S. (1982), Serious illness in the analyst:countertransference considerations. *J. Amer. Psychoanal. Assn.*, 30:365–379.

———(1986), Countertransference, empathy, and the analytic ideal:the impact of life stress on the analytic capability. *Psychoanal. Quart.*, 60:563–575.

Agger, E. M. (1993), The analyst's ego. *Psychoanal. Inq.*, 13:403–424.

Apfel, R. J. & Simon, B., (1985), Patient-therapist sexual contact: Psychodynamic perspectives on the causes and results. *Psychother. Psychosom.*, 43:57–62.

Arlow, J. A. & Brenner, C. (1964), *Psychoanalytic Concepts and Structural Theory.* New York: International Universities Press.

Bachrach, H. & Leaff, L. (1978), "Analyzability": A systematic review of the clinical and quantitative literature. *J. Amer. Psychoanal. Assn.*, 26:881–920.

Balint. M. (1968), *The Basic Fault.* London: Tavistock.

Baranger, M. & Baranger, W. (1966), Insight in the psychoanalytic situation. In: *Psychoanalysis in the Americas*, ed. R. E. Litman. New York: International Universities Press.

Basch, M. (1983), Empathic understanding: A review of the concept and some theoretical consideration. *J. Amer. Psychoanal. Assn.*, 31:101–126.

Baudry, F. (1991), The relevance of the analyst's character and attitudes to his work. *J. Amer. Psychoanal. Assn.*, 39:917–938.

Beiser, H. (1984), Example of self-analysis. *J. Amer. Psychoanal. Assn.*, 32:3–12.

Benedek, T. (1959), Parenthood as a developmental phase. *J. Amer. Psychoanal. Assn.*, 7:389–417.

Bibring, E. (1937), Symposium on the theory of therapeutic results in psycho-analysis. *Internat. J. Psycho-Anal.*, 18:170–189.

Bion, W. R. (1962), *Learning from Experience*. London: Heinnemann.

Bird, B. (1972), Notes on transference: Universal phenomenon and hardest part of analysis. *J. Amer. Psychoanal. Assn.*, 20:267–301.

Blechner, M. J. (1992), Working in the contertransference. *Psychoanal. Dial.*, 2:161–179.

Blatt, S. J. & Behrends, R. S. (1987), Internalization, separation-individuation, and the nature of therapeutic action. *Internat. J. Psycho-Anal.*, 68:279–295.

Blum, H. (1979), Curative and creative aspects of insight. *J. Amer. Psychoanal. Assn.*, 27:41–70.

Boesky, D. (1982), Acting out: A reconsideration of the concept. *Internat. J. Psycho-Anal.*, 63:39–55.

Bollas, C. (1987), *The Shadow of the Object*. New York: Columbia University Press.

Calder, K. T. (1980), An analyst's self-analysis. *J. Amer. Psychoanal. Assn.*, 28:5–20.

Clark, R. (1994), The pope's confessor. *J. Amer. Psychoanal. Assn.*, 43:137–150.

Chused, J. F. (1991), The evocative power of enactments. *J. Amer. Psychoanal. Assn.*, 39:615–640.

Cocks, G. (1994), Introduction. In: *The Curve of Life*, ed. G. Cocks. Chicago: University of Chicago Press.

Colarusso, C. & Nemeroff, R. (1981), *Adult Development*. New York: Plenum.

Dewald, P. A. (1982), Serious illness in the analyst: Transference, countertransference and reality response. *J. Amer. Psychoanal. Assn.*, 30:347–363.

Dorpat, T. (1974), Internalization of the patient-analyst relationship in patients with narcissistic disorders. *Internat. J. Psycho-Anal.*, 55:183–188.

———— & Miller, M. (1992), *Clinical Interaction and the Analysis of Meaning*. Hillsdale, NJ: The Analytic Press.

Dupont, J. ed. (1988), *The Clinical Diary of Sándor Ferenczi*. Cambridge, MA: Harvard University Press.

Ehrenberg, D. (1992), *The Intimate Edge*. New York: Norton.

Eifermann, R. R. (1987a), Interactions between textual analysis and related self-analysis. In: *Discourse in Psychoanalysis and Literature*, ed. S. Rimmon-Kenan. London: Methuen, pp. 38–55.

———— (1987b), Germany and the Germans: Acting out fantasies and their discovery in self-analysis. *Internat. Rev. Psycho-Anal.*, 14:245–262.

———— (1993), The discovery of real and fantasized audiences for self-analysis. In: *Self-Analysis*, ed. J. W. Barron. Hillsdale, NJ: The Analytic Press, pp. 171–194.

Eissler, K. R. (1953), The effect of the structure of the ego on psychoanalytic technique. *J. Amer Psychoanal. Assn.*, 1:104–143.

Engle, G. L. (1975), Death of a twin: Mourning and anniversary reactions. *Internat. J. Psycho-Anal.*, 56:23–40.

Erle, J. (1979), An approach to the study of analyzability and analysis: The course of forty consecutive cases selected for supervised analysis. *Psychoanal. Quart.*, 48:198–228.

——— & Goldberg, D. (1984), Observations on assessment of analyzability by experienced analysts. *J. Amer. Psychoanal. Assn.,* 32:715–737.

Eyman, J. R. & Gabbard, G. O. (1991), Will therapist–patient sex prevent suicide? *Psychiat. Annals,* 21:669–674.

Fenichel, O. (1937), On the theory of therapeutic results of psychoanalysis. *Internat. J Psycho-Anal.,* 18:133–138.

——— (1941), *Problems of Psychoanalytic Technique.* New York: Psychoanalytic Quarterly.

Fenster, C., Phillips, S. D. & Rapoport, E. R. (1986), *The Therapist's Pregnancy.* Hillsdale, NJ: The Analytic Press.

Ferenczi, S. (1955), The elasticity of psychoanalytic technique. In: *The Selected Papers, Vol. III.* New York: Basic Books.

Fleiss, R. (1942), The metapsychology of the analyst. *Psychoanal. Quart.,* 11:211–227.

Freud, A. (1922), Beating fantasies and daydreams. In: *The Writings of Anna Freud,* Vol I. New York: International Universities Press.

Freud, S. (1899), Screen memories. *Standard Edition,* 3:301–322. London: Hogarth Press, 1962.

——— (1910), Future prospects of psycho-analytic therapy. *Standard Edition,* 11:139–151. London: Hogarth Press, 1957.

——— (1912), Recommendations to physicians practicing psychoanalysis. *Standard Edition,* 12:109–129. London: Hogarth Press, 1958.

——— (1914), On the history of the psychoanalytic movement. *Standard Edition,* 14:7–66. London: Hogarth Press, 1957.

——— (1915), Observations of transference love., *Standard Edition,* 12:157–171. London: Hogarth Press, 1958.

——— (1916–1917), Introductory lectures on psycho-analysis. *Standard Edition,* 15–16. London: Hogarth Press, 1963.

——— (1935), The subtleties of a faulty action. *Standard Edition,* 22:233–235. London: Hogarth Press, 1964.

——— (1937), Analysis terminable and interminable. *Standard Edition,* 23:209–253. London: Hogarth Press, 1964.

Friedman, M. (1993), When the analyst becomes pregnant—twice. *Psychoanal. Inq.,* 13:226–239.

Fromm-Reichmann, F. (1950), *Principles of Intensive Psychotherapy.* Chicago: University of Chicago Press.

Gabbard, G. O. (1994a), Commentary on papers by Tansey, Hirsch, and Davies. *Psychoanal. Dial.,* 4:203–213.

——— (1994b), On love and lust in erotic transference. *J. Amer. Psychoanal. Assn.,* 42:385–403.

——— (1995), Countertransference: The emerging common ground. *Internat. J. Psycho-Anal.,* 76:475–486.

——— & Lester, E. P. (1996), *Boundaries and Boundary Violations in Psychoanalysis.* New York: Basic Books.

Gardner, R. (1983), *Self-Inquiry.* Hillsdale NJ: The Analytic Press.

Gedo, J. (1979), *Beyond Interpretation*. Hillsdale, NJ: The Analytic Press, 1993.

———(1988), *The Mind in Disorder*. Hillsdale, NJ: The Analytic Press.

———(1991), *The Biology of Clinical Encounters*. Hillsdale, NJ: The Analytic Press.

Gill, M. M. (1982), *The Analysis of Transference, Vol. I*. New York: International Universities Press.

Gitelson, M. (1962), The curative factors in psychoanalysis: The first phase of psychoanalysis. *Internat. J. Psycho-Anal.*, 43:194–205.

Glover, E. (1937), Symposium on the theory of therapeutic results in psycho-analysis. *Internat. J. Psycho-Anal.*, 18:125–132.

———(1940), *The Technique of Psychoanalysis*. Baltimore, MD: Williams & Wilkins.

Goldberg, A. (1979), New meanings and hidden meanings: Toward a developmental line of meanings. *J. Amer. Psychoanal. Assn.*, 27:627–642.

———(1994), Farewell to the objective analyst. *Internat. J. Psycho-Anal.*, 75:21–30.

Gray, P. (1990), The nature of therapeutic action in psychoanalysis. *J. Amer. Psychoanal. Assn.*, 38:1083–1097.

Greenberg, J. (1986), Theoretical models and the analyst's neutrality. *Contemp. Psychoanal.*, 22:87–107.

Greenson, R. R. (1965a), The problem of working through. In: *Drives, Affects, Behaviors*, ed. M. Schur. New York: International Universities Press.

———(1965b), The working alliance and the transference neurosis. *Psychoanal. Quart.*, 34:155–181.

Guntrip, H. (1975), My experience of analysis with Fairbairn and Winnicott. *Internat. Rev. Psycho-Anal.*, 2:145–156.

Habermas, H, (1964), The hermeneutic claim to universality. In: *The Hermeneutic Tradition*, ed. G. Ormiston & A. Schreft. New York: State University of New York Press, 1990.

Heisenberg, W. (1934), *Philosophic Problems of Nuclear Science*. New York: Pantheon Books, 1952.

Herberlein, T. A. & Baumgartner, P. (1978), Factors affecting response rates to mailed questionnaires: A quantitative analysis of the published literature. *Amer. Sociol. Rev.*, 43:447–462.

Hoffman, I. Z. (1983), The patient as interpreter of the analyst's experience. *Contemp. Psychoanal.*, 19:389–422.

———(1991), Discussion: Toward a social constructivist view of the psychoanalytic situation (discussion of papers by L. Arons, A. Modell & J. Greenberg). *Psychoanal. Dial.* 1:74–105.

———(1992), Some practical implications of social constructivist view of the psychoanalytic situation. *Psychoanal. Dial.*, 2:287–304.

———(1994), Dialectical thinking and therapeutic action in the psychoanalytic process. *Psychoanal. Quart.*, 63:187–218.

Isakower, O. (1974), Self-observations, self-experimentation, and creative vision. *The Psychoanalytic Study of the Child.*, 29:451–472. New Haven, CT: Yale University Press.

Jacobs, T. (1973), Posture, gesture, and movement in the analyst: Clues to interpretation and transference. *J. Amer. Psychoanal. Assn.*, 21:77–92.

—— (1991), *The Use of the Self*. Madison, CT: International Universities Press.

Joseph, B. (1989), Psychic change and the psychoanalytic process. In: *Psychic Equilibrium and Psychic Change*. London: Routledge.

Kantrowitz, J. L. (1986), The role of the patient–analyst match in the outcome of psychoanalysis. The *Annual of Psychoanalysis*, 14:273–297. New York: International Universities Press.

—— (1987), Suitability for psychoanalysis. *The Yearbook of Psychoanalysis and Psychotherapy*, 2:273–297.

—— (1992), The analyst's style and its impact on the psychoanalytic process: Overcoming a patient–analyst stalemate. *J. Amer. Psychoanal. Assn.*, 40:169–194.

—— (1993), The uniqueness of the patient–analyst pair: Elucidating the role of the analyst. *Internat. J. Psycho-Anal.*, 74:893–904.

—— (1995), The beneficial aspects of the patient–analyst match: Factors in addition to clinical acumen and therapeutic skill that contribute to psychological change. *Internat. J. Psycho-Anal.*, 76:299–313.

—— Katz, A. L., Greenman, D., Morris, H., Paolitto, F., Sashin, J. & Solomon, L. (1989), The patient–analyst match and the outcome of psychoanalysis: The study of 13 cases. Research in progress. *J. Amer. Psychoanal. Assn.*, 37:893–920.

—— —— Paolitto, F. (1990a), Follow-up of psychoanalysis five-to-ten years after termination: I. Stability of change. *J. Amer. Psychoanal. Assn.* 38:471–496.

—— —— —— (1990b), Follow-up of psychoanalysis five to ten years after termination: II. Development of the self-analytic function. *J. Amer. Psychoanal. Assn.*, 38:637–654.

—— —— —— (1990c), Follow-up of psychoanalysis five-to-ten years after termination: III. The relationship of the transference neurosis to the patient-analyst match *J. Amer. Psychoanal. Assn.*, 38:655–678.

—— —— —— Sashin, J. & Solomon, L. (1987a), Changes in the level and quality of object relations in psychoanalysis: Follow-up of a longitudinal prospective study. *J. Amer. Psychoanal. Assn.*, 35:23–46.

—— —— —— (1987b), The role of reality testing in the outcome of psychoanalysis: Follow-up of 22 cases. *J. Amer. Psychoanal. Assn.*, 35:367–386.

—— Paolitto, F., Sashin, J., Solomon, L. & Katz, A. L. (1986), Affect and availability, tolerance, complexity, and modulation in psychoanalysis: Follow-up of a longitudinal study. *J. Amer. Psychoanal. Assn.*, 34:529–560.

Kernberg, O. F. (1992), *Aggresion in Personality Disorders and Perversions*. New Haven, CT: Yale University Press.

Kohut, H. (1965), Autonomy and integration. *J. Amer Psychoanal. Assn.*, 13:851–856.

—— (1971), *The Analysis of the Self*. New York: International University Press.

—— (1977), *The Restoration of the Self*. New York: International University Press.

———(1984), How Does Analysis Cure? ed. A. Goldberg & P. Stepansky. Chicago: University of Chicago Press.

Kramer, M. K. (1959), On the continuation of the analytic process after psychoanalysis. Internat. J Psycho-Anal., 40:17–25.

Kris, A. O. (1990a), Helping patients by analyzing self-criticism. J. Amer. Psychoanal. Assn., 38:605–636.

———(1990b), Resolution of conflict. Panel: The nature of therapeutic action of psychoanalysis. J. Amer. Psychoanal. Assn., 38:773–788.

———(1993), Support and psychic structure. In: Psychic Structure and Psychic Change, ed. M. Horowitz, O. Kernberg & E. Weinshel. Madison, CT: International Universities Press, pp. 95–115.

Levenson, E. (1983), The Ambiguity of Change. New York: Basic Books.

Little, M. (1981), Transference Neurosis and Transference Psychosis. New York: Aronson.

Loewald, H. (1960), On the therapeutic action of psychoanalysis. Internat. J. Psycho-Anal., 41:16–33.

———(1979), The psychoanalytic process and its therapeutic potential. The Psychoanalytic Study of the Child. 34:155–168. New Haven, CT: Yale University Press.

Loewenstein, R. (1956), Remarks on some variations in psychoanalytic technique. Internat. J. Psycho-Anal., 39:202–210.

McLaughlin, J. T. (1981), Transference, psychic reality and countertransference. Psychoanal. Quart., 50:637–664.

———(1988), The analyst's insights. Psychoanal. Quart., 57:370–389.

———(1991), Clinical and theoretical aspects of enactments. J. Amer Psychoanal. Assn., 39:595–614.

———(1993), Work with patients and the experience of self-analysis.In: Self-Analysis, ed. J. W. Barron. Hillsdale, NJ: The Analytic Press, pp. 63–81.

———(1995), Touching limits in the analytic dyad. Psychoanal. Quart., 64:433–465.

Margulies, A. (1993), Contemplating the mirror of the other: Empathy and self-analysis.In: Self-Analysis, ed. J. W. Barron. Hillsdale, NJ: The Analytic Press, pp. 51–62.

Meissner, W. W. (1989), Therapeutic action of psychoanalysis: Strachey revisited. Psychoanal. Inq., 9:140–159.

Mitchell, S. (1993). Hope and Dread in Psychoanalysis. New York: Basic Books.

Modell, A. (1976). The holding environment and the therapeutic action. J. Amer. Psychoanal. Assn., 24:285–308.

———(1986), Psychoanalysis in a New Context. New York: International Universities Press.

———(1990), Other Times, Other Realities. Cambridge, MA: Harvard University Press.

———(1993), Affects and the agency of the self. Discussion of papers of Trevarthen, Field, and Stern: First relationships—later therapies: Implications of infant research for theory and treatment. Boston Psychoanalytic Society and Institute symposium.

Natterson, J. M. & Friedman, R. J. (1995), *Primer of Clinical Intersubjectivity.* Northvale, NJ: Aronson.

Novey, S. (1968), *The Second Look.* Baltimore, MD: Johns Hopkins University Press.

Ogden, T. H. (1986), *The Matrix of the Mind.* Northvale, NJ: Aronson.

Oremland, J., Blacker, K. & Norman, H. (1975), Incompleteness in "successful" psychoanalysis: A follow-up study. *J. Amer. Psychoanal. Assn.* 23:819–844.

Pfeffer, A. Z. (1959), A procedure for evaluating the results of psychoanalysis. *J. Amer Psychoanal. Assn.*, 7:418–444.

———(1961), Follow-up study of a successful analysis. *J. Amer Psychoanal. Assn.*, 9:698–718.

———(1963), The meaning of the analyst after analysis: A contribution to the theory of therapeutic results. *J. Amer Psychoanal. Assn.*, 11:224–244.

Pine, F. (1993), A contribution to the analysis of the psychoanalytic process. *Psychoanal. Quart.*, 62:185–205.

Poland, W. (1984), On the analyst's neutrality. *J. Amer. Psychoanal. Assn.*, 32:283–299.

———(1988), Insight and the analytic dyad. *Psychoanal. Quart.*, 57:341–369.

———(1993), Self and other in self-analysis. In: *Self-Analysis*, ed. J. W. Barron. Hillsdale, NJ: The Analytic Press, pp. 219–235.

Pope, K. S. & Vetter, V. A. (1991), Prior therapist-patient sexual involvement among patients seen by psychologists. *Psychother.*, 28:429–238.

Quinn, S. (1987), *A Mind of Her Own.* New York: Summit Books.

Racker, H. (1968), *Transference and Countertransference.* New York: International Universities Press.

Reich, A. (1960), Empathy and countertransference. In: *Psychoanalytic Contributions.* New York: Internal Universities Press, 1973, pp. 344–360.

Renik, O. (1993), Analytic interaction: conceptualizing technique in light of the analyst's irreducible subjectivity. *Psychoanal. Quart.*, 62:523–553.

Ricoeur, P. (1974), Metaphor and the main problem of hermeneutics. In: *Hermeneutics and the Human Sciences*, ed. & trans. J. B. Thompson. Cambridge: Cambridge University Press, pp. 165–181.

Roughton, R. E. (1993), Useful aspects of acting out: Repetition, enactment, and actualization. *J. Amer. Psychoanal. Assn.*, 41:443–472.

Sandler, J. (1976), Countertransference and role-responsiveness. *Internat. Rev. Psycho-Anal.*, 3:43–48.

Schafer, R. (1954), *Psychoanalytic Interpretation in Rorschach Testing.* New York: Grune & Stratton.

———(1959), Generative empathy in the treatment situation. *Psychoanal. Quart.*, 28:342–373.

Schlessinger, N. & Robbins, F. (1974), Assessment of follow-up in psychoanalysis. *J. Amer. Psychoanal. Assn.*, 22:542–567.

——— & ———(1975), The psychoanalytic process: Recurrent patterns of conflict and changes in ego function. *J. Amer. Psychoanal. Assn.*, 23:761–782.

——— & ———(1983), *A Developmental View of the Psychoanalytic Process.* New York: International Universities Press.

Schwaber, E. A. (1990), Elucidating patient's particular experienced psychic reality. panel: The nature of therapeutic action of psychoanalysis. *J. Amer. Psychoanal. Assn.*, 38:773–788.

――― (1992), Countertransference: The analyst's retreat from the patient's vantage point. *Internat. J. Psycho-Anal.*, 73:349–362.

Schuman, H. (1995), Sex, lies and social science: Another exchange. *The New York Review of Books*, 62:55–56.

――― & Kalton, G. (1985), Survey methods. In: *Handbook of Social Psychology*, Vol. I, ed. G. Lindzey & E. Aronson. Reading, MA: Addison-Wesley, pp. 635–698.

Silber, A. in press, Analysis, re-analysis, and self-analysis. *J. Amer Psychoanal. Assn.*

Skolnikoff, A. Z. (1993), The analyst's experience in the psychoanalytic situation: A continuum between objective and subjective reality. *Psychoanal. Inq.*, 13:296–309.

Smith, H. F. (1993), Engagements in the analytic work. *Psychoanal. Inq.* 13:425–454.

Sonnenberg, S. M. (1991), The analyst's self-analysis and its impact on clinical work: A comment on the sources and importance of personal insight. *J. Amer. Psychoanal. Assn.*, 39:687–704.

――― (1993), To write or not to write: A note on self-analysis and resistance to self-analysis. *Self-Analysis*, ed. J. W. Barron. Hillsdale, NJ: The Analytic Press, pp. 241–259.

Spruiell, V. (1984), The analyst at work. *Internat. J. Psycho-Anal.*, 65:13–30.

Spitz, R. A. (1956), Transference: The analytic setting and its prototype. *Internat. J. Psycho-Anal.*, 37:380–385.

Stein, M. (1981), The unobjectionable part of the transference. *J. Amer. Psychoanal. Assn.*, 29: 869–892.

――― (1988a), Writing about psychoanalysis: I. Analysts who write, and those who don't. *J. Amer. Psychoanal. Assn.*, 36:105–124.

――― (1988b), Writing about psychoanalysis: II. Analysts who write, patients who read. *J. Amer. Psychoanal. Assn.*, 36:393–408.

Sterba, R. (1937), Symposium on the theory of therapeutic action. *Internat. J. Psycho-Anal.*, 18:160–169.

Stolorow, R. & Atwood, G. O. (1992), *Contexts of Being*. Hillsdale, NJ: The Analytic Press.

――― Brandchaft, B. & Atwood, G. O. (1987), *Psychoanalytic Treatment*. Hillsdale, NJ: The Analytic Press.

――― & Lachmann, F. (1988), *Psychoanalysis of Developmental Arrests*. New York: International Universities Press.

Stone, L. (1961), *The Psychoanalytic Situation*. New York: International Universities Press.

Strachey, J. (1934), The nature of the therapeutic action of psychoanalysis, *Internat. J. Psycho-Anal.*, 15:127–159.

Sullivan, H. S. (1940), *Conceptions of Modern Psychiatry*. Washington, DC: W.A. White Psychiatric Foundation.

Tansey, M. J. (1994), Sexual attraction and phobic dread in the countertransference. *Psychoanal. Dial.*, 4:139–152.

Treurniet, N. (1993), Support of the analytic process and structural change. In: *Psychic Structure and Psychic Change*, ed. M. Horowitz, O. Kernberg & E. Weinshel. Madison, CT: International Universities Press, pp.191–232.

Twemlow, S. W. & Gabbard, G. O. (1989), The lovesick therapist. In: *Sexual Exploitation in Professional Relationships*, ed. G. O. Gabbard. Washington, DC: American Psychiatric Press, pp. 71–87.

van Dam, H. (1987), Countertransference during an analyst's brief illness. *J. Amer. Psychoanal. Assn.*, 35:647–655.

Waelder, R. (1932), The psychoanalytic theory of play. In: *Psychoanalysis*, ed. S. A. Guttman. New York: International Universities Press, pp. 84–100.

Wallerstein, R. (1986), *Forty-Two Lives in Treatment*. New York: Guilford Press.

Weinshel, E. (1993), Psychic structure and psychic change: a case of inconsolability. In: *Psychic Structure and Psychic Change*, ed. M. Horowitz, O. Kernberg & E. Weinshel. Madison, CT: International Universities Press, pp. 29–56.

Weiss, J. & Sampson, H. (1986), *The Psychoanalytic Process*. New York: Guilford.

Winnicott, D. W. (1954), Hate in the counter-transference. *Internat. J. Psycho-Anal.*, 30:69–74.

———(1965), *The Maturational Processes and the Facilitating Environment*. New York: International Universities Press.

———(1969), The use of an object and relating through identification. In: *Playing and Reality*. London: Tavistock, 1971.

Zetzel, E. R. (1958), *The Capacity for Emotional Growth*. London: Hogarth Press.

Appendices

STUDY OF THE ANALYST'S PERSONAL CHANGE AS AN
OUTCOME OF ANALYZING PATIENTS

The purpose of this study is to explore 1) whether and to what extent
analysts believe that their analytic work with patients has led to personal change for themselves; and 2) when analysts do believe that personal changes have come about as a result of their work with patients,
a) what in the patient–analyst interaction triggered this change for the
analyst and b) what method, if any, the analyst employed to continue
his or her personal work.

Demographic information. Check the appropriate item.

Sex: Male_____ Female_____
Age: under 40_____ 40–49_____ 50–59_____ 60–69_____ 70–79_____
          80 or older_____
Institute Position: Member_____ Faculty_____ Training Analyst_____
Number of years since graduation:_____

For each item check the answer that best describes your experience:

1. Do you believe that your analytic or therapeutic work with patients has led to personal changes for you?

_____frequently
_____sometimes
_____rarely
_____not within awareness
_____not part of the process

More than one answer may apply. Please check all relevant items.

2. If you have recognized changes in yourself, do you believe that these personal changes are the result of (1) self-reflective exploration undertaken in relation to your work with patients, (2) the experience of some affect or area that resonates and opens or expands these experiences for you, or (3) the experience of some affect or area where differences open or expand these experiences for you?

_____yes
_____self-reflective exploration
_____shared affect or area of experience
_____different affect or area of experience
_____other (describe)
_____no

Some or all of the answers to this question may apply. Please check the relevant answers and specify which trigger(s) are the most frequent.

3. Do you think the psychological work was triggered by

_____the patient's pointing out something about you
_____the recognition of a shared area of difficulty
_____the recognition of a shared area of affect
_____the impact of attitudes, values, or beliefs different from your own
_____a transference–countertransference recognition
_____a transference–countertransference enactment
_____other (describe)

More than one answer may apply. Please check all the relevant answers and specify which are your most frequent modes of proceeding.

4. If in your work with a patient, an area of difficulty for you has come to your attention, how have you dealt with this?

_____self-reflection at the time it occurs in the hour and in relation to the patient's work, but not continued self-scrutiny afterward
_____discussion with colleague(s)/personal friend(s)/spouse
_____consultation in relation to the patient
_____self-analytic work
_____consultation for yourself
_____psychotherapy
_____return to analysis
  _____to your former analyst
  _____to a different analyst
_____other therapies, describe
_____other, describe

5. If you have undertaken a self-analytic exploration, how have you done this?

_____by imagining talking with your former analyst
_____by analyzing your dreams
_____by writing down thoughts and associations
_____by writing to someone (whether it is sent or not)
_____by talking to a colleague, friend, or spouse
_____other (describe)

6. If you engage in self-analytic exploration in relation to the treatment, how systematic is it and what is the frequency?

_____daily
_____only when aware of a difficulty being stirred which occurs
_____frequently (every few months or more often)
_____occasionally (once or twice a year)
_____rarely (once or twice in the course of one's analytic work)
_____almost never
_____other (describe)_____

More than one answer may apply. If so, check those answers which apply and explain.

7. The results of self-analysis for you have been
  ____new understanding and/or insight
  ____increased self-acceptance
  ____recovery of memories or previously repressed affect around memories
  ____decrease in conflict and/or distress
  ____change in work with the patient with whom difficulty emerged (describe)_____
  ____change in work with the patient in general (describe)_____
  ____change in other relationships
    ____less conflict
    ____more conflict
    ____greater freedom of expression
    ____greater comfort
  ____return for personal treatment
    ____therapy
    ____analysis

8. Are you aware of a particular transference–countertransference context or affective experience that stimulated your self-analysis?

  ____yes
    ____transference–countertransference context
    ____affective experience
  ____no

9. If you are aware of the particular stimulus to self-reflection, was it in an area

  ____explored previously
    ____in analysis
    ____in some postanalysis treatment
    ____discovered in some other context (describe)
  ____newly discovered

Since more than one answer may apply, check all relevant items.

10. Was the self-discovery or change of self-experience from

  ____an area of shared conflict with patient
    ____similar area defended against by similar defenses
    ____similar area defended against by different defenses

_____similar defenses employed for different areas of conflict or
distress
_____an area of identification or counteridentification with the patient
or a central figure in the patient's life leading to
    _____recognition of disavowed aspects of one's self
    _____recognition of previously unacknowledged attitudes, values,
or beliefs
_____an area of shared painful affect that becomes less personally
painful through analyzing the patient's painful experiences
_____a similar life situation for you now or in the past leading to

    _____recovered affect
    _____recovered memory
    _____discovered affect
    _____new understanding
    _____more self-acceptance
    _____new perspective

_____a difference between you and your patient leads to change in
attitude, value or belief
_____an unfamiliar life situation for you leads to change in attitude,
value, belief, or affect
_____other (describe)_____

It would be helpful to me if you could also briefly describe an example
of a specific transference–countertransference or affective experience
that triggered personal change? Briefly describe what changed and the
process you engaged in that facilitated the change.

Or if there is some other related experience of change that I have not
captured, would you please describe it here.

If you are willing to provide more detailed information or examples, I
would appreciate your contacting me. My intention is to collect 20 illustrations for the data. These examples will be used to convey why and
how we continue the work we undertook in our own analyses. These
vignettes will be written in a manner that assures confidentiality and
shown to each of the participants for their permission before any public presentation. You can call me at 617-738-1689 or include your name
and phone number and I will contact you.

Again, my thanks for your participation.
Please return this completed questionnaire to:

Judy L. Kantrowitz, Ph.D.
334 Kent St.
Brookline, MA 02146

APPENDIX B

Appendix B represents response frequencies for each category of questions 1 through 10 of the survey. Missing data on each demographic variable (i.e., Sex, Age, Institute Position, and Number of Years Since Graduation) are listed in each table but are not included in frequency columns as the missing data did not significantly correlate with any of the other variables.

1. Has analytic work with patients led to personal change?

N = 399	No. of subjects	Frequently	Sometimes	Rarely	Not aware	Not part of process
GENDER						
Men	300	116 (39%)	166 (55%)	17 (6%)	13 (4%)	3 (1%)
Women	81	29 (36%)	48 (59%)	5 (6%)	1 (1%)	1 (1%)
Missing	18					
AGE (YEARS)						
Under 40	9	1 (11%)	7 (78%)	1 (11%)	0 (0%)	0 (0%)
40–49	76	24 (32%)	44 (58%)	7 (9%)	3 (4%)	0 (0%)
50–59	136	66 (49%)	63 (46%)	6 (4%)	2 (1%)	2 (1%)
60–69	111	36 (32%)	70 (63%)	6 (5%)	4 (4%)	1 (1%)
70–79	56	21 (38%)	31 (55%)	3 (5%)	5 (9%)	1 (2%)
80+	9	3 (33%)	6 (67%)	0 (0%)	0 (0%)	0 (0%)
Missing	2					
INSTITUTE POSITION						
Member	32	10 (31%)	19 (59%)	3 (9%)	1 (3%)	0 (0%)
Faculty	132	49 (37%)	72 (55%)	9 (7%)	6 (5%)	1 (1%)
Training Analyst	233	92 (39%)	130 (56%)	11 (5%)	7 (3%)	3 (1%)
Missing	2					
YEARS SINCE GRADUATION						
Under 10 years	95	37 (39%)	50 (53%)	7 (7%)	2 (2%)	0 (0%)
10–19 years	109	42 (39%)	61 (56%)	6 (6%)	4 (4%)	3 (3%)
20–29 years	91	35 (38%)	54 (59%)	3 (3%)	2 (2%)	0 (0%)
30–39 years	69	24 (35%)	40 (58%)	6 (9%)	4 (6%)	1 (1%)
40–49 years	21	8 (38%)	11 (52%)	0 (0%)	2 (10%)	0 (0%)
Missing	14					

2. Have you recognized personal change? What kind?

N = 399	Number of subjects	Yes	Self-reflective exploration	Shared affect or area of experience	Different affect or area of experience	Other	No
GENDER							
Men	300	294 (98%)	263 (88%)	232 (77%)	195 (65%)	37 (12%)	2 (1%)
Women	81	80 (99%)	69 (85%)	71 (88%)	56 (69%)	8 (10%)	0 (0%)
Missing	18						
AGE (YEARS)							
Under 40	9	8 (89%)	5 (56%)	5 (56%)	3 (33%)	0 (0%)	0 (0%)
40–49	76	76 (100%)	68 (89%)	64 (84%)	56 (74%)	9 (12%)	0 (0%)
50–59	136	135 (99%)	120 (88%)	109 (80%)	91 (67%)	16 (12%)	0 (0%)
60–69	111	108 (97%)	94 (85%)	88 (79%)	78 (70%)	12 (11%)	2 (2%)
70–79	56	54 (96%)	49 (88%)	42 (75%)	31 (55%)	8 (14%)	0 (0%)
80+	9	9 (100%)	9 (100%)	8 (89%)	4 (44%)	1 (11%)	0 (0%)
Missing	2						
INSTITUTE POSITION							
Member	32	32 (100%)	29 (91%)	23 (72%)	19 (59%)	5 (16%)	0 (0%)
Faculty	132	128 (97%)	109 (83%)	100 (76%)	80 (61%)	13 (10%)	1 (1%)
Training Analyst	233	230 (99%)	208 (89%)	193 (83%)	165 (71%)	28 (12%)	1 (.0001%)
Missing	2						
YEARS SINCE GRADUATION							
Under 10 years	95	93 (98%)	86 (91%)	74 (78%)	66 (69%)	13 (14%)	0 (0%)
10–19 years	109	109 (100%)	93 (85%)	94 (86%)	79 (72%)	9 (8%)	0 (0%)
20–29 years	91	89 (98%)	78 (86%)	69 (76%)	58 (64%)	12 (13%)	2 (2%)
30–39 years	69	68 (99%)	61 (88%)	53 (77%)	46 (67%)	11 (16%)	0 (0%)
40–49 years	21	19 (90%)	19 (90%)	16 (76%)	8 (38%)	1 (5%)	0 (0%)
Missing	14						

3. Psychological work was triggered by:

N = 399	Number of subjects	Patient point out	Recognition of shared difficulty	Recognition of shared affect	Impact of attitudes, etc.	Transference – countertransference recognition	Transference – countertransference enactment
GENDER							
Men	300	183 (61%)	201 (67%)	177 (59%)	147 (49%)	233 (78%)	193 (64%)
Women	81	48 (60%)	49 (61%)	53 (66%)	47 (59%)	62 (77%)	57 (71%)
Missing	18						
AGE (YEARS)							
Under 40	9	5 (56%)	5 (56%)	3 (33%)	1 (11%)	6 (67%)	3 (33%)
40–49	75	49 (65%)	57 (76%)	47 (63%)	41 (55%)	59 (79%)	57 (76%)
50–59	135	77 (57%)	88 (65%)	87 (64%)	68 (50%)	114 (84%)	94 (69%)
60–69	110	76 (69%)	72 (65%)	70 (64%)	62 (56%)	84 (76%)	72 (65%)
70–79	56	30 (54%)	37 (66%)	25 (45%)	29 (52%)	38 (68%)	30 (54%)
80+	9	4 (44%)	5 (56%)	7 (78%)	2 (22%)	7 (78%)	4 (44%)
Missing	5						
INSTITUTE POSITION							
Member	31	15 (48%)	18 (58%)	17 (55%)	15 (48%)	23 (74%)	14 (45%)
Faculty	131	71 (54%)	86 (66%)	77 (59%)	65 (50%)	101 (77%)	76 (58%)
Training Analyst	232	154 (66%)	159 (69%)	145 (63%)	124 (53%)	184 (79%)	170 (73%)
Missing	5						
YEARS SINCE GRADUATION							
Under 10 years	93	54 (58%)	66 (71%)	56 (60%)	49 (53%)	76 (82%)	61 (66%)
10–19 years	109	72 (66%)	77 (71%)	72 (66%)	53 (49%)	90 (83%)	81 (74%)
20–29 years	90	54 (60%)	61 (68%)	57 (63%)	47 (52%)	71 (79%)	60 (66%)
30–39 years	69	41 (59%)	39 (56%)	38 (55%)	41 (59%)	50 (72%)	44 (64%)
40–49 years	21	12 (57%)	13 (62%)	9 (43%)	9 (43%)	15 (71%)	10 (48%)
Missing	17						

4. Dealing with an area of difficulty in work with a patient:

N = 399	Number of subjects	Self-reflection	Discussion with colleagues, etc.	Consultation about patient	Self-analysis
GENDER					
Men	300	179 (60%)	209 (70%)	132 (44%)	254 (85%)
Women	80	40 (50%)	59 (74%)	42 (53%)	73 (91%)
Missing	19				
AGE (YEARS)					
Under 40	9	4 (44%)	7 (78%)	5 (56%)	8 (89%)
40–49	75	46 (61%)	61 (81%)	48 (64%)	70 (93%)
50–59	135	82 (61%)	102 (76%)	67 (50%)	117 (87%)
60–69	110	60 (55%)	72 (65%)	42 (38%)	96 (87%)
70–79	56	31 (55%)	33 (59%)	14 (25%)	43 (77%)
80+	9	6 (67%)	4 (44%)	1 (11%)	8 (89%)
Missing	5				
INSTITUTE POSITION					
Member	31	17 (55%)	22 (71%)	10 (32%)	25 (81%)
Faculty	131	78 (60%)	90 (69%)	67 (51%)	108 (82%)
Training Analyst	232	134 (58%)	167 (72%)	101 (44%)	209 (90%)
Missing	5				
YEARS SINCE GRADUATION					
Under 10 years	93	51 (55%)	68 (73%)	54 (58%)	86 (92%)
10–19 years	109	68 (62%)	86 (79%)	57 (52%)	96 (88%)
20–29 years	90	49 (54%)	60 (67%)	34 (37%)	78 (87%)
30–39 years	69	40 (58%)	43 (62%)	25 (36%)	56 (81%)
40–49 years	21	14 (67%)	13 (62%)	4 (19%)	16 (76%)
Missing	17				

4. Continued

N = 399	Consultation for self	Psychotherapy	Ret-analysis:	with former analyst	with different analyst	Other therapy	Other
GENDER							
Men	39 (13%)	13 (4%)	29 (10%)	11 (4%)	22 (7%)	3 (1%)	15 (5%)
Women	121 (15%)	2 (3%)	12 (15%)	5 (6%)	4 (5%)	3 (4%)	3 (4%)
Missing							
AGE (YEARS)							
Under 40	0 (0%)	0 (0%)	2 (22%)	0 (0%)	1 (11%)	0 (0%)	0 (0%)
40–49	10 (13%)	2 (3%)	8 (11%)	4 (5%)	2 (3%)	1 (1%)	1 (1%)
50–59	17 (13%)	7 (5%)	23 (17%)	9 (7%)	14 (10%)	3 (2%)	6 (4%)
60–69	19 (17%)	3 (3%)	5 (5%)	1 (1%)	5 (5%)	2 (2%)	6 (5%)
70–79	5 (9%)	3 (5%)	5 (9%)	3 (5%)	4 (7%)	0 (0%)	4 (7%)
80+	0 (0%)	0 (0%)	1 (11%)	0 (0%)	1 (11%)	0 (0%)	1 (11%)
Missing							
INSTITUTE POSITION							
Member	1 (3%)	2 (6%)	3 (10%)	1 (3%)	2 (6%)	1 (3%)	2 (6%)
Faculty	14 (11%)	6 (5%)	16 (12%)	5 (4%)	9 (7%)	2 (2%)	8 (6%)
Training Analyst	36 (16%)	7 (3%)	25 (11%)	11 (5%)	16 (7%)	3 (1%)	8 (3%)
Missing							
YEARS SINCE GRADUATION							
Under 10 years	11 (12%)	4 (4%)	9 (10%)	5 (5%)	2 (2%)	1 (1%)	4 (4%)
10–19 years	14 (13%)	5 (5%)	17 (16%)	7 (6%)	12 (11%)	1 (1%)	4 (4%)
20–29 years	18 (20%)	2 (2%)	8 (9%)	2 (2%)	5 (6%)	1 (1%)	3 (3%)
30–39 years	7 (10%)	4 (6%)	6 (9%)	3 (4%)	5 (7%)	1 (1%)	5 (7%)
40–49 years	0 (0%)	0 (0%)	2 (10%)	0 (0%)	2 (10%)	0 (0%)	2 (10%)
Missing							

5. How have you undertaken self-analytic exploration?

N = 399	Number of subjects	Imagine talking with analyst	Analyze dreams	Write thoughts	Write someone
GENDER					
Men	298	59 (20%)	196 (66%)	51 (17%)	9 (3%)
Women	80	18 (22%)	49 (61%)	20 (25%)	3 (4%)
Missing	21				
AGE (YEARS)					
Under 40	9	1 (11%)	7 (78%)	2 (22%)	0 (0%)
40–49	75	20 (27%)	52 (69%)	13 (17%)	0 (0%)
50–59	135	32 (24%)	93 (69%)	32 (24%)	7 (5%)
60–69	111	17 (15%)	58 (53%)	18 (16%)	4 (4%)
70–79	56	10 (18%)	41 (73%)	11 (20%)	0 (0%)
80+	9	1 (11%)	4 (44%)	1 (20%)	0 (0%)
Missing	4	1 (11%)		1 (11%)	1 (11%)
INSTITUTE POSITION					
Member	31	7 (23%)	19 (61%)	8 (26%)	1 (3%)
Faculty	131	34 (26%)	82 (63%)	20 (15%)	2 (2%)
Training Analyst	232	40 (17%)	154 (66%)	49 (21%)	9 (4%)
Missing	5				
YEARS SINCE GRADUATION					
Under 10 years	93	30 (32%)	67 (72%)	17 (18%)	1 (1%)
10–19 years	109	21 (19%)	69 (63%)	24 (22%)	6 (6%)
20–29 years	90	14 (16%)	49 (54%)	11 (12%)	2 (2%)
30–39 years	69	13 (19%)	52 (75%)	17 (25%)	2 (3%)
40–49 years	21	2 (10%)	12 (57%)	2 (10%)	1 (5%)
Missing	17				

5. Continued

N = 399	Talk to colleague, etc.	Other:	Automatic activity	Thinking	Reading	Writing	Other
Gender							
Men	162 (54%)	162 (54%)	11 (4%)	128 (43%)	10 (3%)	7 (2%)	15 (5%)
Women	48 (60%)	40 (50%)	4 (5%)	32 (40%)	3 (4%)	1 (1%)	3 (4%)
Missing							
AGE (YEARS)							
Under 40	6 (67%)	3 (33%)	0 (0%)	3 (33%)	0 (0%)	0 (0%)	0 (0%)
40–49	44 (59%)	44 (59%)	7 (9%)	34 (45%)	1 (1%)	1 (1%)	1 (1%)
50–59	84 (62%)	69 (51%)	7 (5%)	56 (41%)	2 (2%)	5 (4%)	6 (4%)
60–69	56 (51%)	60 (55%)	0 (0%)	48 (44%)	7 (6%)	1 (1%)	6 (5%)
70–79	29 (52%)	24 (43%)	1 (2%)	18 (32%)	3 (5%)	1 (2%)	4 (7%)
80+	2 (22%)	7 (78%)	0 (0%)	6 (67%)	1 (11%)	0 (0%)	1 (11%)
Missing							
INSTITUTE POSITION							
Member	21 (68%)	11 (35%)	1 (3%)	10 (32%)	2 (6%)	1 (3%)	2 (6%)
Faculty	73 (56%)	56 (43%)	5 (4%)	48 (37%)	3 (2%)	1 (1%)	8 (6%)
Training Analyst	127 (55%)	140 (60%)	9 (4%)	107 (46%)	9 (4%)	6 (3%)	8 (3%)
Missing							
YEARS SINCE GRADUATION							
Under 10 years	54 (58%)	53 (57%)	7 (8%)	42 (45%)	2 (2%)	1 (1%)	4 (4%)
10–19 years	67 (61%)	56 (51%)	4 (4%)	44 (40%)	4 (4%)	2 (2%)	4 (4%)
20–29 years	46 (51%)	49 (54%)	2 (2%)	43 (47%)	2 (2%)	4 (4%)	3 (3%)
30–39 years	36 (52%)	33 (48%)	1 (1%)	26 (38%)	4 (6%)	1 (1%)	5 (7%)
40–49 years	8 (38%)	13 (62%)	0 (0%)	9 (43%)	2 (10%)	0 (0%)	2 (10%)
Missing							

6. How systematic and what is the frequency of self-analytic work?

N = 399	Number of subjects	Daily	Only when aware of difficulty	Frequently	Occasionally	Rarely
GENDER						
Men	300	76 (25%)	140 (47%)	131 (44%)	26 (9%)	4 (1%)
Women	81	16 (20%)	36 (44%)	40 (49%)	12 (15%)	1 (1%)
Missing	18					
AGE (YEARS)						
Under 40	9	0 (0%)	6 (67%)	6 (67%)	0 (0%)	0 (0%)
40–49	76	21 (28%)	26 (34%)	31 (41%)	7 (9%)	0 (0%)
50–59	136	36 (27%)	64 (47%)	69 (51%)	15 (11%)	2 (2%)
60–69	111	28 (25%)	50 (45%)	41 (37%)	14 (13%)	1 (1%)
70–79	56	7 (12%)	31 (55%)	31 (55%)	2 (4%)	1 (2%)
80+	9	2 (22%)	5 (56%)	1 (11%)	3 (33%)	1 (11%)
Missing	2					
INSTITUTE POSITION						
Member	32	6 (19%)	16 (50%)	18 (56%)	4 (12%)	0 (0%)
Faculty	132	29 (22%)	60 (45%)	57 (43%)	15 (11%)	2 (2%)
Training Analyst	233	58 (25%)	106 (45%)	105 (45%)	22 (9%)	3 (1%)
Missing	2					
YEARS SINCE GRADUATION						
Under 10 years	95	25 (26%)	38 (40%)	47 (49%)	4 (4%)	1 (1%)
10–19 years	109	31 (28%)	51 (47%)	55 (50%)	12 (11%)	1 (1%)
20–29 years	91	20 (22%)	37 (41%)	34 (37%)	16 (18%)	0 (0%)
30–39 years	69	11 (16%)	43 (62%)	32 (46%)	7 (10%)	2 (3%)
40–49 years	21	5 (24%)	8 (38%)	9 (43%)	1 (5%)	1 (5%)
Missing	14					

6. *Continued*

N = 399	Almost never	Other	Thinking	Reading	Writing	Other
GENDER						
Men	4 (1%)	18 (6%)	128 (43%)	10 (3%)	7 (2%)	15 (5%)
Women	0 (0%)	11 (14%)	32 (40%)	3 (4%)	1 (1%)	3 (4%)
Missing						
AGE (YEARS)						
Under 40	0 (0%)	6 (67%)	3 (33%)	0 (0%)	0 (0%)	0 (0%)
40–49	1 (1%)	6 (8%)	34 (45%)	1 (1%)	1 (1%)	1 (1%)
50–59	1 (1%)	10 (7%)	56 (41%)	2 (2%)	5 (4%)	6 (4%)
60–69	1 (1%)	12 (11%)	48 (44%)	7 (6%)	1 (1%)	6 (5%)
70–79	2 (4%)	2 (4%)	18 (32%)	3 (5%)	1 (2%)	4 (7%)
80+	0 (0%)	0 (0%)	6 (67%)	1 (11%)	0 (0%)	1 (11%)
Missing						
INSTITUTE POSITION						
Member	1 (3%)	1 (3%)	10 (32%)	2 (6%)	1 (3%)	2 (6%)
Faculty	2 (2%)	8 (6%)	48 (37%)	3 (2%)	1 (1%)	8 (6%)
Training Analyst	2 (1%)	21 (9%)	107 (46%)	9 (4%)	6 (3%)	8 (3%)
Missing						
YEARS SINCE GRADUATION						
Under 10 years	1 (1%)	12 (13%)	42 (45%)	2 (2%)	1 (1%)	4 (4%)
10–10 years	1 (1%)	3 (3%)	44 (40%)	4 (4%)	2 (2%)	4 (4%)
20–29 years	1 (1%)	10 (11%)	43 (47%)	2 (2%)	4 (4%)	3 (3%)
30–39 years	2 (3%)	3 (4%)	26 (38%)	4 (6%)	1 (1%)	5 (7%)
40–49 years	0 (0%)	1 (5%)	9 (43%)	2 (10%)	0 (0%)	2 (10%)
Missing						

7. The results of self-analysis for you have been:

N = 399	Number of subjects	New understanding	Increased self-acceptance	Recovery of memories	Decrease conflict	Change in work with patient	Change in other relationships
GENDER							
Men	300	245 (82%)	214 (71%)	125 (42%)	177 (59%)	228 (76%)	173 (58%)
Women	81	70 (86%)	56 (69%)	30 (37%)	48 (59%)	58 (72%)	54 (67%)
Missing	18						
AGE (YEARS)							
Under 40	9	6 (67%)	5 (56%)	1 (11%)	6 (67%)	6 (67%)	5 (56%)
40 – 49	76	62 (82%)	59 (78%)	33 (43%)	49 (64%)	61 (80%)	40 (53%)
50 – 59	136	112 (82%)	102 (75%)	56 (41%)	86 (63%)	106 (78%)	87 (64%)
60 – 69	111	95 (86%)	73 (66%)	42 (38%)	57 (51%)	85 (77%)	65 (59%)
70 – 79	56	46 (82%)	35 (62%)	21 (38%)	24 (43%)	36 (64%)	31 (55%)
80+	9	8 (89%)	7 (78%)	3 (33%)	7 (78%)	4 (44%)	8 (89%)
Missing	2						
INSTITUTE POSITION							
Member	32	26 (81%)	21 (66%)	11 (34%)	20 (62%)	19 (59%)	16 (50%)
Faculty	132	97 (73%)	92 (69%)	53 (40%)	73 (55%)	93 (70%)	72 (55%)
Training Analyst	234	205 (88%)	167 (71%)	91 (39%)	136 (58%)	186 (80%)	147 (63%)
Missing	1						
YEARS SINCE GRADUATION							
Under 10 years	95	79 (83%)	74 (78%)	43 (45%)	60 (63%)	71 (75%)	54 (57%)
10 – 19 years	109	89 (82%)	85 (78%)	40 (37%)	72 (66%)	86 (79%)	70 (64%)
20 – 29 years	91	72 (79%)	61 (67%)	37 (41%)	50 (55%)	71 (78%)	54 (59%)
30 – 39 years	69	61 (88%)	38 (55%)	23 (33%)	30 (43%)	47 (68%)	36 (52%)
40 – 49 years	21	17 (81%)	16 (76%)	8 (38%)	11 (52%)	13 (62%)	15 (71%)
Missing	14						

7. *Continued*

N = 399	Less conflict	More conflict	Greater freedom	Greater comfort	Return treatment	Therapy	Analysis	Other
GENDER								
Men	115 (38%)	12 (4%)	131 (44%)	128 (43%)	35 (12%)	17 (6%)	21 (7%)	2 (1%)
Women	33 (41%)	6 (7%)	38 (47%)	35 (43%)	13 (16%)	5 (6%)	9 (11%)	0 (0%)
Missing								
AGE (YEARS)								
Under 40	3 (33%)	0 (0%)	2 (22%)	3 (33%)	2 (22%)	1 (11%)	1 (11%)	0 (0%)
40 – 49	26 (34%)	3 (4%)	29 (38%)	28 (37%)	9 (12%)	3 (4%)	7 (9%)	0 (0%)
50 – 59	59 (43%)	9 (7%)	67 (49%)	63 (46%)	21 (15%)	10 (7%)	11 (8%)	3 (2%)
60 – 69	40 (36%)	5 (5%)	45 (41%)	49 (44%)	11 (10%)	5 (5%)	7 (6%)	0 (0%)
70 – 79	18 (32%)	2 (4%)	27 (48%)	23 (41%)	6 (11%)	3 (5%)	5 (9%)	0 (0%)
80+	7 (78%)	0 (0%)	4 (44%)	6 (67%)	0 (0%)	0 (0%)	0 (0%)	0 (0%)
Missing								
INSTITUTE POSITION								
Member	13 (41%)	1 (3%)	14 (44%)	16 (50%)	4 (12%)	1 (3%)	3 (9%)	0 (0%)
Faculty	44 (34%)	4 (3%)	47 (35%)	49 (37%)	21 (16%)	10 (8%)	11 (8%)	0 (0%)
Training Analyst	97 (41%)	14 (6%)	113 (48%)	107 (46%)	23 (10%)	11 (5%)	17 (7%)	2 (1%)
Missing								
YEARS SINCE GRADUATION								
Under 10 years	33 (35%)	5 (5%)	40 (42%)	43 (45%)	10 (11%)	5 (5%)	6 (6%)	0 (0%)
10 – 19 years	51 (47%)	7 (6%)	54 (50%)	46 (42%)	16 (15%)	4 (4%)	12 (11%)	1 (1%)
20 – 29 years	32 (35%)	4 (4%)	37 (41%)	40 (44%)	10 (11%)	8 (9%)	4 (4%)	1 (1%)
30 – 39 years	22 (32%)	3 (4%)	26 (38%)	26 (38%)	9 (13%)	3 (4%)	7 (10%)	0 (0%)
40 – 49 years	12 (57%)	0 (0%)	12 (58%)	11 (53%)	1 (5%)	1 (5%)	1 (5%)	0 (0%)
Missing								

8. Awareness of particular transference–countertransference context or affective experience:

N = 399

	Number of subjects	Yes	Transference–counter-transference context	Affective experience	No	Other
GENDER						
Men	300	240 (80%)	199 (66%)	168 (56%)	39 (13%)	12 (4%)
Women	81	74 (91%)	61 (75%)	44 (54%)	2 (2%)	3 (4%)
Missing	18					
AGE (YEARS)						
Under 40	9	7 (78%)	6 (67%)	6 (67%)	0 (0%)	0 (0%)
40–49	76	68 (89%)	58 (76%)	48 (63%)	4 (5%)	3 (4%)
50–59	136	111 (81%)	95 (70%)	71 (52%)	19 (14%)	6 (4%)
60–69	111	85 (77%)	70 (63%)	59 (53%)	16 (14%)	5 (5%)
70–79	56	45 (80%)	31 (55%)	30 (54%)	8 (14%)	2 (4%)
80+	9	7 (78%)	5 (56%)	2 (22%)	0 (0%)	0 (0%)
Missing	2					
INSTITUTE POSITION						
Member	32	27 (84%)	23 (72%)	17 (53%)	3 (9%)	1 (3%)
Faculty	132	104 (79%)	85 (64%)	76 (58%)	17 (13%)	2 (2%)
Training Analyst	232	192 (83%)	157 (68%)	122 (53%)	27 (12%)	13 (6%)
Missing	3					
YEARS SINCE GRADUATION						
Under 10 years	95	78 (82%)	66 (69%)	58 (61%)	9 (9%)	5 (5%)
10–19 years	109	94 (86%)	82 (75%)	62 (57%)	13 (12%)	4 (4%)
20–29 years	91	74 (81%)	60 (66%)	52 (57%)	12 (13%)	4 (4%)
30–39 years	69	53 (77%)	39 (57%)	32 (47%)	8 (12%)	3 (4%)
40–49 years	21	17 (81%)	13 (62%)	8 (38%)	2 (10%)	0 (0%)
Missing	14					

9. Was the stimulus to self-reflection an area:

N = 399	Number of subjects	Explored previously	In analysis	In postanalysis therapy	Other context	Newly discovered	Other
GENDER							
Men	298	199 (67%)	185 (62%)	49 (16%)	60 (20%)	148 (50%)	7 (2%)
Women	80	51 (64%)	45 (56%)	9 (11%)	12 (15%)	39 (49%)	2 (2%)
Missing	21						
AGE (YEARS)							
Under 40	9	7 (78%)	6 (67%)	1 (11%)	0 (0%)	3 (33%)	0 (0%)
40–49	75	57 (76%)	55 (73%)	12 (16%)	11 (15%)	24 (32%)	2 (3%)
50–59	135	100 (74%)	87 (64%)	22 (16%)	29 (21%)	70 (52%)	4 (3%)
60–69	110	60 (55%)	58 (53%)	13 (12%)	26 (24%)	61 (55%)	1 (1%)
70–79	56	29 (52%)	27 (48%)	14 (25%)	9 (16%)	31 (55%)	2 (4%)
80+	9	4 (44%)	5 (56%)	1 (11%)	1 (11%)	5 (56%)	0 (0%)
Missing	5						
INSTITUTE POSITION							
Member	31	15 (48%)	15 (48%)	4 (13%)	6 (19%)	15 (48%)	2 (6%)
Faculty	131	92 (70%)	86 (65%)	20 (15%)	23 (18%)	55 (42%)	4 (3%)
Training Analyst	232	149 (64%)	137 (59%)	39 (17%)	47 (20%)	125 (54%)	3 (1%)
Missing	5						
YEARS SINCE GRADUATION							
Under 10 years	93	74 (80%)	71 (76%)	8 (9%)	15 (16%)	32 (34%)	2 (2%)
10–19 years	109	73 (67%)	68 (62%)	22 (20%)	26 (24%)	58 (53%)	5 (5%)
20–29 years	90	60 (67%)	53 (59%)	15 (17%)	16 (18%)	49 (54%)	0 (0%)
30–39 years	69	30 (44%)	28 (41%)	11 (16%)	14 (20%)	36 (52%)	2 (3%)
40–49 years	21	12 (57%)	13 (62%)	4 (19%)	3 (14%)	13 (62%)	0 (0%)
Missing	17						

10. Was the self-discovery or change of self-experience from:

N = 399	Number of subjects	Shared conflict	Similar area/similar defense	Similar area/different defense	Similar defense/different area	Area of identification	Recognition disavowed	Recognition unacknowledged	Shared pain
GENDER									
Men	298	209 (70%)	138 (46%)	136 (46%)	49 (16%)	186 (62%)	129 (43%)	102 (34%)	128 (43%)
Women	80	57 (71%)	39 (49%)	35 (44%)	14 (18%)	43 (54%)	31 (39%)	25 (31%)	23 (29%)
Missing	21								
AGE (YEARS)									
Under 40	9	5 (56%)	5 (56%)	2 (22%)	3 (33%)	4 (44%)	1 (11%)	2 (22%)	3 (33%)
40–49	75	58 (77%)	32 (43%)	41 (55%)	15 (20%)	48 (64%)	32 (43%)	23 (31%)	33 (44%)
50–59	135	105 (78%)	73 (54%)	68 (50%)	25 (19%)	82 (61%)	56 (42%)	48 (36%)	56 (41%)
60–69	110	68 (62%)	48 (44%)	41 (37%)	16 (15%)	63 (57%)	44 (40%)	38 (35%)	43 (39%)
70–79	56	34 (61%)	21 (38%)	20 (36%)	9 (16%)	34 (61%)	25 (45%)	17 (30%)	17 (30%)
80+	9	6 (67%)	7 (78%)	5 (56%)	1 (11%)	5 (56%)	4 (44%)	3 (33%)	4 (44%)
Missing	5								
INSTITUTE POSITION									
Member	31	19 (61%)	14 (45%)	11 (35%)	3 (10%)	13 (42%)	11 (35%)	7 (23%)	9 (29%)
Faculty	131	88 (67%)	62 (47%)	56 (43%)	18 (14%)	74 (57%)	43 (33%)	37 (28%)	56 (43%)
Training Analyst	232	168 (72%)	110 (47%)	109 (47%)	48 (21%)	148 (64%)	107 (46%)	86 (37%)	91 (39%)
Missing	5								
YEARS SINCE GRADUATION									
Under 10 years	93	66 (71%)	44 (47%)	43 (46%)	18 (19%)	55 (59%)	35 (38%)	28 (30%)	42 (45%)
10–19 years	109	88 (81%)	58 (53%)	58 (53%)	18 (17%)	66 (61%)	44 (40%)	33 (30%)	47 (43%)
20–29 years	90	64 (71%)	45 (50%)	38 (42%)	16 (18%)	56 (62%)	40 (44%)	38 (42%)	33 (37%)
30–39 years	69	32 (46%)	24 (35%)	24 (35%)	10 (14%)	39 (57%)	29 (42%)	21 (30%)	23 (33%)
40–49 years	21	15 (71%)	10 (48%)	10 (48%)	5 (24%)	11 (53%)	8 (38%)	6 (29%)	7 (33%)
Missing	17								

10. Continued

N = 399	Similar life situation	Recovered affect	Recovered memory	Discovered affect	New under-standing	Greater self-acceptance	New perspective	Difference leads to change	Unfamiliar life situation	Other
GENDER										
Men	158 (53%)	79 (27%)	47 (16%)	38 (13%)	119 (40%)	116 (39%)	107 (36%)	118 (40%)	75 (25%)	16 (5%)
Women	47 (59%)	14 (18%)	12 (15%)	12 (15%)	33 (41%)	30 (38%)	27 (34%)	24 (34%)	19 (24%)	2 (2%)
Missing										
AGE (YEARS)										
Under 40	4 (44%)	3 (33%)	0 (0%)	0 (0%)	2 (22%)	3 (33%)	1 (11%)	1 (11%)	2 (22%)	0 (0%)
40–49	35 (47%)	18 (24%)	11 (15%)	9 (12%)	24 (32%)	30 (40%)	25 (33%)	23 (31%)	15 (20%)	3 (4%)
50–59	77 (57%)	38 (28%)	21 (16%)	22 (16%)	58 (43%)	55 (41%)	53 (39%)	43 (32%)	35 (26%)	5 (4%)
60–69	62 (56%)	26 (24%)	19 (17%)	15 (14%)	47 (43%)	41 (37%)	40 (36%)	50 (45%)	32 (29%)	5 (5%)
70–79	27 (48%)	9 (16%)	7 (12%)	5 (9%)	21 (38%)	18 (32%)	15 (27%)	27 (48%)	14 (25%)	4 (7%)
80+	7 (78%)	1 (11%)	1 (11%)	1 (11%)	5 (56%)	4 (44%)	5 (56%)	3 (33%)	0 (0%)	1 (11%)
Missing										
INSTITUTE POSITION										
Member	14 (45%)	6 (19%)	1 (3%)	4 (13%)	13 (42%)	11 (35%)	9 (29%)	9 (29%)	8 (26%)	2 (6%)
Faculty	64 (49%)	31 (24%)	20 (15%)	14 (11%)	46 (35%)	49 (37%)	42 (32%)	43 (33%)	25 (19%)	5 (4%)
Training Analyst	134 (58%)	58 (25%)	38 (16%)	34 (15%)	99 (43%)	91 (39%)	89 (38%)	97 (42%)	65 (28%)	11 (5%)
Missing										
YEARS SINCE GRADUATION										
Under 10 years	47 (50%)	24 (26%)	15 (16%)	13 (14%)	34 (37%)	38 (41%)	31 (33%)	27 (29%)	19 (20%)	4 (4%)
10–19 years	59 (54%)	32 (29%)	15 (14%)	17 (16%)	46 (42%)	46 (42%)	41 (38%)	36 (33%)	27 (25%)	3 (3%)
20–29 years	50 (56%)	24 (27%)	20 (22%)	12 (13%)	35 (39%)	36 (40%)	33 (37%)	40 (45%)	26 (29%)	5 (6%)
30–39 years	34 (49%)	11 (16%)	5 (7%)	6 (9%)	26 (38%)	17 (25%)	23 (33%)	32 (46%)	20 (29%)	4 (6%)
40–49 years	16 (76%)	4 (19%)	4 (19%)	3 (14%)	13 (62%)	10 (48%)	8 (38%)	9 (43%)	3 (14%)	2 (10%)
Missing										

APPENDIX C

Significant Correlations with Analyst's Age

	Age (r)
Analyst Seeking Consultation for Self	−0.27*
Discussing Work with Colleagues	−0.20*
Stimulus to Self Reflection Previously Explored Area	−0.21*

*(p < 0.05). Point-biserial correlation, Bonferroni corrected t.

Index